REA

5-20-70

Damn the Torpedos!

Damn the Torpedos!

The Story of America's First Admiral:
David Glasgow Farragut

by
Christopher Martin

Abelard-Schuman
London   New York   Toronto

Library of Congress Catalogue Card Number: 73-85799
Standard Book Number: 200.71622.0

LONDON	NEW YORK	TORONTO
Abelard-Schuman	Abelard-Schuman	Abelard-Schuman
Limited	Limited	Canada Limited
8 King St. WC2	257 Park Ave. So.	200 Yorkland Blvd.

An Intext Publisher

Printed in the United States of America

ACKNOWLEDGMENTS 1540495

The principal sources for this book are *Admiral Farragut* by Captain A. T. Mahan, USN. (New York, D. Appleton and Co., 1897); *Twelve Naval Captains* by Molly Elliot Seawell (New York, Charles Scribner's Sons, 1897); *Midshipman Farragut* by James Barnes (New York, D. Appleton and Co. 1896); *David G. Farragut* by John Randolph Spears (Philadelphia, George W. Jacobs and Co., 1905); *The Life and Naval Career of Vice Admiral David Glascoe Farragut* by Rev. P. C. Headley (New York, William H. Appleton, 1865); and above all, Charles Lee Lewis's two remarkable volumes on Farragut: *David Glasgow Farragut: Admiral in the Making* and *David Glasgow Farragut: Our First Admiral*, published by the United States Naval Institute in 1941 and 1943 respectively.

As a biographer one might say that Mr. Lewis did all the work; his is the fine bibliography, the finely annotated study of Farragut and the period. If one were to find a fault with the Lewis books, it would be that they tend to be indiscriminate in the study of boy, youth, young officer, senior officer, and admiral, and that as much attention is paid to the detail of navy life and navy work at the various times as to Farragut's part in these. But for the purposes intended, there could scarcely be validity in such a cavil. For the general reader, the books might be regarded as a bit too special, and thus derives the author's excuse for writing a biography about a figure whose story has been dug out thoroughly from the navy files by another.

American naval biography is a much neglected subject since the days of "Preble's boys" and a select handful of other heroic figures. One reason is the paucity of naval wars in American history. The War of 1812 produced some historic moments, as did the Barbary wars, but until the Civil War the American Navy waned almost steadily from the signing of the Peace of Ghent. Farragut has long interested this author as a little-understood and authentic American naval hero whose light was submerged by an almost purposeful ignoration by the Grant administration and succeeding administrations, and then by a hearty neglect of American naval affairs almost up to the moment of the Spanish-American War. Farragut's works and Farragut's deeds have been better-known to foreigners than to Americans. Admiral Mahan, the finest of the navy's historians, paid him the courtesy of a biography, but Mahan was concerned almost entirely with Farragut's strategies and Farragut the naval thinker. It took Lewis to bring out Farragut the man, and the Lewis research is invaluable.

The author is very much indebted to various librarians at the Navy Library in Washington, to many at the Library of Congress, the United States Naval Academy, and to librarians at Yale University.

CONTENTS

1. THE FARRAGUTS

The American naval tradition is usually considered hand in hand with the tradition of the British Navy. On both sides of the Atlantic Ocean there is a tendency to oversimplify naval history, a tendency which has led to the common belief that the American Navy is like its British counterpart, except for the British denial of alcoholic beverages and the American claim of a longer recognition of the humanity of the men below decks, or "sailors' rights." Most Americans and most Britons do not know that the first American admiral was descended from the tradition of the Armada, not the tradition of Lord Nelson, or that he was a second generation American, the son of a Spanish father. David Glasgow Farragut was his name. In Spain's Balearic Islands, from which his father came, the name was Ferragut. One Don Pedro Ferragut had been active in the campaign of James I of Aragon to expel the Moors from Majorca. Another Ferragut had been historian of Majorca and had drawn the official maps of the island for the royal government. The family history named soldiers and priests and even bishops. Ferraguts sailed with the Armada, and their adventurous history included the tale of one wealthy ancestor, Antonio Ferragut, who was carried off from his Minorca estate by the Turks in 1558 and was held in Constantinople until ransomed by his family.

The American branch of the family descended from Jorge Antonio Magin Ferragut, of Minorca, who was sent as a child to the city of Barcelona for education, but who opted early for life as a sailor. Very early, indeed, for at the age of ten the boy shipped out to join the merchant service. Eight years

1

later, in 1773, Jorge Ferragut came to the Caribbean, and by 1775, not yet twenty years old, he was captain of a small merchant ship. The ship traded between Havana and Vera Cruz, with occasional stopovers at New Orleans, then a Spanish possession. When "the shot heard round the world" rang out at Concord on April 19, 1775, the news traveled as swiftly as the rivers flowed to New Orleans and was heard by Captain Ferragut. He sailed to Port-au-Prince, sold his cargo for a load of cannon, muskets, and ammunition, and headed north to join the American colonists in their struggle against England. Jorge Ferragut had grown up hating England. Although he was a Spaniard by language and family and tradition, he had, for a time, been a subject of King George III. Minorca had been ceded to Britain by the Treaty of Utrecht in 1713, and when Jorge was born, in 1755, it was still a British colony. France succeeded Britain as master of Minorca during Jorge's childhood. The Minorcans hated both usurping powers and were eager for revenge. So Jorge Antonio sailed to Charleston with his precious cargo and quickly became George Anthony Magin Farragut, lieutenant aboard an American privateer of twelve guns which cruised the Atlantic coast and down into the British waters off the Bahamas.

George Farragut was short and chunky. He had bushy black hair with a widow's peak, framing a heavy, ruddy, but good-humored face, a broad face with dimpled chin and strong straight nose under beetling black brows and deep-set eyes. George Farragut was quick to laugh and quick of temper, the manner of his native — not his enforced — allegiance.

Soon this fiery young man became a lieutenant in the navy of the colony-state of South Carolina. In 1778, Farragut superintended the construction of galleys in Charleston and fought against the British at Savannah, escaping when the port was captured by the British and returning to Charleston to fighting there in the siege. Unfortunately, it was not long before the British reduced the naval might of South Carolina. George Farragut was made commander of a battery of his galley guns and transferred to the army and fighting on land. He was captured by the British at Charleston in 1780, but was exchanged and soon sailed from Philadelphia aboard a privateer. He was wounded in an engagement with a British vessel. His wound healed, he returned to the land battles, fighting under General Francis Marion in South Carolina. He fought at the Battle of Cowpens, among others. In 1781, Farragut commanded a battery of artillery; then he transferred to the cavalry, and ended his war as a Major of Horse in the North Carolina State Service.

At the close of the Revolutionary War George Farragut went to sea again, for soldiering was his only means of livelihood. He sailed for seven more years, then secured an appointment as Major of Militia from an old acquaintance named William Blount, who had been made governor of the South Western Territory (which would become Tennessee). In 1793 and 1794, Farragut's military labors for his adopted country began to bear fruit. He received several land grants in Knox County, amounting to more than six hundred acres, and was on the way to becoming a man of some substance, at least enough to be able to marry Elizabeth Shine, an aging maiden of thirty.

Elizabeth Shine also came from a spirited family. Her people were Irishmen, Dubliners, and her father and brothers had also fought with valor against the British. The well-matched pair soon began to raise a family. The first child was William, born in the summer of 1797 in Knoxville, where George Farragut had built a sturdy house of stone and logs. Three years later the Farraguts moved to a section of land (640 acres) on the north bank of the Holston River, southwest of Knoxville. Here George Farragut was awarded a franchise to maintain a ferry, a helpful source of added income.

On July 5, 1801, a second son was born. They named him James Glasgow Farragut. This son would become the admiral; his name would be changed. He was named James Glasgow in honor of George Farragut's friend who had been Secretary of State of North Carolina—and that is how a Spanish-Irish boy got a Scottish middle name.

James could not remember much about his frontier life as a child, but he did remember one encounter with Indians that occurred when he was about five years old. One day when

3

his mother was at home alone, she spotted Indians approaching the house. Indians did not pay social calls on settlers in 1806, and she knew it. She secreted her four frightened children in the loft and parleyed with the Indians, who had no guns and said they would go away if she would give them whiskey. When she opened the door slightly, an Indian slashed at her with a knife. She slammed the door, bolted it, and stood guard with an axe until they left. When George Farragut returned to the house, his Spanish temper flared and he went off to hunt the Indians. It is not recorded whether he and his posse captured the savages, but he was known as a doughty Indian fighter and was much respected in the frontier country.

George Farragut became bored, homesick for Spanish America, and when another friend, William Charles Cole Cliborne, was made governor of Louisiana after the Louisiana Purchase, he was appointed a sailing master in the United States Navy and ordered to duty at New Orleans. (A sailing master in the old navy was the man actually in charge of the working of the ship. The captain or commander was a naval officer, and he might or might not be adept at seamanship. The system was one of the last hangovers of the old ways that began when navies were armies at sea.) He soon left for New Orleans to take command of U.S. Gunboat No. 13, and his wife and children took a more leisurely voyage down the Mississippi, moving the family possessions on a flatboat. As it turned out, the future admiral's first voyage was on the water where he would later win his flag.

The Farraguts moved into a house near Lake Ponchartrain and Sailing Master Farragut was able to live at home. One day, while off duty, Sailing Master Farragut came across his friend Sailing Master David Porter just after Porter had suffered a sunstroke while fishing on the lake. Farragut took Porter to his own house, where Elizabeth took care of the sick man, or tried to, but Porter was suffering from tuberculosis and died of complications. As luck would have it, Elizabeth Farragut became ill while nursing Porter (yellow fever, it was reported). She died on the same day as Porter and both were buried on June 24, 1808, in the Protestant cemetery.

4

Five days before Sailing Master David Porter died in the Farragut house, his son, Commander David Porter, Jr., arrived at New Orleans to take command of the United States naval station. He tried to help George Farragut, who then had five children to care for, by transferring him from command of a gunboat to duties within the station. The problem was soon alleviated when William, the eldest child, received an appointment as a midshipman in the navy. Not long afterward, George Farragut retired from the navy and purchased a nine-hundred-acre plantation on the Pascagoula River, a hundred miles east of New Orleans. The family moved there, and George became a planter.

One day Commander Porter came to visit the Farraguts, ostensibly paying a duty call on the family that had been so kind to his father. But there was a reason for his visit. Porter and his wife had decided to offer to care for and educate one of the Farragut children. George Farragut was not eager to let a child go, but he realized that Commander Porter was a powerful figure in the American Navy, that Porter's sponsorship could be invaluable to a youngster, and that his second son was already eyeing the brass buttons of William Farragut's navy uniform and talking about the day when he too would become a midshipman. He agreed that if the boy wanted to go he could, and James leaped at the chance.

One of the Farragut girls also went to live with the Porters and stayed with them as long as they were in New Orleans. Then she remained with Porter's sister, who had married a navy surgeon.

James and his sister returned home to the plantation frequently. They sailed on Lake Ponchartrain and on the rivers, and the young boy learned much about the waters around New Orleans and much about sailing small boats. His father was a great sailor of small boats; he had once sailed from New Orleans to Havana in a pirogue. Sailing Master Farragut kept a yawl on Lake Ponchartrain and sailed it in every kind of weather. Before he was twelve years old, young Farragut learned how to roll up in a sail on a lee shore in a wind if he was stranded far from home at night and to dig a sleeping pit in the sand to keep warm. He, too, learned to sail a pirogue, and all the while he dreamed of sailing a great ship as an officer of the American Navy.

Young Farragut could hardly have found a protector of more promise for his own career. The young Porter had been aboard his father's schooner *Eliza,* lying in the port of Jeremie, San Domingo, in 1796, when a British press gang attempted to board the ship and take off members of the crew to augment the force of one of His Britannic Majesty's under-manned warships. Captain Porter ordered his men to arms. They had fought off the British in a bloody battle, and to show his approval, President Washington appointed the senior Porter to the post of Sailing Master in the Navy.

At the time of the fight on the *Eliza,* David Porter, Jr., was sixteen years old. He continued as a merchant sailor for a time and was twice impressed by the British. Both times he escaped. Within three years young Porter secured the coveted appointment as midshipman in the tiny American Navy and was serving aboard the frigate *Constellation* during the un-declared war with France when Captain Thomas Truxton took her into action against the French warship *L'Insurgent.* Soon Captain Truxton had a prize and a problem: a shortage of men to take his prize to port. Lieutenant John Rodgers, Midshipman Porter, and a dozen seamen were assigned to guard two hundred French prisoners of war, and to sail *L'Insurgent* into St. Kitts Harbor. A gale blew up, as effectively screening the French from the frigate as if the ships had been a thousand miles apart, and fourteen Americans had to fight the storm and control their two-hundred angry, restless captives at the same time.

Porter was soon promoted to acting lieutenant and made executive officer of the *Experiment,* a sixty-foot schooner of 135 tons, armed with twelve 6-pounders, which became a scourge of the French and the pirates who abounded in the Mediterranean. By the time he was twenty-one years old, David Porter, Jr., had seen as much action at sea as many an admiral. That year he was posted as first lieutenant of the *Experiment's* sister ship *Enterprise,* which went to the

Mediterranean under command of Lieutenant Andrew Sterrett in Commodore Richard Dale's squadron, which was ordered by President Jefferson to make a show of force against the Barbary pirates. Porter distinguished himself in the fight against the Tripolitan polacca *Tripoli,* which mounted fourteen guns and carried eighty men (the *Enterprise* had twelve guns and ninety-four men). In a three-hour engagement in which the *Tripoli* struck her colors twice and then started fighting again when the *Enterprise* quit shooting at her, the polacca was defeated, and Lieutenant Porter led the boarding party. He threw guns and everything of value overboard and sent the ship back to Tripoli with twenty men dead, thirty wounded, including the captain, the mizzenmast gone, an old sail on the mainmast.

Porter became one of the ardent young men known as "Preble's boys," who struck fear into the hearts of the corsairs with their bloodthirsty forays and absolute disregard for personal danger. Porter was wounded twice in an assault on Tripoli, captured with Captain Bainbridge on the *Philadelphia,* made acting captain of the frigate *Constitution* when still a young lieutenant, and eventually given full command of the *Enterprise.* In 1806, Porter was promoted to the grade of master commandant (roughly equivalent to commander).

James Farragut went to school in New Orleans while living in the house of Master Commandant Porter. On June 21, 1810, a few days before his ninth birthday, Farragut was separated from the rest of his family when the Porters left New Orleans (at the expiration of Porter's tour of duty) and the boy chose to go with them. Their destination was Washington, but they sailed first for Havana, aboard the bomb ketch *Vesuvius,* a small sailing vessel that carried eleven small guns and a crew of thirty, so that Porter could claim rewards owed him by the Spanish government for capture of pirates in the New Orleans area during his duty as commander of the naval station. On this voyage the Porters learned of an incident involving British arrogance. A British ship had fired upon the U.S. brig *Vixen* shortly before their arrival in Havana. Porter was furious. His many brushes with the British had raised in him a solid hatred for them, and his anger was communicated to his nine-year-old protégé.

"I believe it was the first thing that caused bad feeling in me toward the English nation," Farragut recalled later. "I was too young to know anything about the Revolution, but I looked upon this as an insult to be paid in kind, and was anxious to discharge the debt with interest."

When the Porters reached Washington, Master Commandant Porter took young Farragut with him to visit Paul Hamilton, Secretary of the Navy. At the meeting James received a promise from the Secretary that he should be made a midshipman as soon as he reached the ripe old age of ten. In this manner were careers promised and begun.

The family remained in Washington for several months while Porter, dissatisfied with his personal fortunes in the navy, negotiated his affairs and made up his mind about the future. Young Farragut was placed in a school. When the Porters returned to the Mississippi to go upriver to Pittsburgh, and then to Mrs. Porter's home at Chester, James went along and was moved to a school in Chester. Then Master Commandant Porter left them to sail on a merchantman to Havana in another attempt to collect his reward money, the navy giving him leave for the enterprise.

While he was gone, Farragut's commission as a midshipman came through, dated December 17, 1810. He had already been on navy rolls in the spring of 1810 as "boy." He became now a commissioned officer, although of the lowest rank, before he was ten years old. The commission marked the new shape of Farragut's life. He was lost to Pascagoula and the plantation forever, and he would never see his father again. His childhood would cease, for he would join a naval warship where there was no place for childhood, particularly not on an American warship in the year 1812.

2. MR. MIDSHIPMAN FARRAGUT

At about the time of his appointment, Farragut took the given name of his benefactor, David Porter, in gratitude. The change was not made legally, but Porter gave Midshipman Farragut a gold watch with the inscription "D.P. to D.G.F., U.S.N.," and thereafter the youngster was known to the world as David Glasgow Farragut.

Early in the month of August, 1811, Master Commandant Porter and Midshipman Farragut journeyed by stage and packet boat to Norfolk, Virginia, where the U.S. frigate *Essex* was lying at anchor, awaiting Porter, who would be the new captain. The ship was undergoing a refit. Porter stayed ashore to attend to a captain's business, but he sent Farragut and another midshipman, David Fittimary, aboard with a note to the first lieutenant, or executive officer, John Downes. Porter asked Downes to take the two young boys under his special care and to send the wherry for him each morning at 9:30, under the charge of Midshipman Farragut.

On the first day, ten-year-old Midshipman David Farragut clambered into the sternsheets of the wherry and ordered a half-dozen burly navy sailors to row for the shore to pick up their captain. He was responsible for timing, landing, and order among the crew. He seemed a small lad even for his age. He was shorter than average and weighed perhaps seventy pounds in his underclothes. His features were a mixture of northern and southern European strains. His complexion was dark, even swarthy, but his hair was brown, not black, and his eyes were hazel. The face was oval, but the lips were thin, with prominent cheekbones and his father's strong jaw. Actually, he had more the look of the Spanish don about him than had his father, whose Latin figure grew heavy early and whose face usually wore a Falstaffian air.

On these trips Midshipman Farragut wore his undress, or working, uniform, which consisted of a short navy-blue coat of wool with the usual standing collar, decorated by a button and slip of lace on each side of the high neck; vest, knee breeches, and stockings all of white cotton; low-cut black shoes (similar to modern patent-leather dancing slippers with pewter buckles), and a cocked hat. For more formal wear, which included ceremonies such as that of the first day aboard ship or an invitation to dine with the captain, Farragut owned a full dress uniform: a blue tailcoat with short lapels and standing collar, but the collar much more splendid than that of the working uniform, decorated with diamonds of gold lace on each side of the neck, slashed sleeves with buttons at the cuff and half a dozen gold buttons down the front; white breeches of better cut and better material than the working pair; an unadorned white vest, on which he would be privileged to wear buttons as he advanced in rank — three for a lieutenant, four for a captain.

On that first day Porter was wearing his splendid dress uniform with its commander's braid, gold-laced cocked hat, and the short curved sword of all naval officers, called a hanger because it was light enough to hang from the dress belt and did not require a special harness.

The wherry came alongside the frigate. Captain Porter came up the starboard ladder amidships, turned aft on the main, or spar, deck, and walked to the quarterdeck where his ten officers and twelve midshipmen were standing at attention. The captain looked forward to where the three-hundred men of the frigate's crew were assembled on the spar deck. The band played, Porter read his orders from the Secretary of the Navy, his flag was raised, and the ship was once again in commission.

The *Essex* was a vital part of the young American Navy. The navy had a bold and brave tradition, but a very short one, for as such the federal navy was scarcely twenty years old when Midshipman Farragut joined the service. A Continental Navy had been assembled during the Revolutionary War, but when the war ended, the Continental Congress would no longer maintain a navy. The new independent governments (that had been the thirteen colonies) saw no reason to donate large sums of money for the maintenance of useless ships capable only of fighting, when there was money to be made with merchant ships and when there was no apparent danger to American shipping. The officers of the navy were dismissed, or drifted away from the service in the manner of George Farragut, and the handful of ships that remained were sold to pay liquidating expenses. In 1786, the new confederation had no defense force.

But even as the navy was being disbanded, the need for an American navy was growing. With the end of the war the American merchant marine began to multiply, since merchants in Boston, New York, Philadelphia, Baltimore, Charleston, and a dozen other port cities were no longer restricted to carrying their trade goods in British bottoms. American ships streamed into the Mediterranean, the Baltic, the Pacific, and every other sea, seeking trade. The incursion of so many American ships disturbed the delicate balance of trade maintained by European merchants, and they encouraged all comers to seize American ships and cargoes. Only too eager to pirate were the warlike Berbers of northern Africa, who for a thousand years had been preying on the European shipping that passed through the Mediterranean and who even ventured out into the Atlantic from time to time. The Moslem rulers of Algiers, Tunis, Morocco, and Tripoli were happy to seize American ships and goods, and needed no encouragement as Americans, to them, were simply another variety of infidels.

The Continental Congress tried to establish friendly relations with the Barbary pirates, but was not particularly successful. The handling of foreign affairs was totally inept. The insular Americans did not even know that the Barbary pirates were vassals of the Sublime Porte at Constantinople and did not send a representative to the Sultan, who might have eased the way of the infant nation. American representatives treated with deys and beys in Algiers, Tunis, and other ports, and scarcely had they signed a treaty with one ruler than the dey or bey was overthrown and the new ruler declared war again on the Americans so that he, too, could be bought off.

Until a national government was established, little could be done to help the merchants. The pressure of those merchants in their own self-interest was a vital factor in securing the establishment of a federal government that had taxing power. As soon as the government was formed in 1789, the merchants pressed for a navy.

When the new government was established, the feasibility of a navy was investigated by Congress and by Secretary of War Henry Knox, who knew nothing about ships or sailors. There was no Navy Department, and President Washington handed the problem of coastal defense and the security of American shipping to the Treasury and War departments. In 1791, Congress said it wanted detailed figures on the expenses of a navy that would be able to stop the Barbary pirates from seizing American ships, merchandise, and sailors. The figures came slowly because Secretary Knox had to find men who knew what they were talking about, and they were widely scattered. On March 27, 1794, however, Congress passed an act authorizing the construction and manning of six frigates, three of forty-four guns and three of thirty-six guns. They would be the *United States, Constitution, President, Congress, Constellation,* and *Chesapeake.*

These ships were called frigates, but they were much larger than European frigates and were double-banked in the manner of larger ships. The Americans could not afford a great diversity of ships, so they developed an all-purpose ship that would be strong enough to fight and destroy anything the Barbary pirates might mount against them and yet fast enough to cruise rapidly and effectively.

By 1798, only three ships were in the water because of the faltering determination to have a navy; war and peace with Barbary waxed and waned several times in the interim.

Then came the undeclared war with France, and there was a rush to complete the order and build more ships, schooners and brigs, cutters and galleys. That year the federal government encouraged merchants to participate in the naval building program, to build ships by public subscription. Five new frigates were built thus, including the *Essex*. The ship was 140 feet long, 37 feet in the beam, and displaced 850 tons. She was called a thirty-two, but by the time she was built the gun capacity of fighting ships was misleading; the *Essex* actually carried forty-six guns—carronades and long guns. The carronade was a British invention to replace the "short gun," or standard British Navy cannon, and it derived its name from the Carron Foundry. Its advantage was its light weight and ability to throw twice as heavy a shot as the long gun of the same weight. The long gun had the advantage of greater range and, if carefully made after the French pattern, of greater accuracy. The long guns were for chase and long-range fire. The carronades were for close-in fighting—broadsides, for the most part.

On the lower, or gun, deck the *Essex* carried twenty-four of the carronades called 32-pounders and two long 12-pound guns. On the spar deck were sixteen 32-pound carronades and four long 12-pound guns.

Essex had been built by the subscription of the merchants and other citizens of Salem, in Essex County, Massachusetts, who had given $75,000 for construction, a sum matched by the government for outfitting.

The ten-year-old Glasgow Farragut, as he was called by his intimates, knew all these facts about his ship and his service by the time he arrived aboard the *Essex*. It was not very many days before he learned the etiquette of naval life aboard a fighting frigate. First, he learned the rigid behavior demanded of all when approaching the quarterdeck, the after section of the spar deck. The officer on duty on the quarterdeck always appeared in full uniform, and he saluted the deck when he came from below or over the ship's side. Beware any "middie" who came on that deck in undress or failed to salute! The least punishment he might expect would be a few hours perched on the masthead, a frequent punishment which served the triple purpose of discipline, exercise, and strengthening of character. No one ever sat down on the quarterdeck, nor was laughter or boisterous talk acceptable there. For exercise or conversation in the evening, the starboard side of the quarterdeck was reserved for the captain and the senior officers; the larboard, or port, side was given over to the junior officers; and the ordinary seamen were not allowed on the deck at all except on duty. If they must pass across the quarterdeck to reach the after end of the ship on business, they passed on the larboard side. Seamen were known "to have a dozen with the cat" for passing on the starboard.

Three hatches opened on companionways that led from the spar deck to the gun deck, and the farthest aft of these was for the use of officers only. The crew usually had business on the quarterdeck when it came to turning the capstan to lift the anchors, or standing wheel watch before the mizzenmast, as the quartermasters did in watches of four. Just a few feet forward of the quarterdeck was the main, or cargo, hatch and atop this hatch was shipped the big lifeboat. The ship's lumber, several boats, and spars were stored in this part of the spar deck, called the booms. Forward of the hatches was the forecastle deck, and that part of the ship all forward on two decks was the seaman's area. In decent weather the men lived atop the forecastle, and the more generous captains sometimes let them sling their hammocks on the gun deck in the hot climate of the tropics.

On the gun deck, the stern section abaft the mizzenmast was devoted to Captain Porter's cabin, which had windows, not ports, on three sides: port, starboard, and stern. The fourth wall was a removable bulkhead: still four carronades hid their unlovely snouts behind the gunports. In time of action the captain's place was on deck, and the gun crews invaded his stripped cabin and fought from there.

From the cabin forward to the mainmast was the half deck, which was for the use of the officers. Before the mainmast was the waist, where the little stalls of the carpenter, tailor, shoemaker, sailmaker, and other artisans were located. Next to the foremast was the galley, which was divided into three parts: the captain's galley, the officer's galley, and the coopers, which belonged to the crew. Forward were the galley supplies, including the pens of farm animals; sheep, goats, pigs, and chickens accompanied any well-found vessel setting out from commissioning. Here also were the pumps, which kept the bilges dry and pumped seawater to cleanse the decks so that the men could holystone them and tar between the planking every day.

The berth deck was located below the gun deck, or three decks down, which meant that the deck level itself was below the Plimsoll mark. Midshipman Farragut's diminutive size was no liability here; the headroom was only five feet and nine inches between deck and deck. Aft on the berth deck was the wardroom, which extended from rudder post to a point forward of the mizzenmast. Here also were ten tiny staterooms, five on each side, each furnished with a government hammock and a bureau. As first lieutenant, Downes had the first stateroom on the starboard side (which was the largest). Next to him was Second Lieutenant James Wilmer; then came Third Lieutenant James Wilson, Fourth Lieutenant William Finch, and Marine Officer John Gamble. On the portside Surgeon Robert Miller had the stateroom corresponding to that of Lieutenant Downes; then came his assistant surgeons, Richard Hoffman and Alex Montgomery, Chaplain David Adams, and Purser John Shaw.

Forward of the officers' quarters was the steerage, where Midshipman Farragut and his eleven seniors slung their hammocks and kept their sea chests and up-and-down lockers. In the middle of the room was their mess table, securely fastened to the floor against heavy weather. When Midshipman Farragut came aboard, the steerage, or gun room as it was sometimes called, was sweltering in the August heat and humidity of Norfolk. A few months later it would be frigid in the Atlantic seas, heated only by a thirty-two pound shot, which could be made red-hot in the blacksmith's shop in the forecastle and then plunged into a bucket of sand to provide a warming spot for the boys.

The midshipmen were cadets. There were several hundred of them in the American Navy, usually the sons of officers or parents who had special influence with the Secretary of the Navy or high-ranking federal officials. A midshipman's specific duties depended almost entirely on his captain's method of training, for the naval regulations stipulated only that he keep a regular journal and deliver it periodically to his commanding officer. Actually, the midshipman had many duties; the command of the boats (such as the wherry) was only one of them. During the working of the ship, two midshipmen were sent to the tops to supervise the men in the rigging. All midshipmen were on deck or aloft during maneuvers, echoing the orders of the officer of the deck. They took the most dangerous posts, especially in heavy weather, as examples to the seamen. At the guns they assisted the officers in charge and made sure that commands were obeyed promptly. They were responsible for the condition of the clothing of the enlisted men and inspected the men once a week. They supervised the issuance of grog and supplies. They assisted the officer of the watch. They did whatever the officers and their captain wanted, and in between times they went to school, learning to manage a sextant and enough mathematics and navigation to chart a course.

Midshipman Farragut was the youngest and smallest of the cadets aboard the *Essex,* and in the beginning he was the butt of the jokes of the others, who were jealous of him because they deduced from the manner of his coming aboard that he was Captain Porter's protégé. Yet nepotism and favoritism were so common in the U.S. Navy then that he was not hated, and Commander Porter made sure that Midshipman Farragut was not babied either.

Farragut needed no babying. One day he was waiting at dockside with the captain's wherry when a handful of dock loungers espied this small boy in his blue coat with brass buttons in charge of a boatload of sailors. They began ragging, and one wag sprinkled him with an old water pot. The seaman in the bow caught the offender with his boat hook, dragged him into the boat, and the sailors began cuffing him. The other loungers leaped forward, the crew jumped out of the boat as if decanted, and the fight moved uptown to Market Square, where the police quelled it and arrested all concerned, including Mr. Midshipman Farragut, who had been dashing about in the midst of it. The result was that the midshipman and his crew were bound over by the authorities to their captain for discipline and ordered to keep the peace in town. But Captain Porter was not outraged, or even annoyed. He was amused, and he told his officers that young Farragut was composed of "three pounds of uniform and seventy pounds of fight." Later, when he had a bit more experience, Farragut became the most adept of all the midshipmen in rigging. As a rather boastful lark he often climbed to the maintop and sat on this pinnacle surveying all beneath him with lofty dignity, claiming that he did it because he liked a breath of fresh air.

3. ACTION IN THE *ESSEX*

Two months after Porter took command of the ship, the *Essex* was refitted and ready for sea. Midshipman Farragut was on the quarterdeck, ready to listen to and repeat the orders the captain might choose to give during the timeworn process of putting a sailing ship to sea.

The hands were piped to station, each man assigned his relatively simple task, which, when multiplied more than three hundred times, achieved the complicated end of moving the ship away from land and out into the ocean breeze. Up the ratlines, onto the lower and upper yards of foremast, main, and mizzen, the crewmen and the midshipmen scampered, and there they waited for First Lieutenant Downes to give the orders. On the gun deck the anchor gang was moving in circles around the capstan, pushing against the bars and thus bringing up the anchors.

Aloft, the topsails were loosed in their rigging and allowed to roll down and flap against the masts, until the first lieutenant gave the command, "Sheet home topsails!" Midshipman Farragut and the other midshipmen on the quarterdeck and the forecastle bellowed out the orders in repetition. The men standing at the braces and the halliards pulled the lines, the white sails snapping taut, filled, just as the forecastle reported, "Anchor's aweigh, sir." The midshipmen carried the chant aft to the nervous first lieutenant and the contemplative captain, who stood watching critically the process of getting under way. On such maneuvers would the reputation of the ship be judged. Captain Porter did not, and should not have had to,

18

speak a word to the first lieutenant, except to tell him quietly at the beginning to get the ship under way. The first lieutenant was responsible for the working of the ship. His chances of promotion, dim as they might seem in the tiny peacetime navy, depended heavily on his reputation as a shipmaster. First Lieutenant Downes turned to the captain and saluted. "Ship's under weigh, sir," he reported, as the *Essex* moved away from her mooring and turned toward Hampton Roads.

In a few minutes the lower sails were loosened and made fast; the water began to boil beneath the ship's forefoot. Soon the ship was under full sail. The men below were manning the pumps and the sailors atop the forecastle were washing away the mud and debris that had come up with the anchors.

They were at sea. The land gear was stowed and the training of the crew began. The *Essex* had come home that summer from a long cruise abroad, which meant that many of the men had left the ship, other old sailors had signed on again with the navy, but there was a large force of landsmen, heavy-handed farmers and butchers' boys who had decided to come to sea. They must be taught to splice and holystone and paint, to handle shot and powder, and to do these things as a matter of reflex so that when they went into battle there would be no hesitation.

In the minds of Captain Porter and his officers it was a question of *when* the fighting would come, not *if*. The coming of war had been heralded four years earlier when the British frigate *Leopard* had caught Captain James Barron and the American thirty-eight-gun frigate *Chesapeake* just as she was making for sea, guns unshotted, stores half-shipped, crew green and unready. The smaller, less heavily armed British ship had raked the *Chesapeake* and hurt her so severely that Barron had run down his flag. From that incident had arisen the wrath of the American people and the American naval men. Never again did a ship make sail out of harbor unless she was ready for sea and war. This very spring of 1811, the arrogant captain of the British frigate *Guerrière* had over-

19

hauled the American brig *Spitfire* just outside New York, stopped the smaller vessel, boarded, and impressed an American passenger on the ship into the British Navy.

Two weeks later Commodore John Rodgers, in command of the forty-four-gun frigate *President,* saw a sail bearing down on him at night. He hailed twice, and the response was a shot that struck the *President's* mainmast. Captain Rodgers unleashed a broadside, the other fired, and he fired again and again. After fifteen minutes the other ship surrendered. It turned out to be the British corvette *Little Belt,* whose captain was not used to answering hails at night, even in American waters. The *Little Belt* had lost nine men and twenty-three were wounded. This action further incensed the American naval men.

Commodore Rodgers was head of the Atlantic Coastal Squadron, which included the forty-four-gun frigate *United States,* the thirty-eight-gun frigate *Congress,* the little eighteen-gun brig *Argus,* and now the *Essex.*

For the *Essex* the first day at sea passed quickly as the new men got down to the serious business of training. The next day began at dawn, when the ship's drums rolled and the night sentries fired off their loaded muskets. The bugler blew reveille, and the boatswain and his mates moved about the berth deck piping shrilly and shouting, "Ahoy, all hands, up hammocks, Ahoy," until the last of the men had moved sleepily from his hammock and instinctively had rolled it up and lashed it. The hammocks were stowed where they might be used as life preservers in case of need. The major work early in the morning was to holystone the decks and scour every working part of the ship that needed readying for another day. At eight bells the men were piped to breakfast, and the midshipmen were aroused by the midshipman of the watch. Hammock boys from the crew lashed the midshipmen's hammocks and stowed them. The midshipmen ate their breakfast at their own table, then went on deck on the larboard side of the quarterdeck for a brief promenade while their quarters were being holystoned and cleaned. At nine o'clock the drums rolled, the ensign was run up to stay all day long, and the guard was changed.

The midshipmen reported to the chaplain in the forward cabin for school. They studied whatever the chaplain or the captain might require, but navigation above all. The lessons went on for two hours. At 11:30, weather permitting, the midshipmen went to the spar deck to "shoot the sun" with their sextants. Then, each day, they worked out the ship's run for the past twenty-four hours, and the noon position as of that day. Meanwhile, the crewmen went about their various duties; mending sails, mending rigging, painting, cleaning, polishing guns, and attending to the thousand-and-one details that needed attention aboard the ship.

At noon the sweepers were piped, the decks were swept, and the grog issued each man was prepared (a gill of whiskey and a gill of water) under the supervision of a midshipman. A midshipman informed the captain that it was noon, the bell was struck, the boatswain and his mates piped the men to dinner, and the midshipmen went down to the gun room to eat their midday meal. This dinner might be rice with salt beef soaked in brine, or hardtack, bean soup, and scouse (a combination of hardtack and salt pork mixed with water and baked).

At one o'clock the deck work resumed and continued until four, when the hands were piped to dinner. Then began the part of the day that the seamen lived for, the time for relaxing, spinning yarns, singing, dancing, and playing musical instruments. The midshipmen could read or stroll on their side of the quarterdeck, or even seek instruction from officers or the men in special arts of seamanship. At sunset the drums rolled, the guard hauled down the colors and raised the night pendant, marines in undress uniform replaced those in full uniform, taking over the guns, and the band struck up.

Half an hour after sunset, as the last strains of the band music reverberated across the deck, the boatswain and his mates piped their flutes shrilly and the cry was passed: "All hands, stand by your hammocks, ahoy." At eight o'clock the drums beat again—a long roll. Then the bell was struck, once, and the bugles blew their night call; another roll of the drums. The sentries discharged the day muskets and were given freshly loaded ones. The ship began to settle down. Lights were gradually extinguished, and just before climbing into his hammock one midshipman went to the wardroom to be sure that all fires were out in the officers' quarters. At ten o'clock the ship was snugged down for the night. The only men on deck were the seamen of the watch, quartermasters, and the marine guards. The only sounds to be heard were those of the night sea: the rushing of the water under the bow, the creaks of the rigging, the whispers of the sails in the wind, and the measured tread of officers and midshipmen of the watch. Each half hour came the striking of the ship's bell and the cries of the sentries, bound to report from their posts in answer: "All's well; all's well."

When the *Essex* joined the squadron, life changed. The squadron had one mission: to prepare to defend American shores against any and all enemies. And off that shore lurked ships of a potential enemy. There was no time to be lost in training, and Commodore Rodgers ordered intensive gunnery practice, without regard for the cost of shot and shell.

Mr. Midshipman Farragut was assigned to a division, along with two other midshipmen, that would help serve the ship's guns when in action. There were six divisions on the ship, and the midshipmen soon grew to know all of them: one on the quarterdeck, one on the forecastle, three on the gun deck and one on the berth deck. All were commanded by lieutenants and the purser, if there were enough lieutenants to go around; and if there were not, the senior midshipman might find himself in command of a gun division. He might find himself in command, also, during a battle, if his lieutenant was killed or injured. The midshipmen, cadets in all else, were put to deadly serious work in the handling of the guns.

There was no simple formula for the number of guns or men in a division; it depended on the captain. Captains of frigates were given much latitude in the rigging and gunning of their ships (and almost uniformly they overgunned them at the expense of the sailing qualities promised by the fine lines of the designers).

Since the *Essex* carried forty-six guns, a division had seven or eight guns to manage, with ten or twelve men to handle each gun, but not all guns were served at once, only the guns on one side. The crew of Mr. Midshipman Farragut's division numbered seventy or eighty men. The normal gun-crew consisted of a captain, two spongers and rammers, two loaders, two train and tackle men, two crow and handspike men, and a powder boy.

After breakfast came the call to general quarters, the distinctive bugle call and the rattle of the drums, which persisted as long as the guns were manned. To the sound of bugle and drum Midshipman Farragut seized a cutlass from the rack on a bulkhead and ran as fast as his young legs would carry him to his station. The gun crews were assembling, the ports were opening, and the gun captains were giving orders in the long drawling voices they used to be sure that every syllable was understood over the enormous noise that descended on the deck of the ship.

The guns were loaded with powder and ball and primed with powder by the loaders, assisted by the rammers. The muzzles were run out by the tackle men, so that the black snouts stuck menacingly well out past the hinged wooden ports hooked up above. They were pointed by the crow and handspike men, who used quoins and iron wedges to place and hold the barrels in the proper elevation. As the crews labored, the marines assembled on the spar deck and in the tops of the masts, ready to begin their sharpshooting, instructed to aim at officers. The powder boys ran back and forth from magazine to gun station, carrying their leather buckets with tight lids to prevent spillage, fire, and explosion. The guns were aimed, singly or in salvo. Quickly the guns were run in, the spongers cleaned out the burned black powder, and the loading process began again.

The call to general quarters came twice each day (morning and evening) and Midshipman Farragut dropped whatever he was doing to rush to his station, cutlass waving. When the drum stopped beating, the alert was ended. Midshipman Farragut then called the roll of his gun crew. At the end of a fight the captain of the ship must know how many men he had left to man the guns the next time. The list was reported to the division lieutenant and then to the first lieutenant and then to the captain. When the lists were in the captain's hands he ordered the first lieutenant to "beat the retreat." The drums began to roll again, and the men returned to whatever they were doing before the call to quarters.

The *Essex* was back in port at Norfolk early in November, taking on supplies. After that they headed for Chester on the Delaware River, where Porter had his home. Then orders came to join the squadron at Newport, and they sailed just before Christmas.

The ship arrived at Newport on Christmas eve and anchored off the Bluffs. The weather was foul for entering the harbor that night. At about four o'clock the next morning the weather grew worse—high winds, sleet, and snow. At first the *Essex* dropped only a single bower, but was soon forced to drop the other, and within two hours had dropped starboard and port sheet anchors had been dropped astern in an attempt to hold the bottom. Captain Porter's efforts were of no use: the wind blew and blew, and the *Essex* dragged her four anchors until she was aground just off the Bluffs. Normally in such a blow the captain would have ordered the "hamper down," and the topmasts would have been dropped to the deck, the yards lowered and braced on the perpendicular to provide the least possible resistance to the wind, minimizing the danger of dismasting or capsizing. But in this wintry storm the spars were glued to the masts with ice and could not be sent down, no matter how many frozen-fingered seamen and middies were sent aloft to undertake the task.

The main topgallant mast was the first to give way. It broke loose with a splintering crash, sending a shower of ice down on the deck. Next the mizzen-topgallant mast came down, and the rigging of the two masts fouled the lower yards. The masts blew over the side and hung in the water.

The *Essex* was grounded on a sandbank, luckily as it turned out, for on her lee lay the forbidding Bluffs, a mass of sharp barnacled rocks that roared their anger in the smashing surf. The ship would not survive five minutes if blown across the bank onto those spiky mountain shards. If the bank gave way, or the ship slid across, there was very little hope for the life of any man, but what hope existed depended on the swift work of captain and crew. They might just survive if they could dismast the ship and let the hulk ride up and down with that much less resistance against the wind, that much less weight atop to drive her sideways in the wind.

The men had been on deck at quarters for hours. Now the seamen were ordered to stand by the rigging and the masts with axes. They could not stay on deck: the winds and snow were too fierce, the ice cut at their hands, the snow upended them, and the slippery decks threatened to catapult them over the side. The men huddled in the galley, ready to rush at the moment of an order, each man knowing what he must do to save himself and his comrades. It was Captain Porter and Lieutenant Downes who took turns on lookout, watching the ship and the shore. No man could stand it long. The snow beat against the eyelashes and froze them tight.

The ship lay for hours on the bank. Sometimes the *Essex* seemed to be on beam ends, but the bank held, and around midday the storm began to abate. The heeling grew less, and when the waves died down, the captain was able to send out boats and kedge his ship away from the cliffs. In the calmer air after the crisis, there was time for the men to look about them. They discovered how fierce the storm had been: one of the seamen was found frozen to death in his hammock.

Captain Porter put his ship into Newport harbor, and there was no question about his missing spars and rigging or the requisitions he made from the navy yard. That same day the U.S. Navy brig *Nautilus* limped into harbor, having been caught in the open sea by the storm, and having weathered it only by sending a dozen heavy guns over the side.

In the three months that followed, the *Essex* remained stationed at Newport with the squadron, cruising out for training, but still allowing time for the midshipmen to attend school ashore. Farragut was lucky: his captain cared enough to be sure that the midshipmen had more than a nautical education; such niceties were not part of the naval regulations and depended entirely on the goodwill of the captain.

Commodore Rodgers soon declared the *Essex* the smartest ship in the squadron, the best sailed and the best at gunnery. The honor did not come by accident. At sea or ashore, Captain Porter kept his men alert. When the men could manage to be ready for action in ten minutes, Captain Porter was pleased. He constantly tested and trained the men with gun drills, fire drills, and boat drills, until the response to emergency became second nature to them.

In the spring of 1812, the American nation was seized by war fever. The men in Congress who wanted war were contemptuously dubbed "war hawks" because of their fulminations against Great Britain. In the Twelfth Congress, which was organizing in Washington as the *Essex* prepared to join the squadron, the war hawks became important factors. Henry Clay, one of the most vocal of the hawks, was elected Speaker of the House. Langdon Cheves, of South Carolina, another war hawk, was chairman of the House Navy Committee. The Foreign Affairs Committee was controlled by John C. Calhoun, still another hawk. So the Americans moved toward war.

War was the business of the officers and men of the *Essex*, and they were preparing for it all spring. On March 28, the Atlantic Coastal Squadron put to sea, and again there were maneuvers and gunnery practice. On June 18, when Congress declared war on Great Britain, the squadron was lying in New York Harbor. The news of war took two days to reach New York, and then most of the ships under Commodore Rodgers combined with another group under Commodore Stephen Decatur to go out and search for the British. *Essex* was not in the group. A survey had shown that the ship needed a new foremast before it was fit for sea, the winter storm had cut deeper than anyone had thought and Captain Porter had believed his ship ready for action. It was two weeks before the old mast had been cut out and the new one stepped.

Captain Porter began readying his crew for swift, bloody action. He called the men together and read the war declaration message to them. He asked if there was any British subject in the crew who wished a discharge rather than fight against his countrymen, and only one man claimed a discharge. (He was found to be an imposter, was tarred and feathered by his own messmates, and then put ashore in New York City.) On July 3, the *Essex* got under way. Mr. Midshipman Farragut, just two days short of his eleventh birthday, was going off to war.

4. TO VALPARAISO

Outside the Narrows, Captain Porter ordered the course set south and east for Bermuda. The weather was fine and the sea tranquil. Just over a week after leaving port the *Essex* encountered the British, a convoy of seven troop transports sailing from Barbados to aid in the defense of Quebec. In short order the *Essex* swooped down on the rearmost transport, the *Samuel and Sarah*. Like a herdsman, Captain Porter cut out this transport in the dark of night, and at two o'clock in the morning she was boarded and captured—ship, crew, and 197 British soldiers.

The British officers taunted Captain Porter, indicating that he was afraid to meet the British frigate that was protecting the convoy, the thirty-two-gun *Minerva*. Porter did not lose his equanimity; he was ready enough for a fight. The British did not know their "Preble's boys," and they had no idea of the depth of the enmity of a man who had twice been shanghaied aboard British men-of-war. Porter was eager to engage the *Minerva* and called the men to general quarters early on the second morning. He bore down on the convoy and hove to within gunshot. Porter and his men expected the *Minerva* to respond to the challenge, but the *Minerva* did not. The captain of the *Minerva* rushed the ship back through the convoy. The American crew, from First Lieutenant Downes down to the lowest hammock boy, was spoiling for a fight. A deputation from the lower deck came to Captain Porter, asking that he attack the convoy in broad daylight. Porter said it would be foolish and refused. To attack, even if he won, would have been to take on a tremendous and dangerous job of shepherding. He was looking for a fight, not for prisoners.

Within a matter of hours the men of the *Essex* had removed all the arms aboard the British brig and forced the officers and men to declare that they would not fight against the United States. Having elicited this parole, Porter turned the enemy loose, with the promise that they would pay a ransom rather than be captured or sunk. Even if the British did not expect to honor the ransom during the days of war, it would become a matter for settlement in the claims made at the end of the war.

The freeing of the *Samuel and Sarah* also freed Captain Porter to speed along on his course of depredation. Two days after what the crew would recall as the day of cowardice of the *Minerva*, the *Essex* captured the British brig *Lamprey*, laden with a far more usable cargo. The *Lamprey* was carrying rum from Jamaica to Halifax. Captain Porter put a prize crew aboard and sent the brig to Baltimore. Then he turned north toward Newfoundland.

The hunting began again on July 26. In the next two weeks the *Essex* captured six British ships. First came the *Leander*, with cargo so valuable that they were ordered to put in at Cape Ann; then the *Hero*, which had nothing of value and was burned, the prisoners taken aboard the *Essex*; the *Nancy*, which was ransomed for $14,000, and the bond of the captain taken; the *Brothers*, which was made a prisoner-ship and sent to the United States carrying the prisoners from the *Hero*; the *King George*, ordered to Boston port; and the *Mary*, burned.

There was one narrow escape. One day when the *Essex* was flying British colors on the banks off Newfoundland, up came a British ship of the line *Antelope*, which usually carried fifty guns but could conceivably mount as many as seventy. They passed so close that the men of the *Essex* could see the wide ports of the British ship's third gun deck. The frigate hove to, and the *Antelope* sailed on by, quite unaware of the identity of the American ship. It was common enough practice and not in the slightest degree dishonorable for the American ship to sport British colors as a ruse to conceal herself from larger enemies and draw smaller ones within her grasp. The procedure was to hoist the British flag in the morning when expecting to come upon British prizes, to keep the Union Jack up all day, so that any ship on the horizon whose captain had a powerful glass would be persuaded that this was a British frigate. This was practical because Britain firmly dominated the Atlantic all along the American shore. Then, bearing down on a small enemy, *Essex* would strike the enemy colors and triumphantly hoist the Stars and Stripes as she came within range, just before she opened fire. Or, coming upon a behemoth like the *Antelope,* she would stop discreetly, apparently paying homage to the bigger ship, then scurry on about her business, making it a point to go in a direction quite opposite.

On the morning of August 13, *Essex* was sailing along like a lazy warrior who is satiated with battle and is soaking up the sun. A good breeze was blowing and she was in no hurry, so the top sails were reefed and the topgallant masts were housed. The set sails were trimmed loosely, for *Essex* was going no place in particular, but slipping along the coast, waiting for what might come to her. With her upper and lower gunports closed, the deck rail sitting atop a solid bulwark, and the white stripe that crossed them apparently unbroken along the length of the ship, she looked much like a ship-rigged merchantman, which was precisely Captain Porter's intention.

One of the disadvantages of the ransoming system was that the enemy was sure to secure valuable intelligence in time; with the news circulating about Canadian ports after arrival of the *Samuel and Sarah* and the *Nancy,* British merchantmen would be aware of black-hulled, three-masted ships off the American coast and would give them a wide berth. Captain Porter was using high strategy this day.

Suddenly the lookout in the maintop started. "Ship ahoy," he shouted to the quarterdeck.

The crew rushed to the forecastle peak and some men climbed to the ratlines for a look. Off to windward on the horizon was a black speck scarcely larger than a fly. She was heading toward them, off the starboard quarter.

Captain Porter unveiled more of his strategy when he was certain the ship was actually coming in their direction. He ordered sea anchors unshipped astern to slow the frigate, and when the men were rigging them he ordered topmen aloft to raise the topgallant masts, masthead the yards, shake out the reefs and make all available sail, to simulate a desperate merchantman trying to escape a potential enemy.

The black speck on the horizon grew until it became a ship coming down on them with all speed. Satisfied, Captain Porter ordered the crew to general quarters, and the *Essex* was cleared for action, except that all the gunports remained closed and the tampions were left in place, plugging the guns.

As the other ship closed, Captain Porter could see that she was a British man-of-war, a twenty-gun sloop. She was still deceived. The British ship fired one long gun, the shot crossing the bow of the *Essex* and skipping along the water. Still playing the innocent merchantman, Captain Porter ordered the Union Jack hauled down and the Stars and Stripes run up. As the Cross of St. George lowered, the British realized what was happening, gave three rousing cheers, and fired a broadside of grape and canister, aiming to sweep the decks of the American ship and unman her. But coming up on the *Essex* port quarter as she was, the British sloop's broadside struck the solid bulwarks without doing any substantial damage. Captain Porter ordered the helmsmen to put the helm of *Essex* up into the wind, stabilizing her. The gunports were knocked out, and her port broadside fired, tampions and all. The shots rang out, smoke flared to obscure the water between the ships for a moment, and the acrid smell of burned powder hung heavy in the air. The British sloop moved ahead on her line, the distance broadening between the ships, but *Essex* was turning, heading to come about and bring her starboard broadside to bear. The British captain, tricked, saw that Captain Porter was aiming to open fire again. Already three of the British crew were wounded. Wounds or death would not have stopped the captain from fighting, but he was totally

31

outgunned as well as outmaneuvered. If there had been any lingering doubt, the British first lieutenant quickly put it to rights: he reported to his captain that the broadside had holed the hull below the waterline so severely that the ship was taking water and might founder unless action was taken to stop the leak. The captain surrendered. The British sloop ran down her flag as Captain Porter prepared to come alongside once more, the British captain striking his colors eight minutes after firing his first shot.

The ship was the British sloop of war *Alert*. Quickly Captain Porter sent Fourth Lieutenant William Finch aboard the sloop to take possession. Finch found seven feet of water in the hold. In order to save the prize he put the enemy to work immediately. The leak was stopped up with canvas and hammocks, and then shored with wooden battens. The officers were taken aboard the *Essex*, and the *Alert* was taken in tow.

With the coming of the British captain, his officers, and the crew of his gig to the *Essex*, the American frigate's facilities were more than a little strained. Captain Porter was already entertaining the captain of the *Mary*; the officers of that sunken merchantman were distributed in the wardroom and gun room, and the crew was scattered around the berth deck and the gun deck, and most were quartered in the hold that gave onto the spar deck. Under such conditions it was quite impossible to maintain the usual watchfulness, although watchfulness was needed more than ever.

On this night, after all the excitement, Midshipman Farragut, in his hammock in the gun room, awoke suddenly from a deep sleep to see a vague shape standing beside him. In the faint light he made out the figure and features of the coxswain of the captain's gig of the *Alert*, free, on the prowl, and carrying a pistol in his hand. The coxswain looked over the sleeping midshipmen, watching for any signs of wakefulness, which would have been greeted with a hand to the throat or a dirk thrust to the heart. The others snored away, and eleven-year-old Midshipman Farragut held his breath and feigned sleep to save his life.

For what seemed to be an hour the enemy coxswain stood

32

beside his hammock, surveying the quiet scene. Then, satisfied, he moved away to perpetrate what mischief he might make with a sleeping enemy ship under foot. His object was to instigate an uprising. He headed toward the crew's quarters.

When the footfalls ceased and Midshipman Farragut was certain that the man was gone, he slipped from his hammock, quietly, trying not to even rustle the canvas. He stole silently in bare feet along the dark passageways, aft to the captain's cabin. At the door he paused, then screwing up his courage, he crept in and aroused Captain Porter.

The captain awoke and listened to Farragut's whispered report. He leaped from his cot and dashed toward the berth deck.

"Fire, fire," he cried as he ran.

Aboard the *Essex* the cry of "fire" was as important as that of "quarters." For a year Captain Porter and First Lieutenant Downes had been bludgeoning the fear of fire into the heads of the members of the crew. The fire alarm could come at any time of day or night, and when it came each man, automatically grabbing blanket and cutlass rushed to his assigned position—blanket to smother embers, and cutlass to chop away burning debris. But blanket and cutlass could perform another task this night—blanket to confound the enemy as it was thrown in his face, and cutlass to mow him down if he so much as moved a muscle.

The Americans were alert. They rushed to their stations and awaited the orders of their officers. The British prisoners did not know what they should do. The coxswain of the *Alert* had gone to the spar deck and down the hatch to rouse and perhaps even to arm his countrymen. Quickly the captain sent marines and armed sailors to the main hatch to secure the prisoners, and the prisoner mutiny was quelled before it ever really began. The next day Captain Porter eliminated the danger: he disarmed the *Alert*, insisted on the paroles of her officers and men, and put all the British on board the *Essex* onto *Alert*, accompanied by Lieutenant Stephen Decatur McKnight, the fifth lieutenant. McKnight carried a letter from Captain Porter to Admiral Sir J. Y. Duckworth, the British commander in Canadian waters, explaining the engagement—which would save the career of *Alert's* Captain L. P. Laugharne. Porter could spare neither time nor men to bring the *Alert* to an American port, and his gentlemanly gesture followed the highest code of the sea.

Bidding Lieutenant McKnight Godspeed on his delicate mission, Captain Porter turned the head of *Essex* out to sea and continued the search for British enemies. No more were seen. The word of Porter's depradations had gotten about. Early in September he headed for the squadron's home port, New York.

The War of 1812 was soon to become a cat-and-mouse game, as illustrated by Captain Porter's next experience. On the afternoon of September 4, the lookout sighted ships to leeward, and for a time it appeared that they were American and British ships engaged in battle. But Captain Porter had a hunch that all was not as it seemed and, armed with his glass, he climbed the rigging to examine the battle in progress. After several minutes of close watch, he decided he was witnessing a sham battle conducted by a three-ship English squadron, and he deduced that the purpose was to persuade him to stand in and join—so the British ships could close and destroy him. He clapped on all available sail and headed away from the "battle." The validity of his guess was proved immediately: the two frigates and a brig broke off the "engagement" and stood after him, as fast as they could make sail.

The overweening eagerness of American captains of 1812 for battle very nearly cost Captain Porter his ship. The ship, built by Enos Briggs at Salem to the plans drawn by designer William Hacket had been the fastest American frigate afloat, but by the time the war began her captains had made so many changes in the loading, the lines of the ship, and the sail structure that the ship was overweighted and sailing handiness was half spoiled. On this September 4, as the afternoon wore on, Captain Porter became aware of that mournful fact; the British frigate *Acosta* was slowly but steadily overhauling him. Had the *Acosta* been alone, Captain Porter would have been eager to engage, but with the knowledge that not far behind came another frigate of equal size and that as soon as he stopped to fight one, he must turn about to fight two, Captain Porter ran.

As the day wore on into evening, the weather turned foul and foggy, much to Porter's delight, and he displayed the plan he had been considering ever since he sighted one bank of low-lying clouds. He called all hands on deck and explained the program. They would run on in the fog and take in sail so the enemy ship could overhaul them. When she came in sight—and every man jack was to watch out every moment for her—he would tack the ship and smash into the side of the British frigate. They would board and take her. It must be done quietly and quickly for the second British warship could not be far behind, and the third ship was undoubtedly in the train. They would douse all the lights of both ships, and heave to, while their pursuers ran past them in the night.

The details were worked out. The password was announced, and the men were given recognition badges so that no American would kill his fellow by mistake in the bloody skirmish to come. An anchor was hoisted to the main yardarm, to be dropped on the enemy deck and cinched up by its cable to hold the ships together. Grapnels were made ready, to toss into the enemy's hammock nets and bulwarks. The guns were double-shotted, to make a fast hard fight of it if guns became necessary. The desperate plan was put in effect with an order to the helmsmen. Captain Porter headed in the direction in which he had last seen the enemy.

But it came to naught, for in the fog the *Acosta* tacked away and disappeared. When the red-eyed Americans stood on their decks in the bright light of a clear dawn, no sail was in sight.

So far off course for New York had they been sent by the need to fly before a superior enemy that there was no use heading back, even had Captain Porter assumed the British were gone from New York harbor's outskirts. The *Essex* sailed on southwestward and two days later arrived in Delaware Bay.

Captain Porter and Midshipman Farragut were not overly saddened by this change of plan, because they were within easy sailing distance of home, Captain Porter's house Green Bank.

While Porter and Farragut were reunited with the Porter family, the *Essex* took on stores and refitted for a long sea voyage. She had been at sea for ten straight weeks on the last trip and had eaten up many supplies.

While the *Essex* and her crew were waiting for those supplies, Captain Porter suddenly rejoined the ship, bringing along his young midshipman ward, and set out for sea, seeking battle. The reason was a challenge issued to him in the pages of the Philadelphia *Democratic Press*. Sir James Yeo, captain of the British Frigate *Southampton*, had captured an American brig and sent her in to Philadelphia bearing an insulting message: Sir James, in the infuriating manner of the British aristocracy, presented his compliments to Captain Porter and offered to engage in ship-to-ship duel "anywhere between the Capes Delaware and Havannah, where he would have the pleasure to break his own sword over his damned head, and put him down forward in irons."

Captain Porter accepted the challenge in the same publication, saying he would come out under the flag "free trade and sailors' rights" and that if he struck this flag, Sir James might do as he threatened.

The *Essex* went to sea, primed for battle, and cruised in the waters of the Atlantic looking for a fight, but Sir James had gone elsewhere about his king's business and no British warships were to be found. Soon the *Essex* sailed back to Chester to pick up supplies and orders.

The orders came from Commodore William Bainbridge, with whom Porter had served and with whom he had been imprisoned in Tripoli. Porter was to bring the *Essex* to rendezvous with Bainbridge, in the *Constitution*, and go a-raiding British shipping. The squadron would sail to the Cape Verde Islands in the Atlantic and catch British shipping headed for Africa. They would cross back to the Brazilian coast and work the South American shipping lanes, then either move back to

St. Helena or go out into the Pacific and destroy the British whaling industry. The idea was not to engage the British in duels, but to do as much damage to commerce as possible. Therein lay the American naval strategy, a very sensible one, given the American inferiority in naval strength and the British preoccupation with the wars against Napoleon.

The *Essex* sailed at the end of October. Only Porter knew how long and how dangerous the cruise might be. Since there was no certainty that they would find the squadron, they had orders to move from rendezvous point to another until a certain date, when they would be free to proceed on their own.

The first rendezvous was at the Cape Verdes. They crossed the horse latitudes and entered the area of the northeast trade winds. They crossed the equator, and Farragut was initiated into the Noble Order of Neptune by being daubed with soap and foul-smelling unguent, the stuff then shaved off with wooden razor while he was sitting astraddle a spar over a tub of water. He was finally ducked and declared baptized—a shellback, or old salt.

He also had a taste of discipline on this voyage out. When Captain Porter caught his favorite midshipman chewing tobacco, he simply put his hand over the telltale mouth with its brown-streaked corners and ordered the young man to swallow. Farragut swallowed. Thereafter no form of tobacco ever interested him.

The *Essex* had heavy going across the Atlantic in the autumn storms, but twenty-nine days off the Delaware Capes she made her landfall, only to find that the squadron was not there. Porter went on to the second rendezvous, south-southwest to the island of Fernando de Noronha. On this voyage the ship was lucky enough to capture a British packet bearing $55,000 in gold and silver, and Lieutenant Finch was put aboard her with a midshipman and thirteen men as prize crew to sail her home. The *Essex* sailed on and reached the island, only to find that once again she had missed the squadron. So it was on to other adventures, capturing ships of Portugal, England's ally, and a British schooner, but never finding the squadron. On December 20, the ship arrived at St. Catharines Island, five hundred miles south of Rio de Janeiro on the Brazilian coast. Again they had missed the squadron.

Having missed Bainbridge so many times, Captain Porter faced serious problems. In January he summed up: he was short of supplies and it was dangerous for him to enter South American ports, lest a British squadron blockade him. He decided to round Cape Horn and enter the Pacific Ocean. Supplies grew even shorter and the men were put on a half ration of bread. They opened casks of peas and beans and found the worms had gotten to the casks first. The *Essex* was driven by storms. There was one occasion Midshipman Farragut would not forget. He wrote about it later in his journal:

> In going around the Horn, we experienced dreadful weather. We lay off the Cape for twenty-one days. On the morning of the 3rd of March, 1813, we shipped a sea that stove in the ports from the bow to the quarter, carried the weather quarter boat on to the wheel, and took the lee boat off the davits; but by great exertion we saved her. Large quantities of water rushed down the hatchways, leading those below to imagine that the ship was sinking. This was the only instance in which I ever saw a regular good seaman paralyzed by fear at the dangers of the sea. Many of the marines and several of the sailors were seen on their knees at prayer; but in this, as in all other emergencies, most of our hardy tars were found ready and willing to do their duty. They were all called on deck and came promptly, led by a trusty old son of Neptune, William Kingsbury, the boatswain's mate. He was the same who performed the part of Neptune in "crossing the line." Long shall I remember the cheering sound of his stentorian voice, which resembled the roaring of a lion rather than that of a human being, when he told them "Damn their eyes, to put their best foot forward, as there was one side of her left yet." By the exertions of this little bank under the Captain,

First Lieutenant and officers of the watch, the ship was got before the wind, the quarter boat which had been carried away secured, and the decks cleared up.

They went into Valparaiso for provisions on April 29. They captured a big British whaler and learned of the existence of two others. They chased the other ships and found them becalmed. Captain Porter put out boats and sent them rowing across the flat water under command of Lieutenant Downes, with Midshipman Farragut in his boat. After two hours of rowing, at two o'clock in the afternoon the boats were about two miles away from the whalers when the ships hoisted English colors and began firing. The boats pulled up in two divisions and rowed on until they were only a few yards away from the whalers. Lieutenant Downes then hailed the whalers, asking them if they surrendered, and ordered the Stars and Stripes displayed on a pike from his boat. The whaler surrendered immediately. They soon learned why: most of the seamen were Americans pressed into service on the English ships.

That day Captain Porter converted one of the whalers to a cruiser with extra guns, put Lieutenant Downes in command as captain, and sent her to protect American whaling in the area and to injure the British as much as possible. The ships separated, Downes in the *Georgiana* going off to raid, and Captain Porter heading for the Galapagos Islands to replenish his stores.

There Porter decided it would be a good idea to hunt seals, although he had never done so before, and the Americans began a circus chase of seals around the rocks of Charles Island. They found a seal and tried to beat him unconscious with boat hooks, without success. A seaman grabbed the seal by the tail, and the seal dragged the whole crew into the water. Captain Porter fired his musket at the seal, and the seal disappeared, whether hurt no one ever discovered.

Back on the ship, the captain conferred with some of his British prisoners, the whalers, and they instructed him in the gentle arts of seal catching. The men armed themselves with clubs, long knives, and paddles. The idea was to reach

39

the seal, smack him on the nose with a club or paddle, which would stun him, and then stab him to death.

The boats pulled into the same small beach where they had tried sealing before. On their landing in the gig, a large sea lion raised his head, shook himself, and began waddling toward the water.

"Now boys," shouted Captain Porter, brandishing his long knife, "you have a chance to show your American skill. String yourselves along and each man stand ready to give him a blow on the nose. One blow will fix him."

The men got out of the boat and cautiously began approaching the seal, waving clubs, paddles, and long knives nervously before them.

Not Mr. Midshipman Farragut.

He did not like the size or the bristly appearance of that sea lion, and he ran back to the gig and sat down on a thwart to watch.

The captain looked scornfully at the young man. He and the men moved in, forming a semicircle to cut the sea lion off from the water. Slowly they closed the ring, stepping carefully in the sand, raising their clubs.

The sea lion tired of the game. With one great bellow he threw himself forward in a series of jerks, straight at the middle of the semicircle of men, and confronted by that immense bulk, the men gave way to right and left, letting the sea lion through. Captain Porter stood, stunned, gazing into the foam atop the water where the sea lion splashed as he went under.

Mr. Midshipman Farragut began to laugh. Captain Porter, seeing his youthful officer taking his ease in the boat, came over to accuse him of cowardice. Farragut was afraid to stand on the beach like the others, said the captain. Farragut admitted it cheerfully. He didn't know how to kill sea lions, he said, and he never tried to undertake something without believing he could finish the job. The captain had no answer.

Back they went to the ship for more instructions. They soon learned how to kill seals, and the meat supply of the *Essex* was assured for a long time to come. Captain Porter let the men go ashore in groups, and they hunted doves, tortoises, and prickly pears. Farragut managed to go off nearly every day, to hunt and feast ashore, tramp among the rocks and laze away the hours without thought of official duties. It was almost as if this eleven-year-old midshipman were a boy again.

On May 25, the idyll ended. They put to sea in search of more prizes, capturing a pair of whalers within the week. They cruised for three weeks and then moved into the Bay of Guayaquil to take on provisions. They were met on June 25 by Lieutenant Downes in the *Georgiana*, with three prizes in his wake. By this time the *Essex* had quite a fleet of whalers, eight in all, and Captain Porter was thinking about taking them into a South American port. As the Peruvians proved to be most unfriendly, he decided to go to Valparaiso.

One of these whalers, the *Atlantic*, was far superior to the others. She mounted ten 6-pounders and ten 18-pounder carronades and carried a crew of sixty men. She was renamed the *Essex Junior*, and Downes was ordered to take her to Valparaiso to escort four captured British whalers and the re-captured American whaler *Barclay*. Another whaler, the *Greenwich*, was converted to a storeship and mounted with twenty guns. Porter would take that ship and the whaler *Georgiana*, which he wanted to send back to America, and sail to Galapagos. There, or in the Marquesas Islands, the Americans would meet again. This plan was set forth in the last week of June and the first week of July. One might say, then, that Captain Porter gave Mr. Midshipman Farragut a truly memorable present for his twelfth birthday on July 5: young Farragut became captain of a ship.

It was certainly unusual for a twelve-year-old midshipman to be made a commander, but there was little choice. The *Essex* had sailed from America with a captain, five lieutenants, a lieutenant of marines, a sailing master, a dozen midshipmen, and a crew that, with its chaplains, surgeons, specialists and petty officers, made up a total of 319 men. There had been a few deaths from accident and illness, a few replacements of volunteers from among the Americans impressed into the whaling crews, but basically the above was Captain Porter's contingent. Soon a real shortage of manpower was felt. Lieutenant Finch and the senior midshipman had been sent off with the specie ship—the first major prize. Captain Gideon Randall, of the *Barclay* was an American, not an Englishman, and, of course, that is why Captain Porter felt fairly safe in putting the very youngest of his officers in charge of the prize crew. Midshipman Cowan, one of the older midshipmen, was first aboard, but he was sent to a more important post, his eight men left behind, and Mr. Farragut was put in charge as prize master of the *Barclay*.

Captain Gideon Randall, the grizzled old whaling master of the *Barclay*, was informed that he was to navigate the ship and his mate was to remain aboard to handle her, but Midshipman Farragut was to be responsible for the prize crew. When the captain learned that his ship was now to be sent to Valparaiso for inclusion among the other prizes, he was as angry as a sea lion and made noises that were very similar. The instructions were given. Lieutenant Downes dipped his ensign and led the little fleet of whalers out of the Bay—and Captain Randall rebelled against Mr. Midshipman Farragut's authority. He was taking over his ship, he said, and they were not following any damned fleet into Valparaiso or anywhere else—they were going back awhaling.

"You'll find yourself off New Zealand in the morning," he said to Mr. Midshipman Farragut, who was tramping his quarterdeck, such as it might be.

Mr. Midshipman Farragut looked at the fleet, which was fast moving out through the mouth of the bay. His new ship was anchored. He told the captain that he wanted the ship to follow the fleet.

Captain Randall snarled and did nothing. He would take no further orders from Mr. Midshipman Farragut, he said.

The twelve-year-old midshipman was not at all sure of himself, but he mustered his courage and told the captain he wanted the main topsail filled away in order that they might close up with the *Essex Junior*.

The captain flew into a rage. He shouted that he would "shoot any man that touched a rope" without his orders, that he was going his own way, and that he was not going to trust himself to the orders of "a damned nutshell." Having delivered himself of these sentiments, the old captain stumped below to find his pistols.

Mr. Midshipman Farragut called the navy boatswain's mate who had been assigned to handle the crew and told him the problem. He wanted the main topsail filled immediately, he said.

"Aye, aye, sir," responded the boatswain's mate, shrilled on his whistle, and barked out the orders to the men of the *Essex,* who sprang for the ratlines without ado.

With all in motion, Mr. Midshipman Farragut gained the needed courage, and he began striding back and forth issuing the orders necessary to get a ship under sail, as he had seen First Lieutenant Downes do a hundred times aboard the *Essex.* A man was sent below to inform the captain that he was not to come on deck with those pistols unless he wished to be thrown overboard—and when the men of the prize crew, and even of the crew of the *Barclay,* heard those words they smiled and nudged each other. There were a dozen among them who would have been happy to do "the old man" down.

The incipient revolution was ended (one cannot call a captain's rebellion aboard his own ship a mutiny), and the *Barclay* gathered way. Mr. Midshipman Farragut crowded all possible sail on her, and it was not too long before he drew up on the *Essex Junior* and took his place in the convoy. When they anchored for the night, Mr. Midshipman Farragut took Captain Randall in the ship's boat and ordered the men to pull for the flagship. Aboard the quarterdeck he told the story of the attempted overthrow of his authority, and Lieutenant Downes listened carefully.

The old captain harrumphed, laughed hollowly, and tried to convince Lieutenant Downes that it had all been just a joke on the lad, that he had only been trying to frighten him. Lieutenant Downes looked with calm disfavor on a civilian captain who tried to frighten an officer of the United States Navy as he was carrying out the orders of the President, and viewed in that light, the "joke" seemed most unfunny.

Mr. Midshipman Farragut said that in any event Captain Randall had not succeeded in frightening him (which was no more than half-truth) and offered to return to the *Barclay* and proceed to Valparaiso. There was very little chance that anything else would happen because the situation remained the same; Downes, like Porter, was strained to the limit for competent officers. Back to the *Barclay* went the ship's boat, with Captain Randall and Captain Farragut sitting thwart and thwart, and the ears of the former ringing with the understanding put there in terms none too gentle by Lieutenant Downes: Captain Farragut was in command, and Captain Randall was simply the advisor in matters of navigation of the whaler, if and when the ship became separated from the convoy, and not otherwise.

The matter was settled and without further incident the convoy reached Valparaiso.

5. THE END OF THE *ESSEX*

All this while, Captain Porter was wondering what had become of the squadron. Had he known, he would have been cursing his own bad luck to be out of the mainstream of the war, for the *Constitution* and the *Hornet,* the other two ships of his squadron, had not arrived simply because they had been up to their bulwarks in action.

The American naval plan of 1812 called for the small capital force of frigates to be divided into three squadrons and sent about the world raiding British commerce. Strategically, the high-command plan was sound, but it did not take into consideration the high spirits of men who had been trained to consider acts of valor commonplace. Commerce raiding is a difficult business at best, for the raider operates as a corsair. It is inherent in a captain's instructions that he will slink about, avoiding open combat with superiors, and it is even indicated that he ought to avoid his equals in the higher interests of the nation. But few of the American frigate captains were able or willing to avoid a fight; to the contrary, the high spirits that David Porter was inculcating into David Farragut predominated among these captains.

Having established the long list of rendezvous points for the squadron, Commodore Bainbridge, in the *Constitution,* and Captain James Lawrence, in the eighteen-gun sloop *Hornet,* sailed for the rendezvous in the Cape Verde Islands on October 26, as planned. But thereafter nothing went as planned—such were the fortunes of war. The ships sailed together until December 13, when they arrived off San Salvador, where Captain Lawrence challenged the eighteen-gun

British ship *Bonne Citoyen*. The captain of the British vessel refused to fight (because he was carrying home 500,000 pounds in gold and silver), and the *Hornet* stayed outside port to blockade her while the *Constitution* went on. On December 29, the *Constitution* encountered and defeated the British frigate *Java*, which was so badly wrecked that it was burned, while *Old Ironsides* herself was sorely hurt and put home for repairs. Meanwhile, the *Hornet* had blockaded the *Bonne Citoyen* until January 24, when the seventy-four-gun ship of the line *Montagu* came along to chase the little American ship into port, and then sailed away from the area. On February 24, the *Hornet* engaged and sank the British brig *Peacock*, taking so many British prisoners and rescuing so many Americans that her normal complement of 135 men suddenly jumped to 277, and Captain Lawrence put back for home.

Thus Captain Porter and the *Essex* were left alone, and they would never meet the others because the squadron was officially dissolved. The *Constitution* and the *Hornet* were in port for refits and would come out later under new captains.

Leaving the Peruvian coast, Captain Porter sailed back to Charles Island in the Galapagos to wait for his lieutenant and the various prize masters. He was not idle, capturing a number of British vessels and dispatching them home to neutral ports as prizes, or converting them to American warships. Prize Master Farragut delivered his vessel to the authorities at Valparaiso and gladly left the company of the grizzled old pistol-packing Captain Randall to join Lieutenant Downes on the *Essex Junior* and once again become a lowly midshipman. On September 30, the *Essex Junior* rendezvoused with *Essex*, at Port Rendezvous on Albermarle Island, guided by a series of messages left in bottles by Captain Porter in best piratical style. Downes and Porter conferred, and the captain decided to take his flotilla, numbering six ships, to the Marquesas as he had planned. He had done nearly all possible damage to British shipping on the Pacific coast of South America, completely disrupting the British whaling industry there with a loss to the enemy estimated at two-and-one-half million dollars.

For a few days the ships lay in Port Rendezvous. Midshipman Farragut went fishing in one of the ship's boats and caught a boatload full of golden rock cod. He joined a party ashore to stretch his legs, and they caught two large iguanas, which some of the men ate, but Farragut did not. Then they were off on October 2 for the lonely Marquesas, where Captain Porter intended to refit his ship, smoke out her rats, and give the men shore leave in an environment where it was unlikely they would desert, drift away, or be in danger.

He could hardly have been more wrong. The flotilla arrived at Comptroller's Bay on the island of Nukuhiva, and Captain Porter was almost immediately engaged in land warfare. The chief of the local and peaceful Taeeh tribe had been fighting the fiercer mountain men called the Happahs and Typees. Porter promised to protect the Taeehs, the Happahs continued to raid, and soon the marines and armed seamen of the flotillas went out under Lieutenant Downes to suppress the Happahs. The Happahs lost five men. All the tribes of Nukuhiva, except the Typees, came to make peace. Four-thousand natives assembled on the shore and built a village for the American sailors, including a house for Captain Porter and another for his officers. Naval discipline was relaxed, and the officers of the ships came ashore to take up life among the free and easy people of the island. Nearly every officer who wanted one contracted an informal liaison with a Marquesan girl, and life was as idyllic as it could be for a frigate sailor in time of war. They lived on breadfruit and coconuts, fresh pork and fowl, and the work was easy because there were so many men.

The *Essex* was stripped of shot and powder and provisions preparatory to fumigation; the first and most important task was to kill the rats. So numerous and ferocious had the rats become on this voyage into the southern seas that they were cutting through the water casks, even through the skin of the ship, and Captain Porter was fearful for the planking. The rats were big and tough, and if cornered they would not hesitate to attack a man. Dozens of pots of charcoal were brought aboard and placed in every nook and cranny of the ship, and she was thoroughly battened down to allow the smoke to permeate everywhere. The fires were lit. When the fires were out and the ship was opened up, she was clear of rats, except for the fifteen-hundred rat carcasses that the crew picked up and put over the side for the sharks.

Then the refit began. The ship was caulked and painted, the coppering was repaired on her bottom, and native divers were employed, with payment in hoops and tools of iron, to go down and scrape the barnacles from her bottom. The main topmast, rotted and dangerous, was replaced, and the powder and provisions were restored to a clean, clear ship that was ready for action.

During all this activity the younger midshipmen were sequestered, much to their disgust, by a shocked chaplain, who told Captain Porter that no matter how far he was willing to let the officers go with the natives and their libidinous ways, the young must not be corrupted. Midshipman Farragut and the other "youngsters" were kept aboard one of the prizes, where the chaplain instructed them daily in mathematics, English grammar, and the Holy Word, while their older companions disported themselves ashore. "Away from temptation" was how Farragut put it in his journal. But at least, when they were not busy, they were allowed during the daytime hours to go ashore and mingle with the native *boys*. They learned to throw spears and walk on stilts, but above all Midshipman Farragut learned to swim. The youths were indignant when Captain Porter refused to let them go up into the mountains and fight the natives, but they behaved themselves, and Farragut's behavior was so good that when a strange sail was sighted outside the harbor, he was allowed to accompany Lieutenant Downes to investigate in the *Essex Junior*. They sailed out, ready for battle, and discovered that the ship was an American East Indiaman. They sailed back together, and then Midshipman Farragut returned to the *Essex* to learn that he had missed out on a mutiny attempted by the prisoners of war, which was put down without loss of life.

Porter settled back into the routine. Sometimes he was on the *Essex*, sometimes he was on other ships, depending largely on matters of morals. One day four-hundred native women were taken aboard the *Essex*, and the chaplain insisted that the young midshipmen be taken off, although they knew full well what was going on there. For two days midshipmen Farragut, Ogden, and Feltus were sequestered on the chaplain's ship. When the women were removed from the *Essex*, the boys returned.

The Typees continued to be unfriendly, and Captain Porter launched a seaborne expedition against them. It was a disaster, not so much because it failed, but because Lieutenant Downes injured his leg on the expedition. The Typees were put down and forced to sue for peace by a land expedition that marched over the mountains. Farragut had no part in this violence; he was considered "too young" for it. On November 19, he participated in an historic (although long-forgotten) ceremony: Captain Porter raised the American flag over the native-built fort, a seventeen-gun salute was fired, and Porter took possession of Nukuhiva in the name of the United States of America, which made all the tribesmen "Mellekees," as they called themselves proudly.

After some time, the crew was given night liberty. The men became very fond of island life. When the time came it was not an easy task to break them away for the serious business of war. All men were ordered back to the ships. Several men who swam to the beach in violation of rules were put in irons, flogged at the gangway, and set to work with the prisoners. On December 9, the *Essex* was ready for sea. Three prizes were moored in the harbor under guns put ashore for the fort, and, much envied, Lieutenant Gamble, of the Marines, and Midshipman Feltus were to be left behind with twenty-one men to maintain possession of America's newest colony.

It was Sunday, and the men of the ships mingled with their friends on other ships, as was the custom. During the day, a number of sailors of the *Essex* visited the *Essex Junior,* and an *Essex* sailor named Robert White told the open-mouthed men of *Essex Junior* that the ships were about to sail away from the paradise they had been so lucky to find. There was much grumbling on the lower deck, and White began to talk.

He was a slippery sort, an Englishman, an enemy alien who had opted to join the Americans rather than live as a captive. Now he was playing the role of *agent provocateur*. The crew of the *Essex* would refuse to weigh anchor on the next day, he said knowingly, and if compelled to go to sea they would mutiny within three days and sail the ship back to Nukuhiva to live there forever.

The next morning Captain Porter called all hands to the port side of the quarterdeck, and Midshipman David Farragut responded with the others. Knowing his captain, his foster-father, Midshipman Farragut could see that he was in the grip of a strong emotion, that he was virtually shaking. Porter had a cutlass in his hand, a sign of something unusual and threatening. The captain placed the cutlass on the capstan. First he talked of the need for discipline aboard a man-of-war. Then he made a very strange remark: "All of you who are in favor of weighing the anchor when I give the order, pass over to the starboard side; you who are of a different determination, stay on the larboard side."

Every man walked to the starboard.

Captain Porter looked surprised. He called seaman Robert White to step forward.

"How is this? Did you not tell them on board the *Essex Junior* that the crew of this ship would refuse to weigh anchor?"

White trembled visibly, then replied, "No, sir."

"You lie, you scoundrel," shouted Captain Porter. Then he addressed his acting first lieutenant. "Where is the list of the men who visited the *Essex Junior* on Sunday?"

The list was found and the names read off. Captain Porter ordered the first man to step forward and put the question: "Did you not hear of this thing on board the *Essex Junior*?"

"Yes, sir."

The man stood back and another stood forward.

"Did you not hear of this thing on board the *Essex Junior*?"

"Yes, sir."

The third seaman came forward.

"Did you not hear . . ."

"Yes, sir."

Captain Porter motioned the man back, then turned to White.

"Run, you scoundrel, for your life!" he shouted.

White started, then he ran across the deck to the gangway and hurled himself over the side, while Captain Porter made no effort to chase him. The Englishman splashed in the water, began swimming, and was last seen clambering into one of the native canoes that circled about among the ships every day during the daylight hours.

Captain Porter turned back to the crew of the *Essex*. He praised their past bravery and good conduct. He condemned all villainous behavior and this particular villainy, and he warned that he would always act promptly and even harshly. He "would blow them all to hell before they should succeed in a conspiracy."

Without further comment the captain wheeled, ordered the men to man the capstan, and the fiddler, who made music for this work, to play "The Girl I Left Behind Me." The fiddle began to sing, the capstan creaked, the single bower on the bottom came up, the men and boys scrambled up the rigging, the topsails were loosed, and as young David Farragut marveled at the display of discipline he had just seen, the *Essex* began to move and slid out of the harbor, the men quite unmindful of the scores of native girls who lined the shore, waving and chanting. The idyll had ended. They had been brought up short, and now the officers and men knew there was work to be done.

Lieutenant Downes was still commander of the *Essex Junior*. Rendezvous points were arranged between the two ships, and off they went for the coast of Chile, arriving at Valparaiso on February 3.

Coming into harbor, the American frigate exchanged salutes with the Chilean shore battery. Captain Porter paid an official call on the Spanish governor, who returned the call the following day, and then began a round of entertainments. On the night of February 7, Midshipman Farragut and all the other officers dressed in their formal uniforms to be hosts at a gala ball aboard ship. There was punch and dancing to an orchestra, pretty Spanish girls in their long

51

silken ball gowns, tall proud headcombs and mantillas, and here and there were flickers of romance. In order that Lieutenant Downes and his officers might be present, the *Essex Junior* had been called in. It was her task to roam the entrance to the harbor, guarding against surprise attack by the British squadron believed to be nearby, but on this evening Captain Porter ordered Downes to anchor in the bay, at the edge where his ship commanded the sea entrance.

The gaiety continued until midnight, but then the last don and donna, the last señorita and duenna were piped over the side of the *Essex*, and Lieutenant Downes returned to his ship and put out to sea to return to guard duty.

Next morning came the chore of taking down the awnings on the quarterdeck, removing the bunting and the flags, and cleaning up the debris of the night before. The watch was in the process of doing just this, and the men off watch, half the crew, were ashore on leave. Suddenly *Essex Junior* signalled that two ships had come in sight. The *Essex* fired a gun and hoisted the signal "all boats and men to return" to bring the shore party back. The crew began to clear the ship for action, while Captain Porter took his gig to the *Essex Junior* and sailed out to reconnoiter.

At seven-thirty that morning Porter was back aboard the *Essex*, whose decks were cleared, with every man at his station, and every man, but one, was sober—and even he was not so drunk that he could not go to his post.

Around eight o'clock the two ships entered the harbor, and Captain Porter made out that they were a British frigate and a sloop of war. They came steadily in and Captain Porter saw that the frigate intended to pass close by his ship. All hands were at general quarters; the powder boys were standing near the guns they served, slow matches burning in their buckets of sand, ready to fire; the boarders were in position to board the enemy, cutlasses in hand.

The British sloop of war falling off about a half mile away from the *Essex*, the larger ship bore on in, until she reached the quarter of the *Essex*, whereupon the navigator ordered the helm put down and the British ship luffed up on the starboard bow of the American, coming within fifteen feet of the *Essex*.

Why did she do it? One explanation was that the captain of the British ship knew this American was the *Essex* and that Captain Porter was commander. The British frigate was the *Phoebe*; her commander, Captain Hillyar. The two men knew each other from the days when Captain Porter was Bainbridge's lieutenant, fighting the wars of the Barbary pirates. Porter had visited Hillyar's home at Gibraltar, and Hillyar's family had once taken passage in an American man-of-war from Malta to Gibraltar. It was to say hello to his old companion that Captain Hillyar came so close.

But that was not Midshipman Farragut's explanation. The mate of an English merchantman had learned earlier that one watch of the frigate was ashore and that the ball was to be held that night aboard the *Essex*. He had made his way out to the *Phoebe,* which was lying offshore, and told Captain Hillyar that the American ship was nearly defenseless and could be easily taken at anchor. The naval tradition of the British was such that there was a logical conclusion: at the end of a ball many of the British officers might be nearly useless for fighting and a British Navy crew allowed ashore was expected to return with half the men dead drunk, if they returned at all. Consequently, British Navy crews were sometimes not allowed ashore for months at a time. So, said Midshipman Farragut, the British had come so close by intending to attack if the moment seemed propitious.

Whatever the explanation, any misapprehension under which Captain Hillyar was laboring was soon corrected. On the gun deck of the *Essex*, the drunken American sailor saw a British face grinning at him through the port. "My fine fellow, I'll stop your making faces," the sailor shouted through the port and moved to grasp a slow match and fire his gun.

His division officer, Lieutenant McKnight, caught the action from the corner of his eye, whirled, and with a single blow sent the drunk sprawling on deck, averting for the moment an international incident that would have meant battle.

At that moment Captain Hillyar stood up on the after gun

and shouted across the few feet of water. "Captain Hillyar's compliments to Captain Porter, and hopes he is well."

"Very well, I thank you," Porter replied evenly. "But I hope you will not come too near, for some accident might take place which would be disagreeable to you." He waved his speaking trumpet, and at the signal the men standing below the yard-arms hauled on lines, and out to the ends went kedge anchors, ready to drop on the deck of the *Phoebe*, pulling her close enough to be boarded.

Captain Hillyar saw. He also saw the smoke from the slow matches, and the number of faces looking grimly through the ports, the boarders on deck, and the marines in their tops—and if he had been told that the *Essex* was ripe for the taking, he suddenly knew that it was his ship and not the American frigate that was in danger. The *Phoebe* lost her way and fell off from the wind; her bows were swept around toward the *Essex*, and her stern was presented to the *Essex Junior*, whose guns were also run out, ready. Both American ships were ready to give her a broadside, and she could not bring a single gun to bear.

Hillyar braced back his yards and remarked that if he did fall aboard the American ship, it would be entirely accidental. But as he said these words, the *Phoebe's* jib boom, which projected far beyond her bows, swept across the forecastle of the *Essex*.

"Well," said Captain Porter, "you have no business where you are. If you touch a rope-yarn of this ship, I shall board instantly."

Captain Porter looked across the *Phoebe* to *Essex Junior*, trained his speaking trumpet, and hailed Lieutenant Downes, telling him to be prepared to repel the enemy.

The *Essex* at that moment was as ready for action as a rifleman with his finger on the trigger, following a target across a field; and had Porter been another man, the *Phoebe* might have been taken right then and there. As it was, no one knew what would happen next. But Porter would not take the first action to violate the neutrality of the Chileans, whose hospitality he had tasted so often in recent days and whose company he had so recently left. He watched as the *Phoebe* backed clear, not touching a rope although her yards passed over the yards of the American ship. The tension eased as the distance grew between them. When the *Phoebe* anchored some distance away, the crisis was over, and Captain Porter put down his speaking trumpet.

He had just thrown away his greatest possible advantage. As matters stood, the British ships completely outgunned the Americans. *Essex* at this time carried forty 32-pounder carronades and six long 12-pounder guns. The *Phoebe* carried twenty-six long 18-pounders, one long 12-pounder, one long 9-pounder, and eight carronades. It might seem that the Americans had ten more guns than the British, but at any distance at all the Americans had only the six 12-pounders, while the British frigate could fire twenty-eight guns. The Americans were cognizant of the different practices in arming their ships, but they counted on fighting at close quarters, which meant sailing into the teeth of the enemy to begin firing.

As to the lesser ships, *Essex Junior* was a converted merchantman, and while she was rated as a twenty-gun ship, her guns did not compare in range or accuracy with the eighteen 32-pounder carronades, eight 24-pounder guns, and two long 9-pounders of the British sloop of war *Cherub.* At the moment when Captain Hillyar stood atop his gun and looked into the face of the American cannon, and when the drunken sailor tried to fire his gun, the Americans might have beaten the British ship—at least there was no question about it in Midshipman Farragut's mind. "I am convinced that the *Phoebe* would have been ours," he wrote. But the advantage was thrown away, and the port settled down again.

In the next few days, the British ships took on provisions, and the British and American captains met ashore. Captain Hillyar announced blithely that he intended to blockade the American frigate and her tender until a superior British force should come along, and after exchange of words as acrimonious as the slogans the competing ships' crews flew from their mastheads in these days, they parted. The British ships stood out to sea, and then passed back and forth before the mouth of the harbor.

Captain Porter was well aware of his problem; it would be difficult to wage a successful fight against the British ship if she stood off at long range and pelted the *Essex* with her broadsides, which was, of course, exactly what Captain Hillyar proposed to do. One night the Captain called his officers, and they took to the boats, muffling the oars and silently stealing alongside the *Phoebe,* hoping to take her by surprise and board; but they learned that the crew was waiting for them.

Captain Porter did all he could to provoke a ship-to-ship battle, wherein he might have a chance of victory. One day the *Phoebe* stood in toward shore, flying at her masthead the motto flag "God and Our Country! British Sailors' Best Rights!" The *Essex* was flying her own flag: "Free Trade and Sailors' Rights."

The *Phoebe* fired a gun to windward and the *Cherub* ran to leeward. It looked as though the *Phoebe* was accepting the American challenge to a single fight, and in five minutes the *Essex* anchor was up, her topsails and jib pulling. She was cleared for action and moving out to fight. But when the *Phoebe* was two miles away, the Americans saw her bear up, set her studding sails, and run away.

"This I considered a second breach of faith on the part of Hillyar," said Midshipman Farragut, "for by his maneuvers in both instances it was evident that he was either wanting in courage or lacked the good faith of a high-toned chivalrous spirit to carry out his original intention. However, as Captain Hillyar subsequently proved himself a brave man in more than one instance, I shall not deny him that common characteristic of a naval officer, and have attributed his action on these two occasions to a want of good faith. He was dealing with a far inferior force, and it was ignoble in the extreme, on his part, not to meet his foe, when he had the ghost of an excuse for doing so, ship to ship."

Farragut's statement tells more about Farragut than about Captain Hillyar, for the captain was trying to win the war for his country, not trying to be the heroic storybook captain.

He did not share the idealistic bravado of the Americans of the day; he was cold and intensely practical, and he had already told Captain Porter that he had no intention of yielding a single bit of his known advantage over the American ships.

On March 28, 1814, Captain Hillyar showed how he intended to use that advantage. A storm blew up from the south and the *Essex* put out both her bowers, port and starboard. In the storm the port anchor cable parted and the starboard anchor began to drag; the ship was gotten under way to prevent her dragging ashore. The British ships were close into the weather point of the bay, but Captain Porter hoped to run to windward of them. The ship was hauled up, and the topgallant sails were taken in, leaving the topsails set close-reefed. Then a squall struck the ship, carrying the high canvas. The topmen immediately let go the topsail halyards to drop the sails, smash the wind out of them, and decrease the pressure. The yards jammed and the sails would not come down. The pressure forced the ship over until the gunwale was nearly under. The main topmast went overboard, carrying the men on the main topgallant yard, who fell into the sea and were drowned, for there was no chance of going back to rescue them; the *Essex* was fighting for her life. The crew was then able to wear ship, and came about to regain the harbor, but the wind and the condition of the *Essex* prevented them. Captain Porter ordered the ship anchored in a small bay about a quarter of a mile offshore.

Almost immediately it was apparent that the British felt it safe to attack the crippled American frigate, and Captain Porter made ready for the fight to come. Springs were put on the anchor cables so that the *Essex* could be turned to bring her broadside to any direction, and the men stood to quarters with a will. Here is Farragut's recollection of the scene:

> I well remember the feelings of awe produced in me by the approach of the hostile ships; even to my young mind it was perceptible in the faces of those around me, as clearly as possible, that our case was hopeless. It was

equally apparent that all were ready to die at their guns rather than surrender; and such I believe to have been the determination of the crew, almost to a man. There had been so much bantering of each other between the men of the ships, through the medium of letters and songs, with an invariable fight between the boats' crews when they met ashore, that a very hostile sentiment was engendered. Our flags were flying from every mast, and the enemy's vessels displayed their ensigns, jacks, and motto flags, as they bore down grandly to the attack.

It made no difference to the British captain that the American ship was well within the traditional three-mile limit from the shore and under the protection of Chilean neutrality. His task was to attack the Americans when and where he could defeat them—obviously had *he* been holding the lighted slow matches in Valparaiso harbor that earlier day the American would have been shown no mercy.

Poor Captain Porter had tried before sailing to exchange his forty carronades for long guns that had decent range, but he had been turned down. Now Captain Hillyar chose to come within range of his long guns, but not within range of the *Essex's* carronades. Hillyar's object was to stand off and shoot the American frigate to pieces without harm to himself. Perhaps it was not a pretty way to wage war, but it was effective.

The British ship with its long-range guns bore down on the crippled ship armed with short-range carronades. The attack began at 3:54 in the afternoon, the *Essex* riding to anchor with a southerly wind, the *Cherub* coming in on her starboard bow, southwest of her, and the *Phoebe* coming in north, under her stern. Almost immediately the spring was shot away from the *Essex* cable, and she could not turn to bring in her broadside. Three of the long guns were brought aft and directed through the stern ports to give some fire power. The shooting from these guns was effective and the *Phoebe* lost so much of her rigging that Captain Hillyar feared he would drift away from the action and not get back to it. The *Cherub* quickly became uncomfortable at the bow and turned around to a stern attack.

The damage to *Phoebe* was repaired. The two British ships anchored in a position in which they could bring their guns to bear on the starboard quarter of the *Essex*, and the *Essex* could not bring a broadside against them by any means, for the springs of the cables were shot away three times. It was like shooting at a duck with injured wings sitting in a small pond; the first lieutenant of the *Phoebe* told his captain that what they were doing was no better than murder, and urged him to close in and fight. Hillyar, typically, said it was not his business to be gallant but to capture the *Essex*, and he was not going to take any risks.

Seeing his men shot down without a chance to fight back, Captain Porter tried to get under way and managed to set the flying jib, the only sail and rigging left to him. The *Essex* got under way, the *Cherub* fled, and the *Phoebe* moved carefully back to stand off and continue the slaughter.

Finding that he could not fight, Captain Porter attempted to run his ship aground and destroy her. He headed her in and the *Essex* responded, achieving a position within musket shot of the beach when the wind shifted. He left her stranded. The target practice from the *Phoebe* began again.

During this action, Farragut was a busy midshipman. He acted as captain's aide, quarter gunner, and powder boy. He recalled the fight vividly even years later:

> I shall never forget the horrid impression made upon me at the sight of the first man I had ever seen killed. He was a boatswain's mate, and was fearfully mutilated. It staggered and sickened me at first; but they soon began to fall around me so fast that it all appeared like a dream, and produced no effect on my nerves. I can remember well, while I was standing near the Captain, just abaft the mainmast, a shot came through the waterways and glanced upward, killing four men who were standing by the side of the gun, taking the last one in the head and scattering his brains over both of us. But this awful

sight did not affect me half as much as the death of the first poor fellow. I neither thought of nor noticed anything but the working of the guns.

At one point Midshipman Isaacs reported to Captain Porter that a quarter gunner named Roach had deserted his post. Captain Porter looked down at Midshipman Farragut. "Do your duty, sir," he ordered.

Midshipman Farragut knew what that duty was. He picked up a pistol and went to find Roach, to shoot him on sight. He did not find Roach, who with six others had lowered a boat while the other men were fighting and had escaped to shore.

Shortly, Midshipman Farragut learned that gun primers were wanted and he was sent to find them. He was going below, climbing down the wardroom ladder, when the captain of the gun directly opposite the hatchway was struck full in the face by an 18-pound shot and fell back on Farragut, tumbling him down the hatch. The midshipman struck his head, and the body of the dead gun captain sprawled across his hips as he lay at the bottom. Recovering, he rushed back to the quarterdeck smeared with blood. Captain Porter asked if he was wounded.

"I believe not, sir," replied the midshipman.

"Then where are the primers?" asked the captain.

Midshipman Farragut came completely to his senses only then. He scurried down the companionway and sped back with the primers. As he came, he saw his captain fall. He ran up to him and asked if he was wounded.

"I believe not, my son," said Captain Porter. He had been missed by a shot that passed so close it damaged his hat.

Midshipman Farragut went to a gun and helped carry powder like any powder monkey. He would stop and carry a message for the captain, and then go back to a gun again. He was standing near the wheel with an old quartermaster named Francis Bland when he saw a shot coming over fore-yard. He told Bland to jump and pulled him. Just then the shot struck, taking off Bland's right leg and Farragut's coattail. Farragut helped carry Quartermaster Bland below to surgery and then returned to the deck.

Soon the cockpit, the steerage, the wardroom, and the whole berth deck were full and could hold no more wounded. Even dressing the wounded seemed useless because many were killed after their wounds had been cared for. The ship caught fire, not once but several times. Captain Porter's previous fire drills paid off now, and the fires were put out. The bottom was holed and the *Essex* seemed in danger of sinking—Porter would have welcomed sinking if he could get the crew off. When fire broke out near the magazine, the men came rushing up from below with their clothes aflame. Porter sent them over the side, to swim for shore three quarters of a mile away. Boatswain's Mate Kingsbury was so badly burned that scarcely an inch of his body seemed whole; yet he plunged into the salt water, swam for shore, and survived to fight another day.

After two hours of such punishment, Captain Porter decided it would be useless to continue. He called his officers to consult about surrender. To his shock he found that Lieutenant McKnight was the only officer on his feet. Lieutenant Wilmer had been knocked overboard by a shot and drowned; Lieutenant John Cowell had lost a leg; Acting Sailing Master Edward Barnewall had been wounded twice; Acting Lieutenant William Odenheimer had been knocked overboard and was swimming for his life.

Captain Porter sent for Midshipman Farragut, ordered him to find the signal book, and throw it overboard to keep the British from having it. Farragut searched high and low, until he discovered the weighted book lying on the sill of a gunport and threw it into the sea. He and Midshipman Isaacs walked about the decks, throwing small arms overboard to prevent their capture. At twenty minutes after six, Captain Porter gave the order to strike the colors. The Stars and Stripes came down slowly. It was ten minutes before the British stopped shooting, and in that time four more men were killed by Porter's side. Finally the British saw that the Stars and Stripes was lowered, and they stopped shooting. The battle was over.

61

6. CAPTIVES

The British Navy of the Napoleonic period was filled with arrogant young officers who had never known defeat and believed themselves to be both invincible and important. It was Captain Porter's luck that the cold and careless Captain Hillyar had chosen one of them to be boarding officer.

He came leaping onto the quarterdeck, a whirlwind in blue and gold, and demanded to know why Captain Porter had let his men jump overboard; then rushing on, he demanded that Captain Porter surrender his sword.

"That, sir, is reserved for your master," Porter told the foolish lieutenant. He turned on his heel, sought the *Phoebe's* boat, and went aboard to be rowed to the British warship.

Midshipman Farragut remained aboard the *Essex* with the other Americans now destined to become prisoners of war. Emotionalism and heroism ran high. A Negro boy named Ruff ran about the deck asking what had become of his master, Lieutenant Wilmer, and learning that the officer was killed in action, the boy ran to the side of the ship, jumped over, and deliberately drowned himself. A seaman named Benjamin Hazen went below to the berth deck at the end of the fight, put on a clean shirt and jerkin, told his messmates that he could never submit to capture by the British, and leaped into the sea.

The chivalry, the belief in the right of their cause, the intense personal involvement of the American seamen were beyond the ken of the British. British naval historian William James wrote that the Americans were mostly dead drunk all through the battle and that open buckets of spirit were scattered about the decks (a fact noted by none of the others who wrote about the fight). But if liquor was brought out after the fight, perhaps it was to assuage the pain of the maimed and wounded, for they were many, and the comparison with British losses showed how unequal a fight it had been: The *Phoebe* lost four killed and seven wounded, and the *Cherub* lost one killed and three wounded, but the *Essex* lost fifty-eight men killed, thirty-one missing (most of them drowned), thirty-nine severely wounded, and twenty-seven slightly wounded—a total casualty list of 155 out of a ship's complement of 255 men.

The scenes and poignancies of the battle struck home to David Farragut. One thing on which he mused that night of misery and silence after the battle was the death of his friend, Lieutenant Cowell, a death symbolic of the gallantry of the young Revolutionary Americans of the infant navy. Cowell's leg had been shot away above the knee, leaving a twisted mess of tissues and blood vessels that dripped his life away. When he fell, he was near Farragut, and he addressed the youngster by one of his nicknames. "Oh, Gatty," he said in anguish, "I fear it is all up with me."

And then Lieutenant Cowell was carried below with the other wounded. The surgeon noticed him and offered to stop work on an enlisted man to care for the officer's wound.

"No, no, Doctor," Cowell said. "None of that! Fair play is the jewel. One man's life is as dear as another's and I would not cheat any poor fellow out of his turn."

When Cowell's turn came, an hour had passed, and it was too late to save him.

"Thus died," said Farragut, "one of the best of officers as well as the bravest of men."

Those words came from Farragut's own account, *Some Reminiscences of Early Life*, written many years later when he was a captain in the United States Navy. They indicated the exalted spirits of these young men of America who went out to fight and die so gladly for their country. In this battle, on the quarterdeck and on the gun deck, men died with patriotic sayings on their lips. Seaman John Ripley lost his leg, and bleeding, shouted, "Farewell, boys, I can be of no use to you," and flung himself over the side. Seaman John Alvinson took an

18-pound shot through the body and said, "Never mind, shipmates, I die in defense of Free Trade and Sailors' Rights"; then he died, the word "Rights" trailing from his lips.

It was a remarkable display of patriotism, repeated hundreds of times on other ships, and it is too simple to deride the accounts by claiming they were romanticized by men writing long after the fact, for neither Farragut nor the others tried to minimize the indications of cowardice, such as that of Quarter Gunner Roach. Farragut, in later years, even questioned the judgment of his captain, his foster-father, in the fight. He felt the *Essex* had had a chance to escape, if Captain Porter had not erred by trying to retain the anchorage after the fore-topgallant mast was carried away:

> I think we should have borne up and run before the wind. If we had come in contact with the *Phoebe,* we should have carried her by boarding; if she avoided us, as she might have done by her greater ability to maneuver, then we could have taken her fire and passed on, leaving both vessels behind until we replaced our topmast, by which time they would have been separated, as, unless they did so, it would have been no chase, the *Cherub* being a dull sailer.

As to the method of fighting, once the decision was made to run in:

> . . . the ship should have been run ashore, throwing her broadside to the beach, to prevent raking, and fought as long as was consistent with humanity, then set on fire. But, having determined on anchoring, we should have bent a spring on to the ring of the anchor (seaward end of the cable) instead of to the cable, where it was exposed and could be shot away as fast as put on.

All these words represented hindsight, for at the age of twelve-and-one-half years, Midshipman Farragut was not concerned with strategy; he was a good midshipman who took his orders and did not think above his station. Indeed, later, as a conservative naval captain, he was to sympathize with Captain Hillyar's refusal to accept the personal or ship-to-ship challenges thrown out by Captain Porter. Hillyar, he was to note, was a man of fifty, while Porter was thirty-two; Hillyar had already gained his reputation by several ship-to-ship combats and was sticking strictly to orders—the Admiralty wanted that raider in the Pacific taken, and nothing less than success would suffice; this was war, not a duel, and the British government was too experienced in 1814 to look upon war as an expression of chivalry. Captain Hillyar quite believed that any course but the one he had pursued against the arguments of his young lieutenants would bring him disapprobation by the Admiralty and might even threaten his career. Vice Admiral Berkley, who had been responsible for the Chesapeake-Leopard affair in 1807 had been quietly retired by the Admiralty by the simple method of never giving him another assignment because he had exceeded his instructions.

However, in 1814, Mr. Midshipman Farragut subscribed to the popular feeling of the Young Turks of the navy that war was a glorious business, and he was so "mortified" at the capture of his ship that he cried openly.

On the morning of March 29, the captives were transferred to the *Phoebe* and taken to the steerage, where the British midshipmen lived. Considering his sad plight, Midshipman Farragut broke into tears again, but was roused from self-pity by a shouting English voice: "A prize! A prize! Ho, boys, a fine grunter, by Jove!"

It was a midshipman, about his own size and age, and under his arm was Murphy, the pet pig of the *Essex*. Midshipman Farragut jumped up and claimed the animal.

"Aha," said the British midshipman, "but you are a prisoner, and your pig also."

"We always respect private property," retorted Midshipman Farragut, wrenching his pig away from the other.

They wrestled for the pig for a moment, while the older British midshipmen crowded around to see the fun. The arbiter of the group sang out: "Go it, my little Yankee! If you can thrash Shorty you shall have your pig."

"Agreed," said Midshipman Farragut. He dropped the pig and squared away.

A ring was formed. by the other midshipmen in the open

space of the steerage, and the two youngsters began to fight. It quickly became apparent that Farragut was a master of the art of pugilism and the English boy was beaten.

A shred of honor, at least, was rescued, and Murphy the pig was saved from the gullets of the ravenous British.

Later in the morning Midshipman Farragut was called to the captain's cabin, where Hillyar was serving breakfast to his enemy Captain Porter. The midshipman, as Porter's ward, was asked to have some breakfast. His lip quivered. He could not think of eating; his chagrin at being in the hands of his enemies was too great.

"Never mind, my little fellow," said Captain Hillyar, "it will be your turn next, perhaps."

Midshipman Farragut brushed back the tears that were just below the surface and, without thought for the lack of grace of his muttered remark that he hoped so, made his escape from the hated enemy's presence.

The battle won, Captain Hillyar proved a gentle and generous victor. The officers and midshipmen of the *Essex* and *Essex Junior* were placed on parole and given the freedom of Valparaiso. The wounded of the crew were taken ashore for hospitalization and nursing, while the hale members of the crew were placed aboard a Spanish merchant vessel that Captain Hillyar hired.

Midshipman Farragut could not stand idleness. He volunteered his services to the surgeon as orderly and nurse, and worked faithfully at the unpleasant task. He rose at dawn and arranged bandages and plasters until eight in the morning, then went to work with the wounded for the rest of the day. This service continued until April 27. Porter and Captain Hillyar agreed that the *Essex Junior* should be disarmed and used to transport the Americans to New York. The ship set sail, bearing 130 officers and men, all that remained of the *Essex.*

The voyage was calm and pleasant this time as the *Essex Junior* sailed through the waters where *Essex* had lain hove to for three weeks in evil winds. Seventy-three days out from Valparaiso the *Essex Junior* reached Sandy Hook below New York harbor and encountered the effective British blockade, in the form of the British razee (a ship of war downgraded by the removal of its upper deck) *Saturn,* Captain Nash commanding. The captain treated Captain Porter very courteously and gave him oranges and newspapers. The boarding officer examined only the captain's passport and then allowed the ship to proceed.

But apparently Captain Nash had second thoughts about the explanations he would have to make to his superiors, for two hours later the *Essex Junior* was overhauled by the *Saturn* and boarded by an arrogant young officer who reexamined the papers and sent men into the hold to check the cargo. He said the *Essex Junior* would have to be detained because Captain Hillyar had no authority to make any such arrangements with the Americans. Captain Nash ordered the *Essex Junior* to remain under the lee of the *Saturn* for the night. Captain Porter said that this demand released him from his parole to Captain Hillyar and that he now considered himself Captain Nash's prisoner. Captain Nash refused to take Porter's sword, but Porter reiterated his statement, and next morning he escaped in the armed whaleboat. The *Essex Junior* shielded him, a fog settled in, and Porter got clean away. The *Essex Junior* tried to escape in the fog, but was overhauled and boarded again. The British man-of-war had been seen coming up, and the *Essex Junior's* sails had been taken in and clewed down so that she looked like she was drifting all the while.

The boarding officer, whom Farragut described as "an upstart," was sarcastic. "You drift quite fast," he said. "We have been going nine knots for the last three hours, and yet we find you abeam with your main topsail to the mast."

"Yes," Downes replied flatly.

"And that was Captain Porter who left the ship in a boat, I suppose?"

"It was," said the first lieutenant evenly.

The British officer exploded in anger. "Then, by God, you will soon be leaving too if we don't take your boats away from you."

Downes kept his temper, but with difficulty. "You had better not try that," he said.

The young officer reddened. He was furious. "I would if I had my way," he said.

Downes lost his temper and advanced on "the upstart."

"You impertinent puppy," he shouted, "if you have any business to do here, do it; but if you dare to insult me again, I shall throw you overboard," and he heaved his hands toward the rail in a gesture that could not be misunderstood.

The young officer jumped into his boat and left. The regular boarding officer soon returned and apologized for the youth's behavior, but the crew was mustered and the passports read off. The British, never seeming to learn about American sailors and what they were fighting for, looked hopefully for Englishmen among the crew but found none they could prove to be English. They went away, finally giving permission for the ship to sail on. *Essex Junior* sailed for Sandy Hook undisturbed until about sunset, when they encountered the British frigate *Narcissus* and had to explain all again.

They made the Hook at about eight o'clock in the evening, a dark and squally night promising, could not find a pilot, and had to go in alone. Opposite the Horseshoe, where a battery stood, they sent a boat ashore with a light to identify the ship, but the light was extinguished and the fort began firing on them. The boat crew put back, got another light and took it ashore, and explained, all the while under fire. Not one shot struck the ship. The crew finally managed to convince the shore battery that they were Americans coming home, and the firing stopped. They remained under this battery for the night and then sailed into New York harbor, to be greeted, even with the Stars and Stripes flying, by shots from another battery on Staten Island. They anchored and went ashore to tell their story. Captain Porter came from Long Island, where he had made his way ashore, and after ceremonies of homecoming, Porter and Midshipman Farragut set off for Chester. They could not fight, or at least Farragut could not, because he was still on parole—even if Captain Porter had relieved himself of parole by surrendering to Captain Nash and escaping. Technically, Farragut was still a prisoner of war when he came home, two days after his thirteenth birthday.

7. THE MAKING
OF A MIDSHIPMAN

There was much excitement in Chester when Captain David Porter and Midshipman David Farragut returned to Green Bank, for a third child had been born to Mrs. Porter—David Dixon Porter—and even without such surprise there was joy, because they had been gone for nearly two years on the adventure to the South Seas.

Porter was soon back in New York, in command of the newest of American naval vessels, *Fulton the First,* an experimental steam-driven man-of-war that was then under construction. Midshipman Farragut could not go with him, for he was not free to serve his country. He was put in an informal school run by a schoolmaster named Neif, who had been one of Napoleon Bonaparte's guards.

At the end of November, 1814, Midshipman Farragut was notified that he had been "exchanged" and was officially released from his parole. Earlier, when the British descended on Washington in force, he had wanted to go south and fight on land, but Porter had refused to take him because he said the boy was too young for the dangers of land warfare. Thus it was not strict adherence to his word to the enemy that kept Midshipman Farragut in school all those months.

On the last day of November, Farragut received orders to join the brig *Spark,* commanded by Master Commandant Thomas Gamble. Farragut was removed from the direct responsibility of Captain Porter for the first time and put on his own. He would still be with Porter, for his foster father had been appointed to command the squadron of which *Spark* would be a part, and go raiding enemy commerce.

Undoubtedly Farragut owed his return to active duty directly to Captain Porter, for many young officers were sitting at home so long they became disgusted and quit the service because there were no ships for them to serve. Farragut's naval career might well have ended in 1814.

He was quartered on the receiving ship *John Adams* while the *Spark* was made ready for sea. Aboard the *John Adams,* young Farragut found it his unhappy lot to be thrown among evil companions. His particular midshipman's mess was dedicated to the dancing of a merry tune. These boys, led by the older midshipmen, decided that the only way to prove they were men was to act like men. To the elder leaders, manlike demeanor meant smoking and drinking and general hell-raising. Farragut was an impressionable youth, and he was soon knee-deep in personal corruption. "And for two or three months," he wrote, "there was scarcely one in the mess except my old shipmate Ogden who ever went to bed sober." He looked back on these high jinks with equanimity, but also with full cognizance of the dangers he ran of ruining a career before it was established. Later he accepted the view of his first lieutenant, William H. Cocke, who said that Farragut was saved by his strict attention to duty. So ingrained was respect for discipline in Farragut after the cruise on the *Essex* that he was able to overcome his sloth and do his duty, hangovers included, until the time came when the squadron had completed fitting out for sea and he was broken away from the other young hellions.

The squadron assigned to Captain Porter was almost ready for sea when the news came that the Treaty of Ghent had been signed at the end of 1814. It was then already 1815, but as it was nearly certain that the war was over, the fitting out stopped. After several weeks of confusion, Midshipman Farragut received orders to go to Boston and join the ship of the line *Independence*, flagship of Commodore Bainbridge's fleet, which was fitting out to sail for the Mediterranean. The *Independence* was a seventy-four-gun ship (carrying eighty-four guns) with three gun decks and a crew of eight-hundred officers and men—a change from any vessel on which Midshipman Farragut had ever served. He was fortunate, again through Porter's influence, to secure the coveted post of aide to Captain William M. Crane. Midshipman Farragut's headquarters became the captain's cabin, on the maindeck, although he messed and slept with the other fifteen midshipmen on the orlop deck, two decks below the main.

It took Farragut a few hours to get the lay of his new ship. She was a three-master, like a frigate; a length of 190 feet and a beam of 50 feet, which were not much greater than an American frigate's; but she stood much higher above the water and her displacement of 2,257 tons was almost three times as great as that of the *Essex*.

The *Independence* represented a new class of ships for the American Navy, an indication that Congress had decided to have a real navy at last. Three more of these big ships were laid down for construction. The navy was willing to experiment with steam-powered vessels like the *Fulton,* but the navy men were not much impressed by steam as a method of moving fighting ships. It was still the age of sail.

The top afterdeck of the *Independence* was the poop and beneath that deck, abaft the mizzenmast, was the commodore's cabin and the spar deck. The quarterdeck was located here abaft the mainmast. The protocol was much stiffer than on a frigate, the starboard side flatly forbidden to midshipmen. A marine guard paced constantly before the captain's cabin, calling out the half-hours from the ship's chronometer, which hung above the captain's door, and announcing all who entered the captain's quarters. The sailors slept on this deck forward; the brig was there, as was the galley for commodore and captain. Below, on the lower gun deck, after, was the wardroom, living room for the eight lieutenants, the captain of marines, and lesser officers, chaplains, surgeons, purser, and even a commodore's secretary. Forward of these were galley, sick bay, and more hammock space. Down again was the orlop deck, the after area of which was occupied by a tin-lined room called the bread room. Next door were the officers' private cubicles. Amidships was the cockpit, or emergency surgery, then the port and starboard steerages, occupied by the midshipmen and the three ship's clerks, and then the rooms of the specialists—the carpenter, sailmaker, boatswain, and gunner. Below this deck was the hold, with forward and after magazines each with its special hatch, and the various rooms for provisions, including the spirit room, which was always under guard.

Fortunately, on the *Independence,* Midshipman Farragut's interest in the spirit room was quickly dissipated. He became friendly with an older midshipman, William Taylor, who showed him by fine example that the course of the rake was not that of the best navy man. Mr. Midshipman Farragut divested himself of his rakish ways quickly and returned to his old worship of manliness and chivalry, tempered after his months of experience among the scapegraces.

The Barbary pirates, encouraged by American preoccupation with survival in the War of 1812, and egged on by the British, had wreaked havoc among American merchantmen during the hard days from 1812 to 1815. Once the Treaty of Ghent was ratified by the United States Senate, President Madison lost no time in declaring war once again—this time a war the Americans could win—against the city-states of Barbary. Madison declared war on March 2, 1815, against Algiers, which was the principal reason for the dispatch of the double squadron selected to put down the pirates of the Mediterranean. Bainbridge's squadron consisted of the flagship, the frigate *Congress,* the sloop *Erie,* the brigs *Chippewa, Saranac, Boxer,* and *Enterprise,* and the schooner *Lynx.* Commodore Stephen Decatur left America in May with another squadron, consisting of the frigates *Guerriere, Macedonian,* and *Constellation,* the sloop *Ontario,* the brigs *Epervier, Firefly, Spark,* and *Flambeau,* and the schooners *Torch* and *Spitfire.* This force was to be commanded by Commodore Bainbridge when he arrived in the Mediterranean, but he was late in sailing and did not actually get away until July 3. When he arrived at Carthagena on August 5, Decatur had already cleared the sea of enemy ships, forced a treaty on the Dey of Algiers, and frightened the rulers of Tripoli and Tunis into promising to leave American shipping alone. Bainbridge really had nothing to do and he did not like it. He cruised around the Mediterranean and then went home in October, after showing his displeasure of Decatur's stealing the thunder.

Home again, Midshipman Farragut was ordered to the frigate *Macedonian,* but he was almost immediately transferred to the ship of the line *Washington,* under Captain John Orde Creighton. He served as aide. Farragut was traveling in fast company now: the *Washington* was Commodore Isaac Chauncey's ship, and Chauncey had been ordered back to the Mediterranean to preserve American interests. Before he left, he called at Annapolis to take aboard William Pinkney, special minister to Naples, to negotiate settlement of differences arising from mistreatment of American shipping during the Napoleonic Wars. At Annapolis President Madison visited the big ship, along with Dolly Madison, the Secretary of the Navy, and two navy commissioners, Commodore John Rodgers and Commodore David Porter, Farragut's foster father (whom he now referred to in a more dignified manner as "my friend Commodore Porter").

Farragut was somewhat embarrassed by this visit, for in the morning he had gone ashore with the market boat to secure provisions ordered for the captain's mess on this special occasion, and on his return he discovered that in tidying up the ship to receive the honored guests, the other midshipmen had moved his sea chest from the steerage to the hold and there was no way he could get at it; so instead of appearing in the splendor of his full dress, he slunk about the edges of the gathering in his shabby second uniform, thoroughly uncomfortable and ashamed.

Captain Creighton understood the circumstances, or he might have been annoyed with his aide, for Creighton was a stickler for discipline and ran the tautest ship in the United States Navy. Admiral A. T. Mahan, the naval biographer and historian, recalled one story about Creighton: when his ship was in port a midshipman in full dress and cocked hat was kept constantly in each boat in the booms, so that no time might be lost in dropping alongside when the boat was called away. A full crew was also apparently kept in the boat at all times, sitting, waiting the captain's, or the commodore's, pleasure.

That was not the worst of it. Captain Creighton ran a terror ship as well as a taut ship. It was not uncommon for the officer of the deck to call up the *entire watch* and give the men two- or three-dozen lashes each for the fault of one man, or for what might have been truly an accident. All hands were sometimes kept from their meals for eight or ten hours, and once, at Algiers, the whole crew was kept on deck all night, not just one night, but several nights in succession, for punishment of minor offenses. So common, so frightful were the punishments meted out to the crew that Farragut, who had lost his journal of the cruise, said later he was glad that he had lost it, because he preferred to forget that captain and those awful days.

For all this, the *Washington* was called a crack ship, modeled on the lines of British ships. Had the men gone sailing with Captain Creighton alone in a frigate or a lesser ship, there might very well have occurred the mutiny he richly deserved to suffer, but Creighton was beyond such service: his was a ship of the line and she traveled in high company. No mutiny was possible. But a lesson was possible, and Farragut learned it; in later years he adopted the Porter approach, not the Creighton approach, to the navy and its men. If having a crack ship meant having an unhappy ship, he would never want a part of one; despite his hot temper, Commodore Porter was loved in the navy because the sailors knew he was fair and even generous. Farragut was able to give Captain Creighton and his officers credit as fine seamen, but when in later years he spoke of the great ones in the navy of his youth, all these men were conspicuous by their absence.

Nor was Commodore Chauncey one of the great ones, as Farragut soon discovered. Chauncey had shown smallness during the war: when Captain Oliver Hazard Perry had been sent to fight the battle of Lake Erie, Chauncey had withheld men from him, sent his own lieutenant to Lake Erie (he nearly lost the battle for the Americans in his attempt at glory-hogging), and had made life generally difficult and uncomfortable for Perry. He was a martinet and a hothead.

One day during winter refit at Port Mahon, the young officers of the *United States* invited three of the *Washington* midshipmen aboard for a ball. They were Commodore Chauncey's son, Midshipman Clinton, his nephew, and Midshipman Farragut. At that time the three midshipmen were aboard the *Ontario*, which they had been given express permission to visit by Captain Creighton. As they had permission to be *out*, they went over to the *United States* without checking back. They were enjoying themselves immensely, when at about midnight an order came from Commodore Chauncey, borne by a *Washington* boat, that the three must return to their ship immediately.

Aboard the *Washington*, they were ordered to the commodore's cabin, where Chauncey and Creighton were awaiting them. First Creighton laced into Midshipman Farragut for daring to visit the *United States* without express permission. Finally exhausting his invective, Captain Creighton sent Farragut below. The boy went outside, put his eye to the keyhole, and watched to see how his companions would fare. He saw young Clinton lying flat on the deck and young Chauncey standing before his father, who was swearing at him. Finally, the commodore struck his son and knocked him down. When the boy got up, he knocked him down again. Farragut hurried down to the steerage then. He was followed shortly by the other two, Clinton talking to young Chauncey.

"Why didn't you do as I did," Clinton asked, "lie still when he first knocked you down? You might have known the old codger would knock you over again when you got up."

Farragut had only the dressing down, but he received suspension from his duties as an aide for thirty days.

In the summer of 1817, David Glasgow Farragut was sixteen years old. He was slender, although not very tall, and his face was developing along angular lines, with broad forehead capped by a thick, long thatch of dark hair, prominent ears, large deep-set eyes under heavy brows and strong cheekbones, a long nose, long upper lip, and long jaw—one might almost have called him lantern-jawed. He gave an overall impression of angularity, boniness, and great energy.

Farragut spent his energy, in these days of peace, studying the subjects he would need for advancement and engaging in the sightseeing available to few other Americans of the period. He traveled to Marseilles, Leghorn, Naples. He saw Mount Vesuvius in eruption. He visited the ruined cities of Pompeii and Herculaneum, and the grottoes and Roman spas along the bay. He boiled eggs in the hot springs at the Baths of Nero. He saw Messina and Syracuse. He observed that Tunis was savage, Tripoli was more civilized, and Algiers was better fortified.

During these two years Farragut endeared himself to Chaplain Charles Folsom of the *Washington,* largely because he was an example of apparent success in the saving of a rake and the making of a scholar. Farragut had come to the *Washington* thoroughly dissolute at the age of fourteen, adept at all the vices a young naval officer might develop, save the use of tobacco, of which he had been cured by Captain Porter, and drinking far more than was good for him. Folsom pointed out to the young man the error of his ways. Farragut heeded, much to the pleasure of the chaplain, who, when he was appointed U.S. Consul to Tunis, asked Farragut to go along.

Farragut's career had been in the balance from the moment he left Chester that last time and headed for New York to go aboard the *John Adams.* Commodore Porter had risen to the highest reaches of the navy, and although his friendship would continue to be valuable to Farragut, it could no longer be said that the young man was under his personal protection. The months aboard the *John Adams* until the young midshipman reached the *Washington* must be accounted very conditional in terms of his career, but he was pulled out of the morass of self-indulgence, and he moved ahead again with a decision to go to Tunis.

Fortunately for Farragut, Commodore Chauncey was favorably impressed with him and acceded to the chaplain's request. On October 26, 1817, they went off on the *Erie* to

Marseilles, where they remained during November, sight-seeing and waiting for transportation. Farragut was often invited to the houses of American merchants in the city, including a Mr. Fitch. After dinner one night at Fitch's, he was called upon to take a hand at whist. He did not like to play cards and consequently was not adept, and soon the others at his table realized as much. But instead of suffering through, as he was doing, they showed bad manners and began making insulting remarks. Finally, one of them threw his hand onto the table in disgust at Farragut's play of the cards. Farragut flamed, threw his cards at the other's head, apologized stiffly to his host, and left the party.

The consul and his protege sailed on December 22 for Tunis. Farragut settled down then to the study of Italian, French, mathematics, and English literature. He was a diligent student, and his command of the languages grew steadily. He visited ancient Carthage (a few miles from Tunis) and in the spring joined Folsom on a trip into the interior with the French and Danish consuls.

Travel in the interior of North Africa was not an affair to be undertaken lightly, and they first secured a passport from the bey, who also gave them a guard of soldiers. They hired a covered cart to carry their baggage and then set out on the adventure.

The first day they traveled to the village of Toar, within sight of Tunis. Here the Carthaginians had built an aqueduct for their water supply, and the party stopped to investigate the ruins. They visited other ruins in the interior and along the seacoast. On the ninth day out they started for Susa, to visit the ruins of the Roman amphitheater at El Jem. It was a hot day, one of the hottest Farragut had ever experienced, and soon the Europeans were seeking the shelter of the covered cart. But the cart could hold only three, and as the youngest member of the party, Farragut rode on in the heat. He wore a large straw hat on his head and tied another on his back; yet at the end of the day he suffered either heatstroke or sunstroke. His tongue became partly paralyzed and he could not speak properly for several hours.

He was overcome with attacks of nausea, and when those waves passed, he was weak with fatigue and hunger.

The hunger could not easily be satisfied. They had sent ahead for quarters for the night and a meal, but the cook had prepared a native supper of *couscous*, which was scarcely to their taste, and furthermore he had dropped the pepper pot into it—probably on purpose, because the natives hated the foreigners. The captain of the guard tasted the concoction, forced the cook to eat a great bowl of it, and poured the remainder over his head. The villagers scowled and referred scathingly to the foreign dogs and sons of dogs who had come to disturb their peace. Farragut and the others were grateful for the bey's guard that day.

Next day as they set out to examine the Roman ruins, Farragut became separated from the others. He was still weak, and having grown tired of carrying his gun, he left it in the hut where they had spent the night, under guard of the soldiers, and took only a pair of pistols for protection. These he shoved into his pockets, where they were hidden from view.

As he was strolling along in the ruins, he suddenly became aware of a Bedouin stalking him. When Farragut moved, the Bedouin moved. When he stopped, the Bedouin stopped and hid. The game went on for some time, then came to its logical conclusion: the Bedouin looked about him, saw no one, and rushed at the foreigner, holding high the heavy club he had been concealing all the while.

Farragut stopped short, drew his two pistols, and pointed them squarely at the Bedouin as he rushed forward. The rush became a walk, the walk ended, and the incipient murderer stopped, looking at those pistols, then turned and fled. Farragut made sure the pistols were ready to fire and went on.

After two days at the ruins, the party continued to Monestin on the seashore, passing cairns of stones as they went. The guard informed them that they represented places where travelers had been murdered by the Bedouins, to which successive travelers added stones as marks of respect for the dead.

They were well received by the sheikh at Monestin, but at the next village to the east they were surrounded by a crowd that threatened to stone them. The captain of the guard drew his sword and led the way through, announcing that if one stone was thrown, the stoner would die on the spot and the sheikh of the village would pay with his head for disregarding the bey's passport. They passed through silently.

Later, when they came to a deserted village where the animals were roaming through the streets, the travelers knew they had encountered plague. They hastened on, not stopping until they reached the outskirts of Tunis, where they took a house for the night. Next day they were home.

Not long after, plague broke out in Tunis also, and people were dying at the rate of a hundred per day. Tunis became boring because they could not go out about the streets. In October Farragut left Tunis to rejoin the squadron. He was glad to be leaving, as glad as Chaplain Folsom was sorry, for in their acquaintance Folsom had grown fonder of Farragut. He realized that Farragut possessed the spark of leadership and that if he continued to apply himself, he would go far.

In the next few months Farragut proved the reasonableness of that contention. On the voyage from Tunis to Sardinia, he saved the Genoese brig on which he and the Danish consul had taken passage, when the captain went to sleep in a dead calm and the ship was drifting onto the rocks off Corsica. When he arrived in Italy and passed through the quarantine required of all who came from plague-ridden Africa, he was introduced to the court of the Grand Duke of Tuscany at Pisa and comported himself as to bring honor on the United States, beginning with his good command of the Italian language, which was unusual among Americans.

In February, 1819, Midshipman Farragut returned to Messina and reported for duty aboard the U.S.S. *Franklin,* another ship of the line, a sister ship to the *Washington.* Again he became aide to the captain, this time Captain Gallagher, and again he distinguished himself officially by his languages. When the Emperor of Austria and the King of

Naples honored the ship with a visit in May, Midshipman Farragut was official interpreter. Except for calling the Emperor "Mister," he met the demands of protocol quite well, and Prince Metternich, who was leading the party, was not annoyed, but rather amused, at the young American's republican slip.

Farragut carried himself well enough, worked hard enough, and made enough friends in the squadron, so that in the autumn, when a vacancy occurred in the brig *Spark*, he was sent as an acting lieutenant. During the winter that followed, he assumed the responsibilities of executive officer of the ship, although he was only eighteen years old.

In the summer of 1820, Midshipman Farragut was ordered back to the United States to take the examination for lieutenant. He took passage on a merchantman, the *America*, at Gibraltar. A few days from the shores of the United States, a sail was sighted and Farragut suddenly found himself involved in a new adventure:

> It was perfectly calm. The stranger used his sweeps and came up with us about 5 p.m. We took him for a pirate, and our Captain was so much alarmed that I assumed command, mustered the crew, and asked them if they would defend the ship. I had determined to compel the enemy or "pirate," if possible, to sink us, rather than allow ourselves to be captured and reserved for some worse fate.
>
> I was impressed on this occasion with the difference between men-of-war's men and merchant men. The latter seemed to be very much alarmed at the idea of resistance, although they had no hope of mercy by surrendering; while the former yielded instantly to my better judgment and expressed their willingness to obey orders. Men trained to arms will never fail if properly led.
>
> By this time the brig was quite near us and hailed us in Spanish. We made arrangements to sink the boat which they proposed to send alongside, but when she reached us I asked the officer if he came as a friend, to which he replied in good English "Yes." I told him to leave his

arms in the boat, which he did and came on board. He proved to be a Mr. Smith, of Baltimore, and offered to supply us with anything of which we stood in need. We took charge of letters for him.

The ship was not a pirate after all, but a Colombian brig of war, preying on Spanish shipping as a part of the South American revolution against the mother country. Farragut was not at all shamefaced, for he had done exactly the right thing. He was impressed with the ease with which a civilian crew might defend itself against such pirates. He had a grindstone and a barrel of tar ready to sink the boat if the occupants proved unfriendly, and even though the precautions were not necessary, the incident livened up the voyage home, taught the midshipman something new, and proved once again his self-sufficiency and his admirable fitness for the profession he had chosen.

8. SERVICE
WITHOUT RECOGNITION

"I was a stranger in my native land, knowing no one but Commodore Porter and his family. I was ordered to New York for my examination, and went in much trepidation, for this was only the second examination which had been held in our naval service, and we had very little information as to what course would be pursued by the board. I felt qualified in seamanship, but doubtful as to mathematics."—David Farragut

The human quality that is called boldness in time of war is often called temerity in time of peace. Regardless of its name, it was one of the key qualities in the character of David Glasgow Farragut, a quality that set him apart from his fellows. In his encounter with the murderous Arab in Africa, his social conquests in Italy, his warning to Captain Porter when the British prisoners tried to take over the *Essex* during the War of 1812, Midshipman Farragut showed boldness. In his attempt now to secure promotion in a peacetime naval service he showed temerity, and his rashness in word and action was to cost him dear.

In Farragut's term of service aboard the *Spark*, his captain had been Christopher Raymond Perry, of the famous family of Rhode Island, whose brothers were Oliver Hazard Perry and Matthew Calbraith Perry, both destined to rise to the top in the naval service. Oliver Hazard, the hero of the Battle of Lake Erie, rose in the service in spite of heavy drinking, but the same habit virtually wrecked the career of Christopher Raymond Perry. Aboard the *Spark* Perry was often too drunk for duty, and thus it was that Midshipman Farragut secured the experience of command of a naval vessel while still in his teens. But having conquered his own indulgences, Farragut was not generous about those of his superior, and he sometimes spoke harshly of his former captain's weakness. In the autumn of 1820, as Farragut waited for the examination to be given in New York, he learned that Perry had been brought back to the United States to be tried for drunkenness. One day Farragut received a message from Captain George Washington Rodgers, another important naval officer, who was also Perry's brother-in-law. The message asked him to call and discuss reports in circulation about Raymond Perry.

Instead of appearing and making the best of a bad situation, Farragut flared. He sent word to the captain that he would be happy to see him at the Farragut lodgings if the captain cared to call. Midshipmen just did not treat captains with such disrespect with impunity, and Captain Rodgers was more than a little annoyed.

Several days later they met in Brooklyn, and Captain Rodgers said that someone had been talking about Captain Perry. Officers should be very careful about what they said about other officers, the captain said.

Even at this point it would have been easy for Farragut either to minimize his own remarks or to take the chiding in stride. Rather, he replied that the captain's remarks did not apply to him. Farragut then said he presumed that officers were always ready to repeat what they had said when called upon. These words, used this way, were nothing less than an invitation to be challenged to a duel. He became more explicit. As for himself, he said, if Mr. Perry had anything to settle with him, he would be ready when called.

Captain Rodgers did not know quite how to deal with this firebrand. He had come to try to resolve the matter quietly and persuade Farragut to keep silent about his brother-in-law. He came as Captain Perry's friend, he said.

"As Mr. Rodgers or as Captain Rodgers?" Farragut asked.

Again George Washington Rodgers was put in a bad position. What Farragut was demanding, was to know whether

Rodgers was speaking as a naval captain, which put a semi-official stamp on the conversation, or as a "friend" of Christopher Raymond Perry, which in this sense meant the carrier of a challenge to duel.

"As Captain Rodgers," he said.

"Then, sir," rejoined the irascible Farragut, "as Captain Rodgers I have nothing to say to you on this subject, but whenever you lay aside your official character and meet me as the friend of Mr. Perry, I shall be most happy to send a friend to settle all difficulties between him and myself."

The two men parted stiffly, but the matter was hardly ended. Captain Rodgers shared lodgings with Captain Samuel Evans, who was to be one of Midshipman Farragut's examiners in the coming tests of his fitness for promotion. It would have been superhuman of Captain Rodgers to have refrained from communicating his irritation with the young officer when he sat in his lodgings talking to his friend Evans. When Captain Evans first met Midshipman Farragut, he already had a poor impression of him, and Farragut complained that on their first meeting Evans indicated that he considered the midshipman a most insubordinate young man.

Under the naval system, the candidate for promotion was examined by three superior officers, with one officer taking the lead. Passage of the examinations did not mean automatic promotion, but failure meant a midshipman could not be promoted.

In essence the examinations consisted of mathematics, which was a matter of answering written questions in a thoroughly impersonal test, and seamanship, in which one of the examining officers posed questions to the candidate and he explained how to handle each problem presented.

Since Farragut had served as first lieutenant of a brig of war, and virtually as commanding officer because of Christopher Raymond Perry's frequent disability, there was absolutely no question in his mind about his seamanship. He had proved it time and again, and had enjoyed one of his greatest personal triumphs in outsailing the British packet brig *Pigeon* in an impromptu race off Malta.

Farragut took his examination in mathematics, and then came up before the board of three officers for his questioning on seamanship. He was dismayed to discover that his examiner would be Captain Evans. He considered objecting to the arrangement, but learned that it was made among the three officers of the board, and there was nothing he could do but submit.

The two other senior officers sat and listened, half idly. At the end of the questioning, Captain Evans remarked that Midshipman Farragut in reefing topsails had neglected to give the orders that would have cleared away the bowlines and that, consequently, the topsails could not be reefed. Farragut demurred. He had included that order, he said, although Captain Evans might not have heard him.

The captain swore and said that Farragut was being insolent. In fact, he added, Farragut was the most insolent young man it was his misfortune to know.

Farragut appealed to the other members of the board. Had they not heard him give the order to clear away bowlines?

The other captains hemmed and hawed. They had not been listening. They had not noticed anything, but Captain Evans would not be so certain that Midshipman Farragut had erred if such had not been the case.

Heatedly, Farragut reminded the board that he had been first lieutenant of a brig of war, and if he knew nothing else about the navy, he knew how to reef topsails.

The officers frowned, and the interview was over. With tears in his eyes Farragut left the room, perceiving at last his mistake in insulting Captain Rodgers rather than conciliating him. As he expected, the majority of the board found that he had failed his examination in seamanship, and even Captain Stewart, who had known Farragut in the Mediterranean and had formed a favorable opinion of him, refused to interpose because Farragut had indeed proved himself insubordinate in his answers and arguments, and Captain Stewart was a stickler for discipline.

Farragut went back to Washington to visit the Porters, who now lived on an estate north of the White House, called

Meridian Hill. He told Commodore Porter about his troubles. Porter was sympathetic, although he did not rush in to order the examination overthrown. The Secretary of the Navy was sympathetic, too, but the decision stood, a lesson to Midshipman Farragut in the necessity for personal diplomacy.

Midshipman Farragut spent several months at the naval station in Norfolk, where he met and courted Susan Caroline Marchant. He applied to take the examinations again and in the fall passed them, twentieth in a group of fifty-three candidates.

Back in Norfolk he became restless and wrote to the Secretary of the Navy asking for sea duty. Nothing happened. He wrote to Porter, who was serving as one of the three navy commissioners. Porter recommended him glowingly. Still nothing happened. Farragut was growing despondent by this time, and began to wonder if he would not have to leave the navy in order to make some kind of career in which he could be happy. His father had died in 1817, and left him an obligation to help support his sisters, who lived on the plantation in Louisiana. On his pay as midshipman, which amounted to nineteen dollars a month, he could scarcely help very much. Also, Farragut was in love and wanted to get married, which seemed an equally futile hope on his pay.

It was not until the end of May, 1822, that he was finally ordered to report for sea duty aboard the *John Adams*, which was about to take the new American minister to Mexico and another official to Guatemala. On the way to Vera Cruz, when the ship chased a suspicious-looking brig, thinking she might be a pirate, Midshipman Farragut was sent with a crew to board and investigate. He discovered that the ship was a Spanish man-of-war.

In Vera Cruz, Farragut was taken by Captain James Renshaw to dine with young General Santa Anna, who had just led the revolution that would establish Mexico as an independent nation.

Farragut was favorably impressed with Santa Anna, but hardly with another adventure that came to him in Mexico.

Joel Poinsett, the American minister to Mexico, went on

to Mexico City to present his credentials to Emperor Augustin, who had been placed on the throne by the general. The *John Adams* was to meet him at Tampico. After weathering a "norther," a serious storm in these waters, the ship arrived off Tampico, which is located on a lake connected to the sea by a river six miles long. On arrival Captain Renshaw sent Midshipman Farragut ashore to make his way to the city and inform Poinsett that the ship had arrived and was waiting.

Farragut was dressed in summer whites. He donned his formal uniform coat, picked up his cocked hat, and stepped into the boat that would take him ashore. The boat landed at a *vigía*, a pilot station, and headed back to the ship because the weather was changing for the worse. Farragut began walking up the beach, looking for someone to direct him to Tampico. He encountered an old man who told him it was three leagues (about ten miles) and rented him a horse for two dollars. By following the beach, he reached the Tampico River in about an hour, but by this time another "norther" was blowing, and he was thoroughly wet and miserable. Further, he discovered that there was not even a hut on his side of the river, and when he shouted across to the village on the other side, his voice was drowned out by the surf and the howling of the wind. He dismounted, took the soft saddle and skins off the horse and spread them out, preparing to spend a cold and wretched night on the ground. But about nine o'clock that night, a boat came across for him and took him to the other side, where he found himself in a village of smugglers. He was rushed into the presence of the head man, Mata. Farragut said he wanted them to send a pilot to the ship and to direct him to Tampico.

"What! Tonight?"

"Yes," said Farragut.

"I'll see if I can find anyone fool enough to accompany you," said the head man.

He went off and Farragut sat self-consciously, awaiting his return. While he waited, he was aware of the intrusion of many inquisitive faces as the members of the smuggling band came to take a look at the crazy American who insisted on going to Tampico in the middle of the night. He was sure that given any pretext at all, the band would rise up and murder him.

Finally a fool was found, with two horses, and at about ten o'clock they set out for a ride of nine miles. But what nine miles! Farragut, who had traveled in the desert of North Africa, said he had never taken such a trip. If they were not brushing through forests of prickly pear, they were immersed in swamp up to the horse's withers.

> Every now and then the guide would turn his horse around with great celerity, utter some oath or imprecation on himself for losing the way, and then try a new route. He did this at least a dozen times, and every time he made the movement I drew my dirk and put myself on the defense, supposing that he had now arrived at a suitable place to rob and murder me.*

But the guide had no such evil intentions. He led on and finally called to Farragut to let the horse pick his own way or he would get his neck broken. Farragut released the reins and sat the horse, instead of riding him. They came down through a hill thick with chaparral, and several times the young officer's cocked hat was knocked askew, and the lace and cockade were torn off. Occasionally the horse would settle back on his haunches and slide fifteen or twenty feet down the hill before he could recover his footing.

At long last they reached a village. It was one o'clock in the morning, and Farragut fell into bed.

The next morning he discovered that all his efforts had been needless. Poinsett had not yet arrived from Mexico. He had, however, sent down thirty Americans released from Mexico City prisons with orders for Farragut to put them on the *John Adams*. Farragut engaged canoes and took them down river, across the bar, and embarked on the ship.

Again he was ordered to Tampico. This time he took a

*Charles L. Lewis, *David Glasgow Farragut: Our First Admiral* (Annapolis, United States Naval Institute, 1943), p. 87.

sword and pistols for protection, but when he arrived at Pueblo Viejo, he discovered that he was to be entertained instead of threatened. He began learning Spanish and occupied himself with long rides in the countryside.

Two weeks later Poinsett arrived, accompanied by more released American prisoners, and they went down to the bar. They found fog and a heavy surf running. They could not see the ship, but they knew she was out beyond the breakers. Poinsett asked Mata to take them out. Mata agreed to try to find the ship and put them aboard for 150 pesos. One of the party argued that they should not pay so much and should not put themselves in Mata's hand, but Poinsett replied that there was no use arguing with a man who held the only means of transportation and that if he, a professional, was willing to run the risk of crossing the bar, they ought to trust him. Farragut added another bit of common sense to his education. They found their ship after a frightening passage.

On December 24, they set sail for home, arriving at Norfolk on January 23, 1823. The cruise had lasted five months and had added immeasurably to Midshipman Farragut's experience. By this time he was the most traveled and most experienced midshipman in the navy, and as far as he was concerned, that was the rub: he was still a midshipman.

9. PIRATE HUNTING

While Midshipman Farragut had been off in Mexico, a force under Commodore James Biddle had sailed down into the Caribbean to suppress the pirates who were becoming ever bolder in these waters. The trouble was aggravated by the steadily worsening relations between the United States and Spain over Cuba and the continuation there of the African slave trade, in spite of promises by the Spanish government that the trade would be ended.

Biddle had captured more than thirty pirate ships but had not ended piracy, by far. To the contrary, the pirates were so bold that a gang of them attacked a boarding party from the U.S. Navy schooner *Alligator* in Cardenas Bay at the very time that Farragut was wining and dining with General Santa Anna and his friends. Lieutenant William Howard, of the *Alligator*, was killed in the fight, along with three of his men.

Biddle could not run his frigates *Macedonian* and *Congress* into the shallow waters of the keys where the pirates lurked. He came back to report to the Navy Department that a different kind of war must be waged to stamp out the piracy in the area. The Secretary took the matter up with President Monroe, and the President viewed the *Alligator* affair with such concern that he made a special message to Congress. Within three weeks after the session began Congress authorized Secretary Smith Thompson to fit out a special squadron of small, shallow-draft ships that would sail south and wipe out the pirates. On February 1, 1823, Commodore David Porter was appointed to command the squadron. Almost immediately after his return from Mexican waters, Midshipman

Farragut saw an opportunity again to distinguish himself on active duty and perhaps have a chance to win the promotion that he wanted so badly. He applied officially for service with the squadron, and he asked Commodore Porter to be sure that he went along.

On February 5, Midshipman Farragut was assigned to the sailing schooner *Greyhound,* commanded by Lieutenant John Porter, the commodore's brother. The *Greyhound* was one of eight such vessels, sometimes called bay boats, which the commodore had bought in Baltimore for the task ahead. She displaced sixty-five tons and carried a crew of thirty-three and three guns, one of them a "Long Tom," a long gun of considerable accuracy. Once again Farragut occupied that strange position in the navy known as "purgatory" among the professionals. He was a passed midshipman but not yet a fully qualified officer. He held his rank by warrant and not by commission. He was qualified for a commission and all its privileges, but as long as he was a midshipman he had to mess in the steerage, his only mark of difference being a single gold star in the gold-lace diamond on his collar to signify that he had passed his examinations. On a small vessel such as the *Greyhound* his life was simpler and easier than on a bigger ship, for there was not much room for formality.

On a cold, windy day in February, the squadron sailed from Norfolk, immediately running into a gale. Midshipman Farragut was the only officer on the *Greyhound* who had ever served on a schooner, and his superiors quickly showed their ignorance. For a time all vessels of the squadron took in sail, but the wind died down a bit and Captain Porter ordered the crew to clap the sail back on, with only two reefs in the mainsail and the square sail. Soon the little schooner ran away from the squadron and began skipping from wave to wave.

"She does not rise to the sea," Farragut said cautiously to Captain Porter.

"If she can't carry the sail, let her drag it," the captain said airily.

So they sped on, Porter on one side of a trunk aft, sitting wrapped up in his boat cloak, Farragut on the other side, bundled up against the storm and holding an umbrella over his captain to shield him from the worst of the rain as the ship pounded and labored under her excessive sail.

Farragut was convinced that he would never live to see daylight, for the ship dashed along like a flying fish, barely touching the water. The rigging groaned and the ship heeled in every straying breeze. Porter sat, soddenly, apparently quite ignorant of their danger.

Finally, about eight o'clock the captain went below to escape the rain and left Farragut on deck with orders to look after the vessel, making or shortening sail as he saw fit without coming below to confirm changes. The captain was scarcely down the hatch when Farragut was shortening sail and soon had her under the foresail, scudding through the gale like a duck, but safely.

Well in front of the rest of the squadron, the *Greyhound* ran south, headed for the Mona Passage between Haiti and Puerto Rico. Not far from there, still alone, she encountered an English squadron consisting of a frigate, a sloop, and a brig. The English wanted to know what ship this might be, and the flagship made a signal to the brig, which hauled out of line and moved to intercept the schooner, firing a shot to bring her to heave to and wait for a boat from the English warship.

Captain Porter was again as foolhardy as he had been in the matter of sail during the storm. "Beat to quarters," he shouted, and when the men scurried to their battle stations, he gave orders that if the English ship fired at them again, they were to return the fire without another command.

The English ship did fire again. "Fire!" shouted the captain, disregarding his own previous order, "but don't hit her."

The brig came on, within musket range, and from the deck of the *Greyhound* Farragut could see the officers in their white uniforms on the poopdeck. The Long Tom fired, and the shot went whizzing above their heads. Farragut noted mildly that it seemed "rather a saucy proceeding on our part," since the schooner mounted at least sixteen guns to their three, to say nothing of the forty or fifty guns of the frigate and the armament of the sloop.

The English captain was near enough to fire a broadside and literally blow the *Greyhound* to pieces. But instead, he slapped his hand down on his thigh and hailed the schooner.

"None but a Yankee would have done that," he told his officers. "What ship is that?" he shouted across the water.

"A United States vessel of war," shouted Captain Porter in reply.

The English captain said that he regretted the mistake of firing the second gun and that he would send a boat with an officer to present his apologies and explain. The boat came alongside; the officer clambered up the ladder and was received. In the course of the conversation, Porter indicated that he was sick. When the English boat returned to the brig, the captain sent it to the *Greyhound* once more, this time bearing fruit. The English coxswain handed it up, saying to the American boatswain's mate who received it: "Here is some fruit for the shot you sent us."

The boatswain's mate looked down on him coolly: "We have a gun apiece for you, and are always ready to fight or eat with you."

The *Greyhound* joined the squadron, and they moved to San Juan, where the harbor guns fired on one of the schooners as she entered port, causing the death of the captain of the *Fox*. Commodore Porter protested this action, and the Spanish apologized, but the apology was not really acceptable to the navy men, and another issue was created between Spain and the United States.

The squadron was divided into two groups, with the *Greyhound* going south to patrol around the southern coasts of Haiti and Cuba. Nothing was found. The squadron reassembled at Key West, and Lieutenant Lawrence Kearney was transferred to the command of the *Greyhound,* a lucky break for Farragut, who might have ended up quarreling with Porter because he was obviously the captain's superior in seamanship and experience.

Kearney knew his business. They sailed south again, around the Isle of Pines and down to Cape Cruz. Kearney took the boat ashore and was fired on by pirates hidden in the woods. No harm was done, but Kearney was determined to go after them. At three o'clock on the following morning, Farragut led a landing party of seventeen men from the *Greyhound* and her sister ship the *Beagle*. As the men assembled in the darkness, the plan was outlined. The schooner would be warped in toward shore past the outlying rocks to cover the landing.

It was totally strange territory and they had no guides, which made the task most difficult. Farragut had little choice but to land his party and forge ahead into the chaparral growth. They landed on a narrow peninsula that was separated from the mainland by a lagoon and had to hack their way through the brambles to reach the mouth. As they emerged onto the beach again their appearance was so ragged that the ships almost fired on them, but Captain Kearney recognized Farragut's epaulet in time.

> My pantaloon stuck close to my legs, my jacket was torn to pieces by the brambles, and I was loaded with mud. The men under [Lieut.] Sommerville saluted me as their chief; but the sight was too much for their risibility and they burst into a loud laugh as I stepped on shore literally covered with mud and rags.[*]

Captain Kearney set out in a boat in search of pirates and was fired on by a 4-pound swivel gun ashore. Farragut was ordered to attack the pirates in the rear as the schooners moved in on them from the front.

Over rocks so sharp they cut the men's regulation shoes to ribbons Farragut led his men in to the attack. They plowed through thickets of cactus and scrub brush that they had to cut back with their cutlasses. They advanced about half a mile into the thick underbrush and waited for a signal from the ships. They were frightened by noises coming from the rear. Farragut grouped his men to repel an attack before he

[*]*Ibid.*, p. 158

learned that the attackers were land crabs, ten thousand of them making their way through the brush.

On the other side, Kearney had the ships towed inshore by the boats and opened fire on the bluffs, where the pirates were concealed. The fire was effective, and the pirates began to scatter. Farragut and his force moved forward in the intense heat; one man fainted. They captured only two old men and a black monkey, which bit the young midshipman on the arm.

They did not catch pirates that day, but they discovered their lair and captured an immense cave filled with loot from pirate expeditions. The cave contained saddles and clothing and equipment, from English and Spanish ships. The sailors also found a dozen boats and several large houses, which they burned and plundered.

That incident was the end of the *Greyhound*'s success in pirate hunting. The rest of the cruise was uneventful, although the remainder of the squadron encountered much more action and cleaned out one important nest of pirates. The squadron returned to Key West.

At the base Farragut met his brother William, a navy lieutenant, whom he had not seen for thirteen years, and they spent some time on the same ship after William was transferred to the *Greyhound*. Then Glasgow (as David was known) was transferred to the steamer *Sea Gull*, which was Commodore Porter's flagship, and they parted again.

Farragut had distinguished himself, and received a letter of commendation from Lieutenant Kearny, which added to his record. On the flagship, Commodore Porter came down with yellow fever as did a number of other men. Infection was common. The naval offices did not know what caused yellow fever in those days and the men slept in the open without mosquito netting. Porter took the *Sea Gull* north to recuperate and steamed to Washington. En route, Farragut came down with a light case of fever and suffered chills for some time. He accompanied Porter back to the West Indies about six weeks later, in February, 1824.

Then it was back to duty, searching for pirates and keeping the sea-lanes clear. Farragut secured leave and visited his family in New Orleans, seeing his sister Nancy and his foster mother. When he returned to Key West, he was appointed to command the schooner *Ferret*, although still a midshipman. He secured the appointment strictly through merit because Commodore Porter, fearful that he would be accused of favoritism, had hesitated to give Farragut the ship and did not until the captain of the fleet interceded and said that Farragut should have her.

At twenty-three, Midshipman David Farragut had his first command. The duty was light, consisting mostly of escorting ships through the dangerous waters of the Gulf of Mexico. He hunted pirates, but, frightened by the coming of the American squadron, they were lying low. For many weeks the *Ferret* cruised in these unhealthy waters and many of the men came down with yellow jack. One midshipman died of it, after refusing to let Farragut treat him because Farragut was not a licensed physician.

In the spring of 1824, he was ordered to Nassau, where he became involved in an incident reminiscent of the bad days of 1812. Because of the prevalence of yellow jack in this season and the knowledge that it was always worse ashore than at sea (although they did not know why this was so), Commodore Porter had given strict orders that the men were not to be given liberty in Nassau. The gunner's mate wanted desperately to get ashore for reasons of his own, and when Captain Farragut told him he could not go, the man grew sulky. He was not a native American, but had come to the American Navy as had many, by deserting from a British ship, the *Pandora*. In spite of the harsh British laws covering deserters, the gunner decided to get even with Farragut and hailed an English surveying ship near the *Ferret*'s anchorage. He informed the officer of the deck that he was a deserter and that he wanted to return to English naval jurisdiction.

Farragut, learning of this action, immediately got the *Ferret* under way, ran outside the port and out of English waters, flogged the gunner's mate for his violation of naval discipline, and came back into port.

At first he was determined not to give his man up to the English. He expected them to come searching, in the manner of boarding parties in the days of his boyhood. But the English were not interested in this man, and nothing happened. Meanwhile, Farragut learned that an English man-of-war had entered Havana, found American ships there, and had promptly turned over to the senior officer an American deserter who had joined one of their ships. That put a different face on the matter, and Farragut must be equally generous. He decided to turn over the gunner, valuable as he was to the ship, to the English commodore in Nassau.

The commodore was not so sure. He greeted Midshipman Farragut gravely and in a most friendly fashion, but he said the English had really had quite enough of such fellows. Times had changed drastically from the days when Napoleon was scourging Europe, and Britain needed every man she could find to work her ships. If a man deserted in 1824, the authorities were not particularly anxious to find him.

But Midshipman Farragut insisted, not so much from the viewpoint of giving the English back their man as to punish a man who had caused him a good deal of trouble. Finally the reluctant commodore took the seaman back, and Farragut administered the coup de grace: he told the gunner that he would get nothing in pay because he had refused to fulfill his contract with the United States government.

The trip to Nassau was very nearly the end of Farragut's service with what came to be called the Mosquito Squadron, because of its size and the unpleasant insect that dominated life in that area. He headed for Washington. As the ship passed up the Potomac, Midshipman Farragut came down with his first severe attack of yellow fever. As soon as they docked, he was taken to the hospital, where he spent many weeks. Command of the *Ferret* was given to Lieutenant C. H. Bell. Farragut offered to give Lieutenant Bell instruction in the peculiar sailing qualities of these schooners and the

Ferret in particular (they were capable of mounting more canvas than they could safely handle), but Lieutenant Bell was not interested in the advice of an inferior in rank. He said he would soon learn the qualities of the schooner as Farragut had done himself.

The *Ferret* pulled out and went back south during the stormy season of the Caribbean. Before he could learn much of anything, Lieutenant Bell presided over the capsizing of the *Ferret*, which went down with eight members of the crew in the waters off the north shore of Cuba.

10. THE VERSATILE LIEUTENANT

Midshipman Farragut rose from his Washington hospital bed yellow and thin, with a medical report advising the navy that he should not at this time return to the squadron for further service in the West Indies. Shakily, he headed for Norfolk again, to visit Miss Marchant. Before leaving for the West Indies station, Farragut had persuaded her to marry him, hoping that when he returned from the war against the pirates he would have his lieutenancy. Even without the promotion, the young couple decided to marry immediately. On September 2, 1824, they were married at Trinity Church in Portsmouth, and very shortly thereafter he took his young bride to visit the family he considered to be very much his own, the David Porters, at Meridian Hill outside Washington.

Commodore Porter was then at home on leave, convalescing from yellow fever himself, and the reunion was a happy one. All too soon, however, the commodore deemed himself well enough to go back to duty and resumed his command of the Mosquito Squadron. In November, when one of his officers was insulted by the Spanish at Fajardo, Puerto Rico, he took the insult as an affront to the American flag, landed a punitive force, and secured apology from the Spanish authorities. When the naval authorities at Washington learned of his action, he was brought to trial by court martial, and in the teeth of the evidence was found guilty of disobedience to orders and conduct unbecoming an officer. He was sentenced to six months' suspension from the service—a light punishment, considering the verdict—because there were friends in the navy who believed Porter had done exactly as he should have done. He was certain of it, and so outraged at what he considered to be an unfair verdict that he resigned from the naval service. Consequently, Farragut was deprived of the assistance of his one great champion in the United States Navy, a blow which might have caused him to leave the service had he not in the same winter already received the good news that he was finally promoted, commissioned a lieutenant after fourteen years of service as midshipman.

The promotion was offset by the failure of the navy to employ him, which meant that the new lieutenant received only half the forty dollars a month to which he was entitled when on active duty. In the spring he was occupied with whatever he could do to help Porter at the inquiry and testifying at the trial. In June he was offered new orders to duty on the storeship *Decoy,* but since she was bound for the West Indies, he pleaded ill health and the orders were revoked.

There was further delay while Lieutenant Farragut's status was clarified, but finally he presented a medical report showing that he was fit for duty but recommending that he stay out of the West Indies because of fever. On August 9, he was assigned to the new frigate *Brandywine,* which had been built especially to convey the Marquis de Lafayette home to France after his final visit to the United States. She was a big ship by frigate standards, larger than the *Constitution,* displacing 1,700 tons and carrying a crew of 480 officers and men.

It was a mark of some distinction that Farragut should be assigned to this ship, for the voyage she was about to undertake was given great importance by the United States government. Lafayette's tour of the United States had been in the nature of a triumphal tour by an old friend and maker of the nation. He was honored wherever he went. He was given land and valuable gifts, needed, in fact, to help restore fortunes much eroded by the changes in France in the past third of a century. Lafayette visited former presidents Monroe, Madison, and Jefferson in Virginia, and was guest of honor at one last great state dinner given by President John Quincy Adams on September 6, and then took steamer passage down the Potomac to where the *Brandywine* lay at anchor ready to receive him. The party was piped aboard with full honors. Captain Charles Morris and the navy had selected the officers to represent as many different states as possible and as many Revolutionary families as possible.

It was the *Brandywine's* maiden voyage, and in a way this proved embarrassing to Captain Morris. She sailed very well, but almost immediately developed a bad leak because the oakum worked out of the seams. Several thousand shot were thrown overboard to lighten her and reduce the pressure, but the leak continued until the planks began to swell from immersion and offset the loss of caulking. For a day or so it was touch and go; she might have to turn about and go back into drydock for a refit. But then the pumps gained the upper hand.

Farragut saw little of Lafayette, who was confined to his cabin with seasickness and the gout for most of the voyage. There was some concern that the French authorities would refuse to receive the old general, because in his absence from France Louis XIII had died and Charles X had come to the throne. Since Charles detested republicanism, Captain Morris was worried about the safety of his passenger. On arrival off Le Havre on October 5, the American consul and some members of the general's family came aboard and assured the captain that all was well. He sent Lieutenant Farragut ashore to double-check and to arrange for Lafayette's landing. The landing on the next day was ceremonious and without event to mar the old gentleman's homecoming. Captain Morris accompanied him to Paris, and the *Brandywine* set sail for England to stop the leak and make the ship ready for the voyage into the Mediterranean. Lieutenant Farragut spent several days visiting resorts and seeing the sights of England's Isle of Wight.

In the fourth week of October, the *Brandywine* was ready and sailed for Gibraltar. They took on a pilot to take them out of Cowes, and as officer of the deck, Farragut offered to take the pilot's boat in tow so that they would not lose track of her. The pilot scoffed at the youthful lieutenant. His boat would go through the Solent and the Needles, round the western coast of the island, and intercept the frigate there. Farragut warned the pilot that unless the captain hove to off the Needles and waited, the pilot boat would never catch them.

The pilot scoffed, for no frigate sailed that well, but he was no longer scoffing when they dashed through the Spithead and rounded the western coast. His boat was nowhere in sight. He asked to be placed aboard a passing waterlogged vessel, but he could not sail it and had to be taken off by another ship. Farragut met a definitely embarrassed pilot much later at Gibraltar, where he was taken by his rescuers.

From Gibraltar the *Brandywine* sailed to the Balearics, where they wintered, and in the spring they returned to America, landing at New York in May, 1826. Lieutenant Farragut joined his wife at New York and went on leave, using this time to take Susan to Connecticut, where she sought the services of doctors at New Haven for neuralgia.

Farragut was detached from the *Brandywine* at his own request and spent the next four months in New Haven while his wife was treated by Dr. Eli Ives, who was supposedly the most learned physician in America. In his letter asking for leave of absence, Farragut sited the delicate condition of his own health; he was very nervous and his eyes bothered him exceedingly. He attributed his troubles to the sunstroke he had suffered in North Africa, as he attributed his growing baldness to the same cause. At Yale he attended lectures and tried to do some reading, but found it difficult to concentrate; his eyes bothered him so much that he could not read more than a page or two at a time.

The four months at New Haven did not do as much good for Mrs. Farragut as the young couple had hoped. Farragut sought shore duty in order to take care of his invalid wife. He was assigned to Norfolk and to the receiving ship *Alert*.

What memories that new assignment evoked! *Alert* was the sloop-of-war that he had helped Captain Porter capture at the outbreak of the War of 1812. It was the coxswain of her captain's gig who had stood silently at the young Midshipman Farragut's hammock in the gun room of the old *Essex*, pistol in hand, watching the young boy's breathing, while the petri-

102

fied Farragut feigned sleep and yearned to warn his captain. Fourteen years had passed, and he again trod the decks of the *Alert,* but what a change. She was a storeship now and in three years would be broken up.

Captain Kennedy, commander of the *Alert,* was an understanding man and he allowed Lieutenant Farragut to bring his wife aboard in order to care for her. Farragut's duty was to establish a school for the boys, the apprentice seamen of the naval station. Most of the boys had joined the service at a very young age and could neither read nor write. Farragut did an excellent job. His school became a point of especial interest in the tours conducted by Commodore James Barron, commander of the Norfolk Navy Yard, and on one occasion Secretary of the Navy Samuel Southard complimented Farragut on his work.

Biographer Charles Lewis noted that while Matthew Calbraith Perry is given credit as the founder of apprentice training in the navy, Farragut was conducting his school a year before Perry first wrote to the Navy Department about the need for such training and nine years before Perry's program was put into effect in the Brooklyn Navy Yard. The Perry letter and the Farragut school were both marks of the growing sense of responsibility of the times. Earlier it had been believed sufficient that a seaman be able to learn his trade without benefit of book studies. But steam was invading the sailing ship navy, and had been since the War of 1812, although it was slow coming. Steam meant new technology and many improvements in the service. It also meant that education was becoming more important and not simply a privilege of the moneyed.

Progress was slow. How slow is indicated by an incident reported by Farragut in his reminiscences. Some years after his tenure as schoolmaster, Farragut encountered a tall well-dressed young man on the street in Norfolk and learned that he was one of his more recalcitrant students of years gone by. The young man had left the navy in his teens and joined an East Indiaman. On the voyage the captain had died at Batavia, and the chief mate had died on the trip home. The young man had learned enough mathematics from Farragut to navigate the ship and brought her home safely. The owners were so pleased with him that he had advanced rapidly in their service and seven years later was commanding a ship in the Charleston trade. Even a tiny bit of education went a long way in this early day.

Farragut spent two years at Norfolk on this tour, and while they were gratifying years because he was able to be with his wife, he knew very well that such duty did not bring advancement in the service. He could not hope for very rapid advancement in the peacetime navy, but as he must go to sea periodically for his record, he began applying for sea duty. In October, 1828, he was ordered to the *Vandalia,* a small sloop that carried eighteen guns. She had been launched recently at Philadelphia and was fitting out there for sea. Farragut had several weeks in which there was enough spare time for him to make visits to Green Bank on the Delaware, to talk over old times with Mrs. Porter. The Commodore, having left the navy, had gone into the service of Mexico and was away from home.

In December, the *Vandalia* sailed for Brazil, a voyage that was uneventful except for a squall that came up one day when Farragut was officer of the deck, when he again showed his superb mastery of the arts of seamanship. Soon the ship was in Rio de Janeiro, then in Montevideo, and then in Buenos Aires. He was witness to history, not once but many times. He saw the Civil War of 1829 in Argentina. He accompanied Commodore Creighton on a visit of state to Emperor Dom Pedro I of Brazil. But a year after his departure, his eyes were irritating him so much that he requested to be sent home.

The waters of the Americas were hardly safe in the days of the 1820's, and on the voyage home, aboard the merchant brig *Barnegat,* they were followed by pirates off the Cape St. Roque and most certainly would have been attacked, had the wind not suddenly freshened and carried them away from their shadower. During this crisis, Farragut assumed military command of the merchantman and prepared with grave confidence to fight her. There was not much with which to fight:

four 18-pound carronades that would be accurate only at very short range, a few musket balls and nails, but no shot, and twenty-four pounds of powder. For wadding, the men he assembled from the crew tore up their flannel shirts, and when the pirate came within two miles of them before the wind came up, Farragut had the six men and the merchant ship's officers all primed for a fight.

Home in 1830, Farragut went again to a receiving ship, the *Congress,* in Norfolk harbor, and again was allowed to keep his invalid wife with him. Later he moved to the *Java* with the same duties, on the same station.

In the summer of 1831, Farragut and the other officers of the naval station prepared to defend the station against an attack from shore. In Southampton County the Negro preacher Nat Turner had rebelled against enslavement and led a band of Negroes for a brief moment of murder and mayhem, followed by an ignominious death and a long silence in history. The death of the Turner band put an end to the momentary fright, and Farragut turned again to his own troubles.

There were enough of them. Most serious was the continuing illness of Susan Farragut, who was confined to bed and wheelchair. Farragut's patience and understanding with his wife brought him an almost sainted reputation among the ladies of the navy yard. He took care of her needs, and when he thought there was any hope, he took her searching for medical assistance. In the summer of 1832, he took her to Philadelphia to see more doctors. The cholera epidemic broke out while they were there, and they fled to Frederick, Maryland, where they felt much safer than in the cities. New York suffered terribly, and the people who could afford it deserted the city in droves. The situation in Philadelphia was only slightly less worrisome.

During this troublesome period Farragut was well-treated indeed by the navy. He was forced to ask for several leaves in order to help his wife and to seek relief for his own painful eyes. The Secretary of the Navy granted these leaves and revoked sea orders for him to join the *Vandalia.* Finally, on December 4, he was ordered to the eighteen-gun sloop

Natchez as first lieutenant, and immediately, again he was precipitated into the mainstream of history. This was the era of the struggle between President Andrew Jackson and southern firebrands over the South Carolinian policy of nullification. The idea was actually an old one, but John C. Calhoun and South Carolina emerged in 1832 as the forces ready to test the theory that the federal government might not try to enforce laws or collect taxes when the state government involved disapproved of the laws. The issue came over the federal tariff on imported goods, and when South Carolina indicated that it would resist the collection of taxes by the federal authorities at Charleston harbor, army and navy forces were sent to the area, among them the *Natchez*.

It was a rough passage from Norfolk to Charleston harbor, for the ship was towing the ten-gun schooner *Experiment*. The towline broke twice, and then the ships ran into a gale in which *Natchez* lost her jib boom. She was hit by a terrible sea that displaced her weather sheet anchor, the quarterboat and the davits, and she was nearly struck by lightning, the crack deafening the men. After the *Natchez* reached Cape Romaine and the pilot came aboard, the ship grounded three times on the bar getting into harbor but finally came to anchor in the way so properly named Rebellion Roads.

But overall the stay in Charleston was more than a little pleasant, and Farragut recalled it as consisting very heavily of entertainment at the homes of Charleston's most prominent citizens. The people of the city were especially grateful when a fire broke out in the downtown district and the *Natchez* sent men to fight it. Farragut went off with the launch and the first cutter and fifty men to help put out the flames.

They stayed in harbor until the troubles ended with the capitulation of South Carolina's legislature to the national government. They returned to Norfolk, giving passage to General Winfield Scott, the army commander, who was in haste to return to duty in Washington. Before they left, Commodore Jesse Elliott took his flag down from the masthead and went ashore to the Charleston Navy Yard, having first ordered a salute and three cheers in his own honor. Elliott rubbed Farragut the wrong way, just as Elliott rubbed Oliver Perry the wrong way at the Battle of Lake Erie in his attempt to hog glory at the expense of his commander and the American fleet, and as Elliott had rubbed Stephen Decatur the wrong way, and even as he had become the enemy of Commodore Porter and had been a member of the ill-advised court that had forced Porter to quit the navy.

After short leaves for the officers and men of the ship, the *Natchez* was dispatched to the Brazil station again, in company with two other ships under the pennant of Commodore M. T. Woolsey. Farragut was soon known in the squadron as the fairest and finest of first lieutenants, and the *Natchez* was a happy ship. He was a disciplinarian but he never forgot what he had learned aboard the *Washington* when Captain Creighton had made life so miserable for all the men. The *Natchez* was the best-worked ship in the squadron, but the men were not tortured into performing; they worked with a will for the first lieutenant they called Little Luff (Luff being a diminutive for lieutenant, and Farragut being a very diminutive lieutenant).

It was not long before Lieutenant Farragut secured his second real command. The little ten-gun schooner *Boxer* had recently been assigned to the Brazil station. But she had come from East Asia for the new assignment, and her officers and men were due for home leave. They were sent home on other vessels and the *Boxer* was remanned from within the squadron, Farragut assuming command on March 7, 1834. There was much ceremony and some excitement and satisfaction for Farragut in the next few weeks in Rio de Janeiro harbor. He was invited to a levee aboard a Brazilian warship on a day when the emperor and his family came aboard. Late in March came Commodore John Downes, his old first lieutenant of the *Essex* and prize master in the days of the war against the British whaling fleet. Commodore Downes was on his way home from a voyage around the world in the forty-four-gun frigate *Potomac* and stopped off at Rio. Farragut went aboard and spent an afternoon yarning with his old first lieutenant. Downes was particularly pleased to see that Farragut had advanced in the service. Here, at least, was another officer from the good old days on whom Farragut might count for friendship if it was needed.

For the next few months Farragut alternated between the waters of Rio de Janeiro harbor and the La Plata, carrying information on the politics of South America from one American base to the other. Then, at the end of July, the ship returned to Norfolk and Farragut was relieved of command.

There was no personal reflection in his relief but rather a general reduction in the activities of the United States Navy. The navy had been created belatedly to protect an expanding United States Merchant Marine. In the 1830's, the merchant marine continued to expand but required very little protection. All but one ship of the line and a handful of frigates were laid up in a mothball fleet, as later navy men would call it. For nearly *four years*, Lieutenant Farragut was kept in Norfolk at the home he and Susan had established, waiting for orders. To amuse himself, Farragut took up carpentry and became adept at the art of cabinet making. He also had quite enough to do to nurse his wife, who had grown so ill, with what must have been arthritis, that she could not walk alone. He carried her about in his arms.

Farragut's pay was a hundred dollars a month, which he augmented somewhat by sitting on courts-martial. He spent nearly all the time at home, making one brief trip to Washington, but coming back quickly because Susan's illness would not permit him to be away for long. He sat and waited. By 1837, he was seventieth on the list of lieutenants, but there were not enough berths on active duty for the seventy. There were other reasons for the inactivity, and the most irritating of these was the corruption within the navy itself. Commodore Alexander J. Dallas was one of the worst offenders (although he could not have continued his activity without the supine acquiescence of Navy Secretary Mahlon Dickerson). Commodore Dallas flatly ignored the matters of rotation and seniority and kept a staff of favorites about him. Lesser officers did the same, until finally the matter became so scandalous that it came to the attention of Congress. Changes were made then, and among them was the ordering to active duty of Lieutenant Farragut. He was ordered to join the *Constellation* at Pensacola.

He joined in April, 1838, immediately received leave to go to Mississippi, visited his youngest sister Elizabeth for the first time in more than a quarter of a century, and hastened back to his ship for a cruise to Tampico. During the cruise, he proved himself a competent officer and on return was assigned to command of the sloop *Erie,* eighteen guns, with a crew of 140 men.

The *Erie* was sent to Tampico to watch a French squadron that stood off the coast, blockading the port (and the rest of the Mexican coast) in a dispute about claims of French citizens arising from the unrest that had troubled Mexico after the revolution against Spain. Farragut's responsibility was to safeguard American interests. He traveled south to Vera Cruz and found more French ships in that harbor. He called on the French Commodore Bazoche, and on Vera Cruz' Mexican governor. A French bark arrived short of water and he gave the Frenchmen four-hundred gallons as an act of mercy because they could not land on Mexican soil. He made soundings in the harbor and elsewhere for his own information about anchorages, and occupied himself with the language and study of the international politics of the moment. In mid-September, Lieutenant Farragut learned of a revolution at Tampico. He sailed for that port again. At Tampico he was delayed for some time by the revolution. He went ashore at the end of September and made his way by horseback toward Tampico, but the fighting cut him off. He went to Pueblo Viejo, where he finally made contact with the American consul. He took money and American passengers to New Orleans, then went on to Pensacola, but directly returned to Mexican waters.

The *Erie* was in Vera Cruz harbor when the French attacked the castle in the city. Admiral Baudin, an old Napoleonic commander, led the assault and, since he was equipped with a plan of the castle, he had a great advantage. The battle began early in the morning and lasted until night-

109

fall, the French fleet firing 7,700 shot, 177 shells, and 302 bombs at the defenses. The shells, which penetrated and then exploded, did more damage than the solid shot or the immediately explosive bombs.

Farragut observed the battle carefully and learned much about modern warfare. The Mexicans capitulated at the end of the day. Farragut went aboard the French flagship to congratulate the admiral, and to learn what more he could about the battle. He was particularly interested in the reduction of a land fort by warships without support of an army, and he had seen it before his eyes. The castle had 186 guns, thick walls, and was surrounded by shoal water, yet it fell to the shot and shell of a naval force, and the French lost only four men killed and twenty-nine wounded.

Lieutenant Farragut spent some time aboard the French warships, particularly the *Iphigénie*, which had been in the front of the battle and had taken 150 shot in her hull from the fortress. He saw the French improvements in guns, much more modern than the American guns, and he wrote home to his superiors about the superiority they showed in action. He said flatly that his own navy was equipped for a War of 1812, but not for a modern war, and that American ships could not win battles against such frigates unless the American Navy paid more attention to improvements. These were strong words.

As result of this battle, General Santa Anna came to the area to replace the commander who had capitulated to the French, and Farragut engaged in a most interesting conversation with his old acquaintance.

"You must tell President Van Buren and Mr. Forsyth [Secretary of State] that we are all one family and must be united against Europeans obtaining a foothold on this continent," Santa Anna said. A foothold was precisely what France wanted, as would be seen a few years later when the Americans were too much occupied with civil war to prevent French invasion.

Santa Anna set about making amends for the disgrace heaped on Mexico by the French. He told Farragut that all

Americans and American property would be protected by the Mexican Army and that in case of loss the Mexican government would be responsible. As for Santa Anna, he would not surrender the town to Admiral Baudin. Instead, he was investing it with all the troops at his disposal.

Admiral Baudin's price for the defeat of the Mexicans at the Castle of San Juan de Ulloa had been the removal of all Mexican troops, except a thousand men, to a point ten leagues from the seacoast. Santa Anna was disregarding the order.

Admiral Baudin gave Santa Anna a few hours in which to submit to French rule. At six o'clock on the morning of December 5, not receiving a reply, the French landed 1500 men, who attacked Santa Anna's headquarters. They almost captured him; he escaped only in shirt and trousers. The Mexicans made a stand at the barracks in the city, however, and the French, who knew they could not hold the town long, retreated. The Mexicans pursued them to the harbor, and nearly succeeded in killing Admiral Baudin. In the battle, Santa Anna received a wound that cost him his left leg. Finally, the French were declared victors, the Mexicans agreed to their terms of settlement, and the undeclared war ended. Farragut sailed to Tampico, then to Pensacola, where he turned over command of the *Erie* to Commander Joseph Smoot and returned to Norfolk.

Farragut had learned much about the conduct of modern warfare in the battle at Vera Cruz. Soon he learned as much about the dangers of expressing a public opinion: He had written a letter for the New Orleans *Commercial Bulletin* describing the battle but casting some doubt on the method by which the French had achieved victory. Admiral Baudin, he said, had violated his promise about the hour at which he would attack Santa Anna. He questioned whether the enterprise was worth the trouble and cost in terms of trade. Admiral Baudin was insulted, called Farragut a liar, and a diplomatic incident was in the making. The Secretary of the Navy called Farragut to account, disapproving of the lieutenant's remarks about the admiral of a friendly (but not very friendly) power. The Secretary also warned Farragut against talking to newspapermen. There the matter ended, probably because the distinguished admiral could not bring himself to quarrel with a lowly lieutenant, but for a time Farragut's career hung in the balance. He certainly learned the lesson of silence.

The offending letter was published in January, 1839, and was the cause of Farragut's remaining idle for nearly a year. At the same time, Susan Farragut's illness grew more desperate day by day, and on December 27, she died.

11. COMMANDER

In February, 1841, Lieutenant Farragut received orders to join the U.S.S. *Delaware* as executive officer. This post was indeed a promotion, for the *Delaware* was a ship of the line, seventy-four guns, 2,600 tons, and a crew of 820 officers and men, every one of whom, except the captain, bore some share of responsibility to the executive officer.

Farragut took the ship at the Norfolk Navy Yard in March and began re-rigging her. He did not forget the lessons he had learned in visiting other ships of other countries, and some of these lessons were brought to bear in the *Delaware*. He devised a new method of rigging the tops which cut the time to a fraction of the old. He brought the rest of the crew aboard on May 7. The others, old sailors, had been helping ready the ship, but this last batch represented men in every state of training, from old salts to the rawest landsmen. The day they boarded, Farragut began rubbing the raw edges off and making a crew of them. A week later the ship dropped down river between the two defending forts, and three weeks later the ship was towed to Hampton Roads. Lieutenant Farragut spent two hard months drilling the men in seamanship and gunnery before he was satisfied that the *Delaware* had a crew of which she could be proud.

Farragut was not pleased with the old method of handling powder on a large ship. He devised a new one, which involved the use of a revolving belt system with hooks to hang the powder boxes so they could be moved up between decks quickly. By July 12, he was ready to try a call to general

113

quarters, and for the next two weeks he called general quarters twice a week to test the crew.

By this time the captain was aboard. On July 23, he called for three broadsides, which would give the crew its first test under realistic battle conditions. Now was the time for Lieutenant Farragut to show how well he had trained this crew.

He gave his first order—assuming that they were a ship of the line cruising under battle conditions, and that the guns would be loaded and ready to fire. The men went through the motions of firing and swabbing. Then came the order to pass the powder from the magazine, and the gun captains were to load and fire as quickly as possible.

In four minutes the main deck divisions had fired three broadsides; the firemen, boarders, pikemen and small-arms men had all been exercised, and the latter had fired half a dozen to a dozen times. Fifteen minutes after the first gun was fired, the guns were cleaned and secured, and the retreat was beaten. It was a record of which any crack ship could be proud.

The ship sailed to Annapolis and lay there receiving visitors, perhaps two-thousand people coming aboard every day. On August 14, Secretary of the Navy Badger and a number of other cabinet officers visited the ship. The captain went ashore and returned on August 27, bringing that most welcome gift, Farragut's promotion to commander, which came sixteen years after he had achieved his lieutenant's rank, or almost thirty years since he had set out on the first cruise with Captain Porter in the *Essex*. Farragut was not an old man by any means, just forty, but he was certainly an old-time sailor by 1841.

There were more ceremonials that autumn, and then the *Delaware* sailed for the Brazil station. Nothing unusual occurred on the passage, except that the copper sheathing of the hull, used to protect her from boring worms (and useful to protect her against attachment of boring mines in wartime) was stripping off. It was placed over felt those days, an innovation of some unnamed naval architect, and Farragut was annoyed. He knew something about construction and knew that felt would not work. The old system had been to put the copper over a coat of turpentine and tallow. He had watched at Norfolk when the old *Guerrière* had been stripped after twenty-five years, and the wood had been as fresh as the day the bottom was treated. In the case of the *Delaware,* the felt swelled in the water, started the nails on the upper edge of the copper, and then the pressure of the sea did the rest, stripping the copper away. To Farragut it was another example of the wasteful, foolish effort of dockyard men and civilian contractors who did not know their business.

In December, after arrival and ceremonies, he took the ship into dock and began a general overhaul. Six more months, and he was detached from the *Delaware* and given command of the sloop *Decatur*, sixteen guns and 150 men; a new, fast ship, which made him pleased and proud. For the next few weeks he conducted a training program. Then he sailed for the La Plata and to Buenos Aires. Commodore Morris transferred his pennant to the *Decatur*, which made her flagship of the squadron and brought Farragut into constant contact with the officials of the countries visited and the officers of other navies. They spent much time visiting ashore, particularly the houses of Governor Rosas. They went to parties and bullfights and balls. They participated in military ceremonies. They watched an abortive balloon ascension. They were taken to horse shows and riding exhibitions. Then it was time to return to Rio de Janeiro, and on December 15 to go home to the United States.

In peacetime a naval officer's reputation was made in many small ways, and Farragut always chose to enhance his name with praise for his ship-handling. Seven years earlier he had astounded Rio de Janeiro's wharf rats, and even the men who manned the international navy that hung about the harbor, by taking the *Natchez* out of the narrow neck of the harbor with a maneuver that called for the most delicate timing and the utmost faith in the ability and speed of action of his crew, an intricate design of movement called "box-hauling," which enabled a square-rigged ship to move out of harbor against a headwind. English and French captains and their officers had lined the decks of their ships as Farragut undertook the maneuver, scorn on their faces, waiting to see the Yankee fail. He had not stayed around to see what they said after he succeeded perfectly.

Again, in the *Decatur*, Commander Farragut decided to show off a little.

> Getting under way was rather a difficult maneuver with us, having Rat Island on our starboard beam, a Brazilian frigate on our larboard, a sloop of war on our starboard quarter, but nearly astern, and a large merchantman on our larboard quarters; the tide running flood, wind south, and lying in eleven and a half fathoms of water. The great difficulty to be apprehended was that in such a depth of water the tide would sweep us into the hawse of the sternmost vessels before we could gather headway, as they were all lying close to us.

What Farragut said here was that he intended to sail out north, surrounded by three ships and an island, with only the area straight ahead of him entirely clear, and the tide and wind running from stem to stern of the ship, so that if he loosed his anchors, he would be swept back into the anchor chains of the other ships.

> We succeeded, however, in the following manner: hove to a short stay, set the topsails, braced the head yards slighta-box on the larboard tack, braced the after yards sharp up on the starboard tack, and, as soon as the anchor was aweigh, fell off to port; hove the anchor briskly up to the bows, braced around the head yards, boarded the main tack, and hauled out the spanker; boarded the fore tack, eased off the main sheet, and just cleared the stern of the frigate; so we lost nothing. Then we proceeded to cat and fish the anchor, and get all sail set, continuing to beat out of the harbor. About sunset we cleared Santa Cruz [the point of the harbor]. . . .

Like many other American naval officers, Commander

Farragut took a strong interest in affairs in Latin America. Actually, the navy showed a much more vigorous interest in hemispheric affairs than the political departments of the nation. Part of the reason was that the United States was then adopting a very precise view of the Monroe Doctrine, and the American naval forces in Rio de Janeiro harbor and in the La Plata River were there to be sure that neither France nor England attempted to suborn a government and secure a new colony. The danger was real if not readily apparent to Americans at home, because the revolution was still in progress. General Rosas, at whose home and in whose company Farragut spent many pleasant hours in Buenos Aires, was the dictator of the region, which was made up of several of the states that would eventually separate into South American nations. Rosas was a bloody dictator, but the Americans took the position that such was necessary in this day to bring order out of chaos. Farragut attended one ball in honor of the victory of a Rosas admiral over a stray revolutionary named Garibaldi, who had been a seaman, a teacher in Montevideo, and then a naval commander who fought a valiant but losing engagement with the Rosas navy before burning his ship and disappearing into the brush.

Farragut's interest in the South American countryside led him to make a stop at Para and, in the company of the American consul, to go upriver to visit a plantation and spend two days wandering among the cocoa and rubber plants. Then it was back to sea, an adventure with an earthquake that shook the ship severely for five minutes, and an otherwise uneventful voyage back to Norfolk. The *Decatur* arrived on February 18, 1843, and Farragut gave up command to go ashore.

With his experience, having achieved the rank of commander, Farragut had the feeling that his star was beginning to rise in the navy, and after a few days of idleness ashore, he made a trip to Washington to propose that he be given command of the *Decatur* once again. The Secretary of the Navy, Abel Upshur, found Farragut's proposal laughable—and with good reason. The *Decatur* was scheduled to join a squadron under Captain Matthew Calbraith Perry which would cruise off the northwest coast of Africa to try to suppress the slave trade. In all the American Navy only the name of Jesse Elliott was more detested by the Perry family than that of Farragut; perhaps Farragut was hated worse because Oliver Perry had risen above Elliott's attempts to destroy his career, while Christopher Raymond Perry's career had really been destroyed. As families will, the Perry's preferred to blame others for making the drunkard's way difficult rather than blame the character of their relative. It was obviously out of the question that Farragut should have any favor at the hands of a Perry.

The disappointment revealed to Farragut the truth of his own position, that it was not nearly so strong as he expected. He was low on the list of commanders; many men of longer age in grade were ashore, idle, and so would he be under the system that obtained.

The system was in for change, but it was not to come just yet. Other navies were turning to steam and were developing new guns and new methods of warfare, but the United States Navy stubbornly stuck to its old ways, and in the absence of any challenge to the American government in its own chosen sphere of influence, the public was completely unaware of the need for change, and the voices of a handful of reformers led by Commander Mathew Maury were generally unheard.

Farragut spent the summer of 1843 in the Virginia mountains, came back, and asked a new Secretary of the Navy, David Henshaw, for appointment as superintendent of the Norfolk Navy Yard. Henshaw refused, saying that he would never appoint a man who claimed Norfolk as his home to the job. Farragut was furious and went up on Capitol Hill to lobby against the confirmation of this new Secretary by the Senate. Henshaw was not confirmed, and Farragut took some pride in his part in helping prevent it, but the fact was that no naval officer had much to do with Henshaw's failure. The real reason was the struggle for power between President John Tyler and Henry Clay. Clay had left the Senate, preparing for the campaign of 1844 for the Presidency, but Tyler could do no right and his appointments were all scrutinized suspiciously by an unfriendly Congress.

No matter, Farragut felt better for having struck out against one who had injured him, for as a commander he was confident that he would be shown respect and receive command appointments.

It did not happen that way. His next position was as executive officer of a ship of the line *Pennsylvania*, which was then station ship, or receiving ship, at Norfolk. Under the circumstances, Farragut forgot his annoyance at being given less than command; he had married again, Miss Virginia Dorcas Loyall, of Norfolk.

The duty aboard the *Pennsylvania* lasted from April, 1844, until early autumn. His captain was detached and Farragut was made commander of the ship until October, when he was detached and sent ashore as second in command of the naval station he had earlier aspired to head. But the commander was a full commodore, Jesse Wilkinson, which eased the pain of again playing second fiddle.

Farragut was at this time taking a lively interest in American party politics, much more so than ever before, and he voted for the Democratic candidate, James K. Polk, in the election that year. One reason was his dislike of the treatment he had been accorded as a naval officer under an administration that was at least nominally Whig in nature. Another was his belief in the propriety of the annexation of Texas, which was the basic issue. A vote for Texas annexation meant a vote for war with Mexico, and it was not long in coming after Polk's inauguration.

As a careful and observant naval man, Commander Farragut had made it a point to secure a copy of the plans of the Castle of San Juan de Ulloa after the French had secured and used them so satisfactorily. When Captain R. F. Stockton was ordered south to Mexican waters in the steam warship *Princeton*, Farragut gave him the plans and a discourse on the method of conducting the battle he had seen. He also began agitating for a part in the action.

In the summer of 1845, he wrote to Secretary of the Navy

Bancroft, outlining his excellent qualifications for service in the Gulf of Mexico. He spoke the language. He had served there twice previously and knew much of the countryside.

But there was that unfortunate affair of his letter to the New Orleans newspaper, and when the authorities considered Mexico and Farragut, they remembered the case. Furthermore, Matthew Calbraith Perry was back in Washington, applying for Mexican service too, as a captain. He secured appointment as second in command to Commodore David Conner, who took a large squadron to the Gulf with the declaration of war in 1846. Obviously, Farragut's services would not be wanted.

"Old Bruin's" star was in the ascendance, and that is a very good part of the reason Farragut's was not; the Farragut-Perry relationship, combined with the unpleasant ending of his last sojourn in Mexican waters, was enough to make any Secretary of the Navy shy. In October, 1846, Captain Perry led a successful foray up the Tabasco River and emerged a hero. At the same time Farragut was writing the Secretary, pleading to be employed in Mexico and citing his experiences and his intimate knowledge of the area. Finally, when the twenty-gun sloop *Saratoga* came to Norfolk for a refit, destined for Mexican waters, he wrote a final time, asking specifically for command of her, pointing out that he had his proper tour of command duty and that many officers junior to him had been given command posts. He secured command of the *Saratoga*.

Farragut got his ship on March 9, but with it he was bequeathed nothing but trouble. The *Saratoga* had just returned from the Brazil station and needed a refit. Her crew was ready for discharge or long leave, almost down to the last man. Farragut was eager to get to sea. The refit part was all right; he had so many friends at the navy yard that he found it easy to get the work done in less than three weeks, and without raising the particular variety of hell stirred up for everyone at the yard by Captain Perry when he had come back in January with the *Mississippi* and forced Norfolk to do six weeks' work on her in two. But manning was something entirely different, and in spite of his best efforts, Farragut could only get 190 of the 210 officers and men stipulated for her. He had the choice of waiting or sailing. He chose to sail shorthanded, with only one man aboard even rated *seaman;* all others were apprentices, boys, and landsmen—landlubbers all. As usual, Farragut was up to the task of sailing and training, and by the time the *Saratoga* reached Vera Cruz on April 26, his men were sailors and fighting sailors at that, ready to go into battle.

Farragut had long nursed the hope of leading a successful attack on the Castle of San Juan de Ulloa. He believed that he could take the castle with the *Pennsylvania* and two sloops of war like his *Saratoga.* On the way south he had dreamed of persuading Commodore Conner to undertake the attack. When he stood off the harbor, it was a great shock to see the castle wearing the Stars and Stripes—it had been attacked and captured a month earlier from the land.

Inside the harbor, Farragut discovered to his chagrin that he had been completely right; the castle was badly defended and might have been taken from the sea. Instead, the navy had waited for General Scott's army to come and make the assault. Thus, said Farragut, Commodore Conner had blithely passed up the opportunity to become a hero, and an admiral.

Farragut was correct in his assertion about the castle, but not about Conner. The commodore had already been disgraced and replaced. Captain Perry had gone to Washington after raising his furore at Norfolk and had persuaded the Secretary of the Navy that Conner was doing a poor job in southern waters and that he, Perry, could do a better one. Secretary John Mason had sent Perry back to Mexico bearing the orders that would give the captain command of the naval forces and send Conner home.

Farragut's dreams of glory were half collapsed by the sight of the American flag atop his hoped-for target. The collapse was complete when he learned that Conner was no longer in command, but that his enemy Perry had run his broad pennant up the mast of the flagship. Perry's enmity was not long in making itself shown. The order came: Farragut was to take the *Saratoga* to Tuspan, a relatively unimportant port 150 miles north of Vera Cruz. There he was to sit in blockade, with the *Albany*. The duty was perfectly legitimate, and Captain Perry had every right to assign Farragut, but it was a signal of his dislike and Farragut knew it.

The next months—nearly a year—represented the most frustrating and debilitating period of Farragut's naval career until that time. Captain Breese, his opposite number on the *Albany*, was congenial enough. The captain had furnished a landing force for the expedition against Tuspan months earlier, so he, at least, had been in action. More than that, he had participated in all the previous actions of the naval forces in the Mexican war, and he was happy to have the respite. Farragut was aching for a naval fight. He was upset when Perry moved an expedition against Coatzacoalcos without him and the *Saratoga*, and more so when he was not allowed to take part in the expedition against Tabasco in June, although the *Albany* was called to join the fleet for that purpose. The irony of it was that Captain Breese would much have preferred to remain on blockade duty off Tuspan. Farragut fumed at the inactivity.

In his anxiety to go to war, and the need for haste in getting a crew, and with all the good assistance from his friends at Norfolk Navy Yard, Farragut had picked up the dregs of the navy—servants, boat's crewmen, and book-keepers. In the enforced idleness of blockade duty off the Mexican coast, the shortage of disciplined naval men soon began to show. The boatswain and his mates laid on heavily with the colt, the rope knotted at the end which was used for minor punishment, and floggings became frequent and severe. The logbook was first scattered with such reports, then studded with them. Day upon day the officer of the watch would pick up pen and scrawl in spidery handwriting the story of disciplinary failure in an unhappy ship. Drunkenness—a sailor might save up his grog or trade his clothing for more, and there seemed to be endless ways of securing spirits even off an enemy shore; fighting—the men were hot and sick and unhappy in the torpid air off the coast of Mexico; their spirits were lax; their morale was as low as Farragut's for different reasons. Having been dragooned, some of them nearly shanghaied, from soft jobs ashore and promised action and chance for glory against the hated Mexicans, this ragtag crew was set to guarding a nonexistent enemy against a breathless, motionless shore. Linked with these other deficiencies was the worst one of all, result of the others and the forerunner of mutiny: direct disobedience of orders. When one sailor refused to obey a direct order from any officer or subofficer, he threatened the safety of the entire ship; when it happened more than once, the situation bordered on mutiny.

The problem lay with the officers themselves. The first lieutenant was a drunkard and often unfit for duty. One lieutenant and one midshipman were found totally unfit for naval service by character or inclination, and they incited the crew. The sailmaker and two of the ship's gunners—all important posts—were mutinous. And each day as they sat off Tuspan, the heat closed in on them in heavy waves, and the tension grew.

Outright mutiny might have come, and might have succeeded, given the character of the officer force, which made Farragut become even more the disciplinarian than he wished. Fortunately, in July there came a respite. The *Saratoga* was ordered to Vera Cruz. She remained for two weeks, taking on stores and water, and the men had a chance for shore leave, which removed some tension.

Early in August the *Saratoga* was sent to Tabasco with dispatches, returning immediately. She pulled into Vera Cruz at sunset on August 11, and anchored after dark. Farragut's orders were to place himself and his ship at the disposition of Colonel Wilson, the army's military governor of city and port. He knew Colonel Wilson well and they were friends. There being no particular reason to do so, having come in so late, Farragut did not go ashore or send a boat ashore for orders. Had he done so, the army commander might have informed the ship that he had just sent away his boarding

123

officer and had no competent officer to carry out the duty of boarding incoming ships, ascertaining their business, and instructing them in the rules of the occupation.

Next morning at dawn an unheralded steamer arrived in Vera Cruz, and when no one stopped her, she came into port, anchored, and landed the Mexican army's General Parades. Colonel Wilson learned of the landing, much to his embarrassment: What if it had been a company of trained soldiers with orders to blow up the castle? He was worried and upset, and in conversation with Commodore Perry very shortly thereafter, he explained away the problem, in a meeting at which Farragut was present.

"You might have boarded the steamer," the Commodore said to Farragut.

"I did not consider it my duty to do anything of the kind unless requested by the Governor," Farragut replied stiffly. It had been his understanding that the army maintained its own port control; indeed, Colonel Wilson had, even up to the time that Farragut sailed off for Tabasco earlier in the month. But between Farragut's sailing and his return, the colonel's situation had changed.

The commodore seemed to understand the matter and dismiss it. Farragut and Colonel Wilson were quick to tell him that as soon as Farragut learned that the army had no boarding facilities, he had undertaken to board all vessels seeking entrance into Vera Cruz and made it a part of the duty of the ship assigned to the station.

"I will issue a circular to that effect," the commodore said in parting.

In fact, Perry did much more. He went back to his desk and dictated a letter that placed the blame for the landing of General Parades squarely on the shoulders of Commander Farragut. The commander had neglected his duty, the commodore indicated. Strictly speaking, Commodore Perry could make such a claim, but had there not been bad blood between the two men, he would not have done so. A generous commander, dealing with an officer who was not in his black books, would have ascribed the mixup to what it was: a result of one of the sudden changes likely to affect any echelon of any command during wartime. The commodore did not wish to make much of the incident, but neither could he permit the Navy Department to believe that he allowed enemy generals to move back and forth between the lines without even investigating their movements. The letter was addressed, as was all the commodore's important correspondence, to the Secretary of the Navy. The Secretary took direct responsibility for the operations of the navy in those days, and for a long time thereafter. From the Secretary's office in Washington came a story for the newspapers that Commodore David Glasgow Farragut had been officially reprimanded by Commodore Perry for failing to do his duty and allowing General Parades unmolested access to Vera Cruz.

Farragut and the *Saratoga* had been relieved at the Tuspan blockade station by the *Decatur,* but the captain of the *Decatur* reported that yellow fever had broken out aboard ship and was spreading. The captain requested relief from the station so he could take his crew back to Pensacola for treatment of the sick, fumigation, and remanning. Commodore Perry was quick to give his assent to the request from the *Decatur,* and *Saratoga* was ordered to return to Tuspan for the relief.

Farragut sailed for Tuspan, arriving September 1. Soon yellow fever struck this ship as well. Farragut kept the commodore informed about his activities in regular letters, but there was no action to relieve her, no indication that his letters and reports were read. He had been ordered to maintain a routine, and in the absence of relief, he had to maintain it; the ship's duties included regular checks of other shore points near Tuspan, which meant running up and down the coast. Farragut himself fell ill with fever and reported it. There was no response from the flagship.

Captain sick, first lieutenant often too drunk for duty, and two of the officers incompetent and disaffected, the *Saratoga* was a sad warship. The sick list grew to ninety, which meant that more than an entire watch, or half the crew, were not fit for duty. *Saratoga* became a slack ship, where she had started out as a taut one; with so many men down and the need for running in and out of heavy weather, the officers and boatswains took to performing the easy way. Soon the sails were half-clewed, and she was half-tacked, and the lines, left loose for easier access aloft, began to chafe, and the rigging and sails began to give way.

Two months after the *Saratoga's* captain sent in his first reports of sickness, when the sick list had hit ninety-nine, the cold word came from Commodore Perry that she should come to Vera Cruz—obviously for verification of her commander's statements. The *Saratoga* sailed sloppily for Vera Cruz and was kept in harbor for an entire month for reasons that Farragut was never able to understand, beyond believing that they represented the ill will of a commander intent on doing him harm.

Four men dead from fever, her sick list second in number of fever-ridden men only to the great steamer *Mississippi* (which had long since been dispatched home), it would seem that even Commodore Perry would find it embarrassing to keep the *Saratoga* on station and, if he continued, dangerous to his successful career. Yet he was a stubborn man and he did not seem willing to act.

Farragut lost his temper and wrote a letter to the Secretary of the Navy, through channels, a letter that showed more spirit than judgment and far more anger than consideration. He had intended that the letter get results:

> As the time for which this ship was fitted out (twelve months) will expire in March, 1848, and her rigging, which, in my anxiety and at my earnest desire, was unwillingly passed by the surveyors for that period, is already beginning to give way, and conceiving that we have endured all the privations, sickness, etc. incidental to a cruise on the coast of Mexico, in the most aggravated form, having had all my officers, and more than half my crew, down with the yellow fever; and lastly, having failed not only in eliciting from my commander in chief any participation in the more honorable duties of the squadron for my officers and crew, but also, as I

conceive, common justice, having already been kept on the blockade of Tuspan five and a half months out of seven on the station, while the other vessels of the squadron have been very differently situated:

I have the honor to request that, if it is not deemed expedient for the ship to return to the United States within that period for the purpose of receiving a new gang of rigging and a new set of officers, I may be released from the command, as the readiest means of securing to those who remain in her a more favorable consideration. I am fully aware, sir, that great latitude must be given to the commander of a squadron, in order to secure his best exertions; but, if he uses the trust with prejudice or partiality, there is no alternative to the subordinate but the one I seek, viz., to get from under his command, and in so doing I am anxious that those who have shared with me the evils of my command should participate in the pleasure of my relief.

I am, sir, with great respect, your obedient servant,

D. G. Farragut, Commander.

Farragut's letter went through channels, first to Commodore Perry at the navy yard in Vera Cruz, and when it arrived, it created a problem for Perry. Perhaps he had not known that Farragut was ready to lay his career on the line, that the thin-lipped balding commander of such diminutive stature wore such a tight-coiled spring within his breast. It was an open challenge, a statement of Farragut's dislike for his commander, and an open claim that Perry was neglecting his duty by keeping sick men on station. As to the charge that seems most obvious in the middle of the twentieth century, it was by far the easiest to refute. The matter of favoritism of selected subordinates was not one to cause any commander undue worry, even if the flattest charge could be laid and proved to a Secretary of the Navy.

The navy was brimming with nepotism, and had been since its beginnings; Perry was a product of the system, but so was Farragut; the Secretary of the Navy would give no particular weight to the plaint that Perry had favorites and Farragut was mistreated. The records of the navy were filled with correspondence far more acidulous than this letter.

Perry's reply showed the canniness of the man, who had, after all, entered the navy as a midshipman only a year before Farragut, yet was a mighty commodore while Farragut was just clinging to the rungs of command. Perry had been sponsored by his brother Oliver, to be sure, but Oliver in 1809 was merely one of many naval lieutenants, not nearly as prominent as Commander Porter, who had already made his name in the wars against the Barbary pirates. Perry had climbed in the service by shrewdness as well as nepotism and influence, and now he called upon that quality.

> I should have forwarded the accompanying letter from Commander Farragut without comment, did it not ascribe to me a feeling of prejudice to him. In this opinion he is mistaken, as it would be impossible for me to entertain a prejudice against an officer with whom I never before served, and in whose company I do not recollect to have passed twenty-four hours in my life.

A telling blow, that last sentence, particularly to a busy Secretary of the Navy, who had no time to give thought to the manner in which naval officers live and make war. On the face of it, the dismissal of the charge of antipathy seemed complete, but if Farragut had been on station for seven months, why had Commodore Perry so little knowledge of him as he claimed? The same could not be said of one other of his captains. There was more here than met the casual eye.

> As to the service in which he has been employed, circumstances of sickness in the squadron, and the consequent withdrawal of the *Mississippi* and the *Decatur*, made the arrangement absolutely necessary as to the faithful performance of the duties devolving on me as commander-in-chief.

How clever, to cast the mantle of patriotic necessity across the affair! How calculated, to give the Secretary of the Navy

128

the answer he wanted. Secretary Mason wanted no trouble, no congressional investigations of his management of the Navy Department, and as all concerned knew well, a commander in the field must be given latitude for dealings with his subordinates that would never be countenanced in dealings with the enemy or the politicians at home. The facts did not support this contention, but it was a long rough job to bring the facts to light: that *Decatur* was dispatched homeward with only a handful of sick men, compared to the status of *Saratoga* when Farragut was writing his unavailing letters to his stony commander-in-chief; that *Mississippi* was sent home when her percentage of sick to complement of men was perhaps half that of *Saratoga*; and that, given two months warning, it should not have been impossible for him to find replacement for a ship with so many men down. Those were facts, but in glossing over the facts and leaving them, Commodore Perry chose to stand on principle, the principle that the commander can do no wrong, barring a wrong of court-martial calibre. His letter continued:

> The crew of the *Saratoga* have been less exposed to the unhealthy localities of the coast than any vessel of the squadron, and have suffered less, in proportion to number, than most of them.

The statement was untrue to begin with, and the sickness figures of the squadron showed it clearly. Commodore Perry went on to say:

> I leave it to the Department to judge of the propriety of the language and tone of the letter of Commander Farragut.

And there Perry had David Farragut, for the language and tone of his letter was angry and petulant, and gave every evidence that Farragut was feeling sorry for himself. Such a letter was easy to disregard, except to lower the status of the complainer.

The two letters went on their way on December 17 from Vera Cruz. Twelve days passed. Perry thought it wise to act, lest he give cause to the department for serious attention to the Farragut letter. Farragut was ordered to do something he had pleaded to do months earlier: to sail to Pensacola, land his sick, take on stores, and return to Vera Cruz. But when he arrived at Pensacola, he found that the controversy had preceded him and that the impression on the Navy Department in Washington of his first letter had been as poor as might be imagined. Perry, after all, represented establishment and success; if the navy had not glorified itself in the conduct of the war against Mexico, at least under Perry it had committed no blunders that could reflect on the Polk Administration. There was strong pressure for preservation of the status quo and strong antipathy toward a wrong-headed commander who tried to upset affairs.

Farragut tried to strengthen his case with a longer, more detailed letter. The only result was to prolong the controversy and increase the Secretary's necessity to support the commodore. But from the controversy arose one change in plan: Commodore Perry had ordered Farragut to return to Vera Cruz when the *Saratoga* was reprovisioned and remanned, and these orders were countermanded. Given Farragut's state of mind and Perry's obvious dislike, it was probably in the best interests of Farragut's career that he was relieved, although what it meant to him at the time could be understood only by a senior naval officer suddenly deprived of his command without honor. All things considered, it must be said that Farragut chose this escape from Perry, and since he had served nearly forty years in the navy, it could not be said that he was blind to the consequences of his action. On February 19, 1848, Farragut arrived in New York, paid off his crew as was the practice in the navy, and delivered his ship to the Brooklyn Navy Yard. He must have been very glad to get rid of her and the crew, for on the last day his first lieutenant collapsed, drunk, and Farragut had no option but to order him to court-martial for drunkenness on duty. His troubles with Perry had begun many years before in this same place over the same subject: the drunkenness of Perry's brother while commander of another ship. It was fitting that the affair should end thus.

Perry went on to greater glory. The war wound up, he was assigned to New York to superintend the construction of ocean-mail steamships, a task placed very high on the navy agenda because the race for steamship-traffic supremacy was just beginning among nations. Perry would superintend the building of such liners as the great steamer *Arctic* and the *Pacific*, which would compete under the Collins-line colors for traffic with Commodore Vanderbilt, half a dozen others, and the whole British effort, led by Samuel Cunard. The navy was aiding, but the navy was following a movement led by civilians, and Perry's task was largely regulatory, his responsibility to establish standards of safety in building and operating hundreds of ships.

Farragut's status in the navy of 1848 was shown by what happened to him next: he was appointed once again to be executive officer of the Norfolk Navy Yard. He chose to believe that the appointment reflected the good name he still had with Secretary Mason. In a sense this was true, although Mason considered Farragut's letters improper and ill-conceived. Farragut's good judgment was much in question in those days, but he was a technical expert who possessed knowledge few others in the service could claim. He was an authority on ships and docks. This proficiency, combined with the rank he held, undoubtedly saved him from being cashiered or buried in the service. The low point of the Farragut career coincided with a low point in the history of the naval service: the civilian authorities, if not the professionals, were becoming restless about the condition of the naval arm.

12. CAPTAIN

Technical proficiency saved Farragut's career after his misadventures in navy politics, but in 1848 and 1849 the future looked anything but bright for him. His duties at the dockyard were routine and dull. He came down with cholera and, while given up for dead by the navy surgeon, he recovered, and after several weeks of recuperation with his wife and son at White Sulphur Springs, he was able to return to duty. The danger to Farragut's career in this period was that he might be "surveyed" and retired by a retiring board, which met to weed out the unfit or the least-fit officers. His long years of service, his many illnesses, and the dispute with Commodore Perry might well have made him a candidate to be dropped from the navy list, except that he was too valuable an officer to be discarded. He was not, however, in very good standing, which was obvious in November, 1849, when Farragut applied for a simple change of duty. He wanted to exchange jobs with Commander Samuel Barron, who was in charge of the receiving ship *Pennsylvania* at Norfolk. He would take the ship and Barron would come ashore to become executive officer of the yard. The request was not granted.

With the simultaneous development of steam propulsion, extension of American trading around the world, and the discovery of gold in California, the navy began to wake up to its obsolescence. The senior officers were not all ready to accept steam without reservation, but the proof lay in the growing fleet of steamships that sailed the seven seas. In February, 1850, the navy launched the steam man-of-war *Powhatan* at the Norfolk yard; thus Commander Farragut was involved in the infant days of the new steam navy.

In the spring of 1850, Farragut was relieved at the navy yard but not given new duty. He was put on waiting orders, and they might not have come, had it not been for the intervention of Commodore John Sloat, head of the Norfolk yard, who chose Farragut when the chance was offered. The choice was for the post of senior officer of a board that was to arrange exercises for the Ordnance Department of the navy. Farragut returned to Norfolk and served there until March, 1851, when he was ordered to Washington to head a committee in drawing up a book of ordnance regulations. He made several requests for sea duty, but they were ignored, and when the ordnance work was done, the best post he could secure was as ordnance officer at the Norfolk Navy Yard.

Yet wherever Farragut served, those who served with him learned to respect his brains and accomplishments. Commodore Charles Morris was in charge of the Bureau of Ordnance and Gunnery, and he chose Farragut to go to Fort Monroe at Old Point Comfort and supervise tests of different kinds of guns during the summer of 1852. Taking three lieutenants with him, Farragut went to the fort, and lived with his wife and son at the Hygea Hotel. From the experiments came a pamphlet, which was soon forgotten because men of more inventive turn of mind were developing far better naval guns. Farragut did not claim to be an inventor, he was a fighting sailor, but he did know one other way of learning about artillery and that was to watch the developments of foreign nations. When the Crimean War broke out in the spring of 1854, Farragut applied for duty as an observer. He wanted to go to the Crimea to study the workings of the guns of England and France in the war against Russia, and he made a case for himself in a letter to Secretary Dobbin, citing his long service and his mastery of the French, Spanish, and Italian languages. Secretary Dobbin had no interest in the Crimean War, and the request was ignored, but Farragut's long and efficient service as a dockyard man was not.

The discovery of gold in California, abetted by the coming of steam to American shipping, had brought about enormous changes in the responsibilities of the United States Navy.

Before 1850, the navy's interest in the west coast of North America was minor and sporadic. After 1850, it became apparent that the navy had a new shoreline to watch and protect, and the concept of a two-ocean navy came into being. A two-ocean navy meant new bases, and at least one major shipyard where naval vessels could be rebuilt, or built from scratch if necessary. In 1852, a commission of three officers traveled to California and selected a site for a navy yard. They chose Mare Island in the middle of San Francisco Bay.

Commodore Joseph Smith, the chief of the navy's Bureau of Yards and Docks, was one of Farragut's few but ardent supporters; Farragut had shown his superiority in attention to naval detail during a long career as a yard master. In the spring of 1854, when the navy was ready to begin building its new yard in California, he supported the choice of Commander Farragut to head the new installation. It would be the most responsible dockyard post in the navy because the Mare Island yard would be farthest away and the commander must take more upon himself than any other, anywhere. Secretary Dobbin accepted Commodore Smith's proposal, and Farragut got the job, by far the most important he had ever held.

In August, the Farraguts boarded the Vanderbilt steamship *Star of the West* and began the voyage to California. A few years earlier a trip to California meant a voyage around the Horn, but no longer. Vanderbilt and the other steamship men had quickened the process, even if they had supplanted the dangers of the stormy cape with those of fever and bandidos. The Farraguts were comfortable enough on the trip to San Juan del Norte because Commodore Vanderbilt was on a yachting expedition to Europe; when the commodore was in charge, there was almost always excitement on the New York–San Francisco trip. He was either cutting rates, ordering his captains to set new records, if they had to tie down the safety valves to do it, or lowering the quality of food and service to make more money out of each passage. At San Juan del Norte, on the east coast of Nicaragua, the Farraguts transferred to a shallow-draft river steamer, which took them through the fever-ridden Nicaraguan jungle. The river steamer did not have staterooms; the Farraguts staked out a deck space for their baggage and sat on hard wooden benches during the day-and-a-half trip, protected from the hot sun and the night dew only by a canvas awning, and protected from the malarial mosquitos by nothing at all. In the daylight hours, the steamboat glided through dense jungle that grew down to the shore and overhung the banks. The male passengers amused themselves by shooting at the monkeys that chattered in the trees, or the heavy-billed toucans and bright parrots that stared out at them from the green vines and creepers, or the long, low, scaly shapes of the alligators lying motionless on the edges of the river.

At Castillo Viejo rapids, the steamer stopped. During the high-water season the steamboat went up the rapids, but at this particular time of year the water was too low and a portage must be made. The passengers, not the ship, were taken out and around the rapids and embarked on another river steamer for the remainder of the river voyage. It was afternoon when they made the portage in the tropic heat, and evening before the second steamer reached Lake Nicaragua. They transferred to a side-wheel lake steamer, which took them to Virgin Bay on the west shore of the long lake. They spent a second night in the open. Farragut had been ill before he left the United States, had left Washington on a litter, and was still very weak. The voyage from San Juan del Norte was very trying to him and to his family, but the next morning it was over—they believed.

The steamer came within sight of shore. But the shore was flat and the beach long, and the distance was negotiated by an iron barge pulled back and forth by native manpower. The Farraguts and their baggage descended into the barge, jostled and hurried by other passengers, and were pushed and hastened out of it on shore. They walked to the stage depot and their belongings were carried by cart. In his contract with the Nicaraguan government, Commodore Vanderbilt stipulated that he would build a railroad across the twelve miles from the lake to San Juan del Sur, the Pacific port where his steamers connected for San Francisco. But he had never built the railroad, sensing after the early days of the gold rush that the California trade would not always be as lucrative as it was in the beginning years. He had promised—and his brochures illustrated the promise—to install handsome Concord coaches trimmed in the blue and white that were the colors of the Vanderbilt line. That was in 1850. Four years later those coaches still had not arrived, and although he had built a passable road across the mountains, the vehicles were merely canvas-covered wagons, much like the later Conestoga type that crossed the North American plains—huge, tall oaken wagons with great iron-rimmed wheels, drawn in their jerky ride by spans of mules.

It took all day to make the trip across the mountains. The wagons had to stop to rest the mules, and to repair broken harness or a slipped brake, which failure would be fatal on the steep downgrade of the Pacific side.

At ten o'clock at night, in the blackness, the caravan arrived at San Juan del Sur, only to discover that further ignominy faced the travelers. The brochure said there was a hotel, and pictured a handsome dining room with grand chandeliers and glittering table silver. Instead there existed a primitive clapboard hotel, which scarcely deserved the name. The floor was rude and rough, the eating accommodations primitive, the food unpalatable, the rooms so badly lighted one could scarcely see. As for the sleeping accommodations, the brochure promised private rooms and Vanderbilt gave them private rooms: he divided one great room with ropes strung lengthwise and across, and from the ropes hung canvas partitions, and there were the private rooms with four canvas walls and rough-hewn bunk beds with canvas bottoms instead of mattresses and springs.

They waited in the hotel until the steamer came from the north. The brochure indicated that steamers were kept on tap at the harbor, but a sailor could not blame Vanderbilt for his system because San Juan del Sur had no real harbor, at least not one that a sane captain would lie in on a stormy night. After a few days the steamer *Cortez* came round the head of the harbor; the passengers for San Francisco boarded and began the last half of their voyage. Twelve days later they were inside the Golden Gate.

At San Francisco, Commander Farragut and his family boarded the old sloop of war *Warren*, which would be their home for the next few months. The captain's quarters were extended to the mainmast to give the Farraguts a very comfortable apartment. Farragut lost no time in taking control of the flat expanse known as Mare Island, opposite Vallejo in San Pablo Bay. The island was located about thirty miles from San Francisco, in a famous swampy area called the "tule," which connected, or very nearly connected, with the northern shore, but through such ground as to be impassable. Mare Island was three miles long and half a mile wide, and at this time was settled by squatters who lived in shacks. Farragut ordered them off, and the navy's construction work began.

In October, 1855, Farragut received his captain's commission. Ironically, at about the same time, his older brother William was listed by the retiring board as one of the officers who ought to be dropped from the service. William Farragut's naval career had been less than distinguished, but not through his own failures. Serving in the Gulf of Mexico, he had contracted rheumatism and had thenceforth spent more than half his life on sick leave, either in bed or on crutches. The board, examining the record only, found that Lieutenant Farragut was not worth his salt and proposed to drop him from the list. There was no provision for "retirement" with pay in the modern sense of the word, and an officer dropped from the navy was thrown out into a cold world to make his own way. Captain Farragut now came to the defense of his brother and managed to secure Lieutenant Farragut's retention on the naval reserve list, which meant that he did not forfeit all his pay and allowances.

As the senior United States naval officer in the West, Captain Farragut was called upon, in 1856, to involve himself and the federal government in a dispute between state and local authorities in San Francisco. The dispute arose because San Francisco was the roughest city in the Union, and the

137

prospering businessmen of the city found their wealth and welfare threatened by desperados and men of the Barbary Coast, who were apparently uncontrollable by the state authorities. They pleaded with the state for help, did not get what they wanted, and began grumbling about the formation of a vigilante group to preserve law and order. They also considered themselves far superior to the rough men of Sacramento who ran the state government. The problem was further complicated by the argument between northern and southern sympathizers over the issues that beset the entire Union and would soon cause it to dissolve.

The conflict in San Francisco began with the shooting of a state marshal by a gentleman named Cora, and then the murder of James King, editor of the San Francisco *Evening Bulletin,* by another worthy named Casey. At that point, the outraged citizens rose up and formed the Vigilance Committee. Their first action was to find Messrs. Casey and Cora and hang them. Next they rounded up a number of Democrats and others whom they accused of stuffing ballot boxes. They threatened to hang these men, but decided to send them back to the East, or at least to Central America, via the next steamer. Yankee Sullivan, a prize fighter who was numbered among the prisoners, was led to believe that he would be killed, so he hanged himself in his place of confinement.

The Democrats were in control of the state government, the Know-Nothings having polled second place on the ballot in the elections of 1856, and the infant Republicans having taken third place. When the Vigilance Committee of San Francisco seized power in the city and began punishing criminals, Governor Johnson in Sacramento became annoyed, then frightened, and appealed to Captain Farragut to use naval forces to restore the state's authority.

This was easier said than done, even if Farragut had been totally out of sympathy with the vigilantes (and he was really very sympathetic to their aims). San Francisco rapidly divided into two armed camps. The Vigilantes, in June, raised a force of six-thousand armed men and had artillery at their disposal. The state government supporters then formed the Law and

Order party, and attempted to bring in arms of their own to put down what was now called a "rebellion" by both sides.

The Law and Order party managed to secure some guns and put them in the hands of a sailor named Maloney, an old naval storekeeper, who attempted to bring them from Benicia to San Francisco in a sailing ship. But the Vigilantes were ever watchful. Their espionage system was so good that Farragut commented on it especially. They boarded the vessel and took the arms to their headquarters. Maloney and his men were released; however, the Vigilantes apparently had second thoughts and sent men to recapture Maloney.

The storekeeper had gone to the office of Dr. R. P. Ashe, one of the leaders of the Law and Order party and also the Navy Agent in San Francisco. The Vigilantes followed on his heels. They broke in on a meeting of the Law and Order leaders, who included Ashe and Judge D. S. Terry, of the Supreme Court of California.

The Vigilantes moved to take Maloney by the arm, but he asked if they had a warrant for his arrest. No, they did not have a warrant, but he was to come with them anyway. Maloney refused to go.

Dr. Ashe ordered the Vigilantes to leave his offices, and Judge Terry chimed in to strengthen the demand. The Vigilantes left to get reinforcements. The Law and Order men then hastened out of the office and toward the headquarters of their organization to get guns and reinforcements of their own. Some were already armed, including Judge Terry, who was carrying a pistol and a bowie knife in his belt.

The Vigilantes did not have so far to go as the Law and Order party, and just as the latter group came up to the entrance to their headquarters, the Vigilantes came up also in force. Dr. Ashe and the Judge stopped and stepped to the fore to face their enemies. Judge Terry drew his pistol. The Vigilantes rushed forward and made a grab for the gun, and the men began struggling in the street.

A shot rang out—no one knew who fired it. Judge Terry said it was fired at him and came so close he could tell that he was the target. At that moment he was struggling with a

Vigilante named Hopkins, who had the judge by the neck. The judge drew his bowie knife, stabbed Hopkins, and wrenched himself free. In the confusion the Law and Order men escaped to their headquarters, where they locked themselves in. In half an hour the sixteen men inside the headquarters found themselves surrounded by a crowd estimated to consist of three or four thousand Vigilantes.

The Law and Order men were willing to fight it out, hopeless as their cause appeared, but Judge Terry said he would not let them do so because the Vigilantes were obviously after him, and him alone. The sixteen men surrendered and were taken prisoner, to be held at Vigilante Committee headquarters.

The word immediately got out, and the Law and Order men made certain it reached Commander E. B. Boutwell, captain of the man-of-war *John Adams*, which had just arrived in San Francisco from Hawaii. When Commander Boutwell heard that Navy Agent Ashe was under arrest, he wrote a strong letter to the Vigilantes, who released Dr. Ashe on parole. That same day all the other Law and Order men were released on parole as well, except Maloney and Judge Terry.

The Vigilantes said that if Vigilante Hopkins died, they would hang Judge Terry for murder. The Law and Order men said that Judge Terry was protecting himself and that if the Vigilantes hanged the judge, they would hang every Vigilante they saw. The affair was working against the Vigilantes because they had started the trouble and many citizens were now dubious about government by this self-proclaimed committee of action.

Both sides tried to enlist the assistance of the naval forces in the San Francisco area. On June 28, Commander Boutwell sent a letter to the Vigilance Committee, asking that Judge Terry be given asylum on the *John Adams* as a prisoner of war—if the Vigilantes were declaring a rebellion against the United States—or that he be turned over to the state authorities (which meant the Law and Order party). The Vigilantes were so incensed by the letter that they sent a copy to Captain

Farragut, recognizing that he was senior officer in the area (and knowing that he was sympathetic to the committee's original desire to bring law and order to lawless San Francisco).

Farragut replied that he wanted to use the offices of the federal government "to pour oil on the troubled waters, rather than do aught to fan the flame of human passions, or add to the chances of the horrors of civil war." Another letter went to Commander Boutwell chiding him gently for his preparation to interfere in the matter. Privately, Captain Farragut had been more explicit with Commander Boutwell; perhaps he had even told Boutwell of the foray of Commodore Porter into the political sphere in his landing of armed men on the coast of Puerto Rico to avenge an insult to the flag—and how that landing had destroyed Porter's navy career.

However he handled it, Farragut dealt in precisely the proper manner with the ebullient Commander Boutwell, with the Vigilantes, and with the Navy Department. Boutwell apologized for not consulting him before acting, but said he considered himself to be under the orders of the absent Commodore Mervine, commandant of the Pacific Station, and acted without checking only because of the long distance between San Francisco and Mare Island, and the apparent need for speedy action to save Judge Terry. He suggested that he might sail out of the harbor to remove his embarrassing presence, but complained that he still felt he had acted properly under the circumstances.

Captain Farragut was no Commodore Perry, and he did his very best to soothe the ruffled feathers of his junior officer. He told Boutwell he could not leave port, that the services of the *John Adams* might be needed, and that he was to stand by for orders. In another letter, he indicated that he was not going to push the affair in a way that would create trouble for Boutwell:

> It is the duty of the superior officer present to act according to the best judgment for the general good. He alone is responsible, after an appeal is made to him, and not

the junior. That there was ever any disrespect intended by you, never entered my mind. That you are besought by the Government party to blow the town down, I am well aware. But that we should act in our public capacity with unbiased judgment, is only called for the louder. The people on both sides are violent, and it therefore becomes us to be cool and temperate. As to your responsibilities in this case, alluded to in your letter, you shall have the full credit to which they may entitle you; the correspondence shall be forwarded by the next mail to the Navy Department.

Your course may be more approved than mine. If so, be assured my eye will not be evil because you have proved to be right.[*]

Meanwhile, Farragut was not idle. He sent an officer to Seattle, in the far-off Washington territory, by commercial steamer, with a letter to Commander Swartwout, captain of the *John Hancock*, ordering that ship to San Francisco. He made sure the batteries of the *Warren* and the *Decatur* were ready for action, and as he watched the development of affairs over a two-week period, he wrote the Navy Department asking for advice or orders. Calm, but ready to take any action in emergency that he saw fit as a federal officer, Farragut stood by.

The shooting of Vigilante Hopkins occurred at the end of June. July began tensely. On July 20, the United States Circuit Court Judge was in touch with Farragut and the next day the two met in San Francisco. They talked over the federal authority and obligation. Farragut made ready to take and guard four million dollars in gold of the United States Treasury that was then held in the Branch Mint in San Francisco. Judge McAllister said he would issue a writ of habeas corpus for the person of Judge Terry, and when he was convinced that this was legal, Captain Farragut said he would support its enforcement and sent the schooner *Fenimore Cooper* to Commander Boutwell with orders that if he was asked by a

[*]*Ibid.*, p. 183

federal marshal to assist in the enforcement of the writ, that the commander do whatever was necessary. He was ready for action, and he was growing disgusted with the Vigilantes, as he wrote Secretary Dobbin:

> These people have been running riot, and setting all law and the Constitution at defiance, and I did not know at what moment they would seize the money at the Branch Mint. The history of nearly all revolutionary movements shows such to be the result the moment the *canaille* get the upper hand.*

Secretary Dobbin replied in August that he approved of Boutwell's generous and patriotic attitudes, and that he also approved thoroughly of Farragut's prudence. By that time the immediate affair was settled; the Vigilantes released Judge Terry on August 7, and he took refuge on the *John Adams* until the Sacramento steamer came into San Francisco Bay. He boarded the steamer and went on to the capital, where he was received triumphantly by the government officers.

The Vigilantes remained in control in San Francisco, however, and Captain Farragut sought advice from the Navy Department and—through Secretary Dobbin—the President, on his responsibilities and courses of action. But soon the affair died down. The Vigilance Committee was eventually dissolved and the government of San Francisco returned to the hands of the state and local officials. The Secretary of the Navy approved thoroughly of the manner in which Farragut had comported himself. Farragut made sure that Commander Boutwell was not slighted or his record hurt by the difference of opinion, and Farragut himself came out of the affair with the highest honor. If he had behaved as a petulant subordinate in the Perry affair, he retrieved the gaffe in San Francisco and created confidence that he had the good judgment necessary for high command posts.

Ibid., p. 186

13. THE TURNS OF THE CARDS

Farragut's tour of duty at the Mare Island Navy Yard lasted until the spring of 1858, when a new administration and a new Secretary of the Navy were in office. He and his family went back to Norfolk, which he would always consider to be his home. They toured a little, then settled down while the captain awaited his new orders to duty. He was thirty-ninth on the list of eighty-one captains, which meant that although he would not be the first to be employed, he would certainly not be the last, and he had come away from the San Francisco experience with much prestige. His old enemy, Commodore Matthew Perry, died that spring, and the negative past was wiped out.

On New Year's Day, 1859, Captain Farragut took command of the new screw sloop-of-war *Brooklyn* and suddenly found himself catapulted from the world of sail into the world of steam.

How the navy had changed!

The captain who was piped aboard the new steamer was no longer dressed in cocked hat, white breeks, and buckle slippers, but in navy-blue double-breasted coat with nine buttons in each of two rows that ran up and down the front, cutaway tails, a high standing collar with gold lace an inch and a half wide around the top and down the front. The sleeves were now decorated with insignia of rank, which in the captain's case consisted of three gold stripes each three-quarters of an inch wide. He wore blue pantaloons, loose at the bottom to fit over boots or shoes, and as a captain, his were decorated along the outer seams by a gold stripe an inch and a half wide. (White pantaloons were tropical or summer uniform.) There was still a cocked hat, but of entirely different design, and black, not blue and gold. On his shoulders, as a captain, Farragut wore two epaulets of gold embroidered with the design of the eagle and the anchor with a star.

His new ship was changed even more from the old *Essex* than his new uniform. She was 233 feet long, 43 feet in the beam, and displaced 2,600 tons. In other words, although she was called a sloop, she was larger than one of the old ships of the line, the seventy-four-gunners on which Farragut had served.

She was rigged for sail, with a long bowsprit, three masts, and a mizzen boom to carry a fore and aft spanker and fly the ensign, and from a distance she looked like a great under-rigged sailing ship—until one saw the black stack almost directly amidships. The look of under-rigging was deliberate —sail was to be nothing more than an auxiliary for her, a hangover, a last gasp of a navy that was not ready to commit itself to the vagaries of the machine age. The stack was awesome. It was seven feet in diameter and extended fifty feet above the grate bars. The stack was connected to two vertical boilers, which furnished power for the two engines, and these engines connected to the drive shaft, which turned the screw propeller, a monster fourteen-and-one-half feet in diameter. She burned anthracite coal, but so much was yet to be learned about engines, boilers, and hydrodynamics that she was able, with all this, to develop a maximum speed of only eleven knots, while she cruised at seven knots.

The *Brooklyn* was one of six such ships, and one of perhaps twenty modern steamers that had been built in the past ten years by the navy. To Farragut the command was all new; it had been ten years since he was last afloat, and he had never served on a steamer before, except on a very primitive steam vessel, the old side-wheeler *Sea Gull*, which for a time was the flagship of Commodore Porter's Mosquito fleet.

The armament, however, was much the same as on the fighting ships to which Captain Farragut was accustomed.

Guns had changed. Farragut had grown up on 32-pounders, which were 6-inch guns, and the new warships had 9-inch guns. They were still arranged in broadside, eleven 9-inch Dahlgren shell guns on each side, and a heavy 12-pounder and a light 12-pounder as pivot guns.

Farragut had five lieutenants, a surgeon and two assistants, a purser and a marine officer, much as on the old frigates, but he also had a chief engineer and seven assistant engineers, which was an entirely new development.

The *Brooklyn's* trial run was made at the beginning of February, from New York to Beaufort, South Carolina. The ship steamed out to sea, but outside the harbor the captain ordered the sails hoisted and she moved along for a time under full steam with her sails filling also. The use of sails with steam created a new set of sailing problems and some neat calculating. Steamships could travel on straight lines between points, regardless of the wind, so the calculation became a question of when the wind was right for using the sails and when it was best to use the steam alone. After a week, Farragut was growing used to the new ways and his reports were favorable, although as always he had suggestions for rerigging and new arrangements in the ship.

From Beaufort he sailed and steamed to Port au Prince and then to Vera Cruz, where the *Brooklyn* arrived in April. Mexico was torn by civil war, and the American minister, Robert McLane, was informed that the *Brooklyn* was at his disposal. Captain Farragut could be, and was, of considerable help to the minister because of his knowledge of the country and the language, and in June he went from Vera Cruz, which was occupied by President Benito Juarez and the Constitutional party, to the camp of the opposing leader, General Miramon, of the Clerical party, to negotiate for the release of money held up by the Miramon force by General Robles, who was in charge of the camp.

Several months' experience with the new class of ships had taught Captain Farragut that the sloops needed redesigning for comfortable habitation. He wrote the Secretary of the Navy that he had never served aboard a ship where the accommodations were quite so miserable, and that among other troubles, his cabin was almost constantly wet and so dark that he could not see in it at high noon without candlelight. During the summer, he took the ship to Pensacola, and then to New York, where he was to pick up Minister McLane and his family, and take them back to Mexico.

Shore leave in the United States brought its troubles. A young lieutenant named W. N. Jeffers had quarreled with Captain Farragut on a social occasion, and taking umbrage at what he called Farragut's "ill-bred manner," the lieutenant had never again spoken to Farragut or responded to any remark except on official business. In a 233-foot ship, with only half a dozen deck officers, such enmity was bound to create unusual tensions and problems. One day when Farragut was ashore in his undress uniform, wearing an overcoat on which he had forgotten to attach his epaulets of rank, he encountered Jeffers in passing. Jeffers was dressed in civilian clothes, as he had a right to be in peacetime, and while Farragut spoke civilly to his young officer, Lieutenant Jeffers chose to ignore his captain. On return to the ship on the night of October 31, Jeffers was informed by the executive officer that the old man was angry and that the lieutenant was not to leave the ship again except by permission of the captain. Instead of bracing Farragut personally and having the matter out, Jeffers attempted to go over his captain's head and appealed to the commandant of the Brooklyn Navy Yard, charging that Farragut was treating him unjustly.

The commandant, of course, not wanting to get embroiled in any such arguments, immediately referred the matter back to Farragut. On hearing that his lieutenant had attempted to injure him with naval authority as well as being insulting, Farragut lost his temper. He called Jeffers in and dressed him down, and when Jeffers responded with spirit, Farragut told him he was suspended from duty until further notice and ordered him to go below to his cabin and stay there.

The next day, Jeffers wrote a letter to Secretary Isaac Toucey, complaining about Farragut's treatment, and smuggled it off the ship for mailing instead of putting it through channels. The tempest in the teapot began.

But as it was brewing, a far more serious matter occurred.

147

Within a week after the Jeffers incident, as the ship was preparing to leave New York harbor for Vera Cruz with the McLanes aboard, there was a mechanical breakdown in the steam plant, and the *Brooklyn* was forced to anchor off Staten Island while repairs were made. The men below decks managed to smuggle liquor aboard, and a number of them became royally drunk, including Seaman George Ritter, who was so noisy and abusive that he was put in the brig to sober up, and while there began swearing and shouting. The noise was so irritating that a corporal of marines, Charles Cooper, reported to the officer of the deck that Seaman Ritter was completely unruly and was fighting all who tried to control him. The officer of the deck ordered Corporal Cooper to tie and gag Ritter to bring him under control, since he was resisting arrest, and once arrested was trying to tear down the brig. Seaman Ritter was bound and gagged with a wooden gag, thrown back into the brig, and left there. Either the excessive amount of liquor paralyzed his breathing or poisoned him, or the gag strangled him. Seaman Ritter died that day. When the crew discovered that Ritter was dead, some of them grew excited and rushed up onto the main deck shouting about "murder" and demanding that the "murderer" be handed over to them. Hearing the mob, Captain Farragut grasped a cutlass and rushed to the mainmast to confront the angry sailors in the darkness. When the marines and his other officers joined him, the men suddenly realized that they were on the verge of being charged with mutiny and they quieted down. Farragut promised a complete investigation of the affair, and it was left at that.

Although the death had occurred aboard a naval vessel, under the procedures then in effect the matter was placed in the hands of the civil authorities for investigation, and as might be expected, it became thoroughly confused in a few hours. Corporal Cooper was sent ashore to the commandant of the naval yard for protection and duty; the quarantine police arrested him and charged that he was attempting to escape.

Farragut was trying to get away for Vera Cruz to deliver his passengers. The civil authorities were determined to have their own way, and they ordered the witnesses among the men to be brought ashore. Farragut refused to comply, and sailed for Vera Cruz. The civilians were furious. The coroner found that Seaman Ritter had died at the hands of Corporal Cooper, and complained bitterly, and *publicly*, that Farragut had not stopped everything to let the coroner do his work.

In Mexico, Farragut discovered that the situation was more than a little confused, and eventually he brought Minister McLane back, leaving a force of twenty-two men and marines, commanded by Lieutenant Jeffers—which solved the Jeffers problem for the moment.

The final solution came when Jeffers realized that he had gone too far. Farragut had preferred charges against Jeffers for contempt and scandalous conduct, and Jeffers realized that his own deportment would be regarded as most unseemly at a court-martial. First he asked for transfer. Farragut, showing immense good humor under the circumstances, wrote the Secretary of the Navy that "as much as I desire to get rid of Lieutenant Jeffers, I have no disposition to do an injustice to others." Jeffers then asked to withdraw his letter, and although that could not be done under regulations, Farragut agreed to forget the matter, and so did the Secretary. The tempest in the teapot subsided.

But the storm in New York was raging, largely because of the efforts of Horace Greeley, staunch Republican and Democrat-hater, who wanted to embarrass the Democratic administration in Washington. The navy was part of the federal government, Captain Farragut was part of the navy, and thus to Greeley he was fair game.

In March, when the *Brooklyn* was again in New York harbor, Farragut appeared at the trial held to uncover the facts about the Ritter case. Corporal Cooper had been released and disappeared, but the coroner wanted a victim; he chose the sergeant of marines and accused him of complicity in the death. Farragut testified that the use of a wooden gag was forbidden aboard his ship unless he personally authorized it and he had never authorized it to subdue Seaman Ritter.

The press stirred up a mighty holocaust, and for a time it

appeared that Captain Farragut was the murderer—if a murder had been committed. Sea lawyers among the crew had attempted to incite the men, and, failing that, they gave outrageous statements to the New York press.

For Farragut the real threat was the near-panic of Secretary Toucey. The Secretary ordered Farragut's removal from command of the *Brooklyn*, as the case was in progress, and if the order had stood, it would have shown on his record as a sign of the navy's dissatisfaction with his behavior. But having written out the order, Secretary Toucey countermanded it by telegraph while it was in transit and ordered Farragut to bring the *Brooklyn* to Hampton Roads and await orders. Farragut sailed from New York. There was a new difficulty when the pilot missed his boat at Sandy Hook and Farragut took him into Norfolk to land. The Secretary of the Navy chose to regard Farragut's action as a violation of orders and wrote of his disapproval. But in a few days Minister McLane was aboard again, and the *Brooklyn* was steaming for Mexico. Jeffers came back to the ship, sick with rheumatism and much subdued, and the ship remained in Mexican waters for some time under Minister McLane's orders. Later, Farragut gave passage to a naval expedition that wished to explore the Isthmus of Chiriqui in Panama and remained in those waters until the autumn of 1860. When his tour of duty ended on October 20, he turned over command of the *Brooklyn* at Aspinwall (Colon) to Captain W. S. Walker and returned to New York aboard the Vanderbilt steamship *Northern Light*.

His service aboard the *Brooklyn* had been difficult in a difficult time, but professionally it had given Farragut pleasure to have mastered the ways of the new navy, and as an old sailing ship man he did not cease to marvel at the feats he could accomplish in a steamship, such as running into port in a gale. He had successfully made the difficult transition to a new navy.

14. WAR

As had often been the case in Captain David Farragut's naval career, he found himself, in the autumn of 1860, at odds with the officials on whose word, or even whim, depended not only his employment but the future of his career. Although punctilious, his relationship with Secretary Toucey had become exceedingly chilly. The reason was Farragut's objection at being put under the command of a junior officer, when he was told to provide transportation to Captain Frederick Engle for the Chiriqui Survey Party.

When Farragut realized that he was to be at the beck and call of an officer junior to himself, he felt impelled to protest to the Secretary. Perhaps he was correct, in the narrow terms of naval protocol, but it is also obvious that he was oversensitive. Yet, given this high degree of sensitivity by a naval officer who must have been regarded as a typical career man, Secretary Toucey might have mended matters simply enough in replying that the survey mission was a technical project necessary to the good of the navy and that there was no alternative but that Captain Engle be permitted to manage the comings and goings of the ship put at his disposal. If Farragut had proved too touchy, the Connecticut Yankee who was Secretary also proved too stubborn to give in a little and cater to the officer's pride. Secretary Toucey was not very pleased with Farragut anyway, for the incidents involving Lieutenant Jeffers and Seaman Ritter were too fresh in his mind. Farragut did not feel that his objections were satisfied, although he and Engle got on very well and Engle was more than normally complimentary in writing to the Secretary of

Farragut's cooperation and willingness to do anything that was asked of him in behalf of the expedition. At his own request he was relieved of duty in Panamanian waters instead of waiting until the ship returned to the United States.

The trouble of sending a new captain south, and the recollection of all the other unpleasantnesses in connection with Farragut's name did not dispose Secretary Toucey very kindly toward the captain. On November 2, when Farragut arrived in New York, he reported to the Secretary and said he was awaiting orders. There was no answer. A week later Farragut asked if he might go to Norfolk to meet the *Brooklyn* and pick up the belongings he had left aboard. The Secretary replied irritably that Captain Farragut could go anywhere he wished within the United States as far as he was concerned. Certainly that was answer enough for Farragut to the question of employment he might expect from Secretary Toucey. But Farragut knew that the administration of President James Buchanan was living out its last days—the election had occurred between his first and second letters to the Secretary —and Farragut knew that beginning in March he would be responsible to a new Republican Secretary of the Navy. What might come of that change he could not know, but certainly it could not but be an improvement.

Farragut went to Poughkeepsie, where his wife and his son Loyall were staying so that Loyall could attend the Dutchess County Academy. But it soon became clear that he would not secure new orders under this secretary and that he must adjust to living on the $3,000 a year an unemployed naval captain drew. The family moved back to Norfolk.

The Farraguts were living in the heart of Virginia when the Secession Fever struck, with the action of South Carolina in December. Virginia attempted desperately to hold the southern states in the Union, but when it became apparent that the cotton states were going out, Virginia seemed inclined to cast her lot with them. Farragut was in the habit of walking down to a store in the center of town every morning after breakfast to hear the news and talk over what was in the morning papers. During the winter and early spring, Farragut grew more gloomy; he said there would be war between the states. Most of his friends thought he was crazy. They called him a "croaker" because he spoke so solemnly, but as Mississippi, Florida, Alabama, Georgia, Louisiana, and Texas followed South Carolina, Farragut grew ever more pessimistic. When the Confederacy was formed, he predicted that this was the end.

All the while, Captain Farragut considered his own position. He was a Virginian by adoption. His wife was a Virginian, born and bred. What would he do if the rupture came?

If Virginia joined the Confederacy and the country split in half, and if the Confederate States were allowed to go away in peace as they proposed to do, then Farragut decided he would resign his commission and settle down to retirement in Norfolk, to live out the rest of his life among his friends. He had made a little money in California in real estate speculation (buying lots in Vallejo, which soared in value as the navy yard was built at Mare Island). He would never be rich, but he would not starve.

But if Virginia stayed in the Union, as he hoped and expected, and if war came, he would cast his lot with the government he had served so long. "God forbid I should have to raise my hand against the South," he said, but he was prepared to fight against his many friends if the need arose.

In April the Virginia convention met in Richmond and, on April 17, enacted the ordinance of secession. The next morning, Farragut went as usual to the store to talk politics. He was immediately aware that something important had happened. There were no smiles, and the greetings of his friends were grave, if not despondent. When he learned that Virginia was going out, Farragut said he did not approve and that he would vote against it when the issue was referred to the people. But the referendum was set for May, and affairs would not wait that long. When Farragut expressed his disapproval and his support of President Lincoln's call for troops to retake the forts and arsenals captured by the southerners, his old friends warned that a person who held such sentiments could not live in Norfolk.

"Well, then, I can live somewhere else," Captain David Farragut responded, and took his leave of his old friends.

Farragut told his wife what had happened and said that it was his duty to stick to the flag. But for her it might be a different story. All her family, all her friends, lived in Norfolk, and Norfolk had been her life.

"This act of mine may cause years of separation from your family; so you must decide quickly whether you will go north or remain here," he said.*

She decided to go with him.

That very day the Farraguts left their pleasant house on Duke Street. Farragut insisted on leaving immediately. His friends at the navy yard were mostly Southerners. At any moment he might be called upon to report for duty at the yard; he might end up fighting his personal friends and killing them, or being killed by them.

Thus the Farraguts fled their home, leaving their belongings behind them, to side with the country against relatives and old friends. The family went to Grandfather Loyall's house where the tearful good-byes were said. Then the Farraguts and Mrs. Farragut's sister (who was married to Dr. Ashe, of San Francisco) went to the wharf and boarded the steamer for Baltimore. There was a rumor that Farragut might be arrested—but by whom and for what? There was no cause to arrest a man who was doing his duty to his country as he saw it. The Farraguts departed in peace. The steamboat whistled, the paddle wheels began to turn, and they were soon on their way, looking sadly back, not sure when or if they would ever again see Norfolk.

The next day they were in Baltimore, and wondering if they had bettered themselves. Baltimore was aroused, and the Massachusetts troops called up by President Lincoln were attacked by a mob in the streets as they passed through on the way to Washington. The rail line to Philadelphia had

*Ibid., p. 204

been cut with the destruction of the Susquehanna bridge, and life looked grim. But Farragut managed to secure accommodations on a canal boat, which took them to Philadelphia, and then they continued by train to New York. Mrs. Ashe boarded a steamer for California, and the Farraguts traveled to the village of Hastings-on-Hudson, north of New York City. There they rented a cottage, and Captain Farragut waited.

15. NEW ORLEANS

Captain David Glasgow Farragut was sixty years old in the summer that the Civil War began. He was five feet and six inches tall, still trim at 150 pounds, still youthful looking, although his black hair had turned to iron gray, and he vainly sought to conceal his growing bald spot by combing the hair across the top of his head. He had the look of an outdoorsman about him, gained from many years of watch-standing in tropical climates and foul weather. He was mild-mannered and quiet; his eye troubles gave his face a placid sheeplike expression that was belied by the sensitive man beneath the surface. He half feared that his career was over, yet he was prepared to serve the Union as he could, and he wanted to get into the fight.

In the beginning, there was little fight to get into. Farragut applied for a command, but the Navy Department did not seem to hear his cry. He sat in Hastings-on-Hudson, and because he came from Norfolk, the rumor quickly spread around the community that he was a suspicious Southerner. The rumor grew as he took long walks about the countryside, for exercise and to kill time, and soon it was said in the village that he must be watched, for someone suggested that this mysterious figure was preparing to blow up the Croton Aqueduct and create a water famine in New York.

As for the United States Navy, it was thoroughly disorganized and confused by the beginning of hostilities. In January, the Pensacola Navy Yard surrendered to the Confederates, even before there was a Confederacy. The navy was on the defensive from the start.

On April 19, President Lincoln decided that the Confederate ports should be blockaded, but this was easier said than done. The distance from Alexandria, Virginia, to the Mexican port of Matamoros on the Rio Grande was 3,500 miles, but if one measured the coastlines of all the inlets, bays, and islands along the American shore, the distance was 12,000 miles—and that was what must be blockaded. The federal government, in 1861, owned twenty-six steam warships and sixteen sailing ships, but all except three of these were scattered around the world; thus the navy had an effective force of three vessels to carry out the blockade and begin hostilities against the Confederacy.

The Farraguts settled into their half of a double house at 60 Main Street in Hastings-on-Hudson, and Farragut fretted. He wrote to the Secretary of the Navy, Gideon Welles, and told him why he had left Norfolk. A few weeks later he received and executed the oath of allegiance required by the navy, which at that point did not know loyal officers from avowed Confederates. In another few weeks Farragut went to Washington with an idea: he wished to ask for command of a fast ship and go out and engage in battle with the *Sumter,* which had run the navy blockade off the mouth of the Mississippi and was beginning to seek victims among the Union merchantmen. Nothing came of the visit, and he went home again, shortly before the Battle of Bull Run. He did not see Secretary Welles on that visit, for the Secretary was busy trying to put together the ships of a fighting navy, and until he had ships, he had little need of officers to man them.

There was indeed very little naval activity during that first summer of the war, and only one victory of any consequence. Toward the end of August, Flag Officer Silas H. Stringham led a naval force that accompanied an army force under Major General Benjamin F. Butler in capturing Hatteras inlet. As for Captain Farragut, although he watched the mails hopefully, it was not until September that he received an appointment, and then it was to a survey board. The task was important, more important than Farragut believed, because the war brought a new responsibility to the navy to examine the fitness of its officers, and in the case of civil war, "fitness" included unquestionable loyalty. It was a considerable tribute to Farragut that in these times of trial, located so far from the wellsprings in Washington, his loyalty was accepted without question. Farragut was impatient and bored by the work; he wanted a command.

Yet even as he fretted in the daily meetings of the board in New York, his affairs were taking a turn for the better. The change began in the spring of 1861, when the war steamer *Powhatan* was given to Lieutenant D. D. Porter and ordered to Pensacola to relieve Fort Pickens and blockade Pensacola Bay. The commander was David Porter, son of Farragut's great friend and protector, and now a naval officer approaching middle age. Porter and the *Powhatan* were ordered to join the blockade of the Mississippi River. While on duty there, he conceived a plan to attack New Orleans by sea. During the summer he went out to chase the *Sumter,* and chased heartily in his rotten old steamer whose boilers were held together with patchwork, and whose rigging was mended and torn. Finally, in November, he came back to New York for repairs and went down to Washington to talk about his plan. Commander Porter (he was promoted) convinced Secretary Welles and other political leaders that his plan was practicable. It really was not very hard to convince Welles because Porter was lucky enough to see the Secretary on the very morning that Welles learned of the capture of Port Royal, South Carolina, by a fleet of fifty ships that carried 13,000 troops. The force had gone out under Flag Officer Samuel F. DuPont and Brigadier General Thomas W. Sherman. Actually, when Porter came into the office, the Secretary was already considering such a plan, and Porter was then taken into Welles' confidence. The Assistant Secretary of the Navy, Gustavus V. Fox, had served in the merchant navy, and he was sure that New Orleans could be captured without the need of raising and sending a huge army force along with the navy. Porter believed the forts that lay between the mouth of the river and the city must be taken, too, and he thought soldiers would be needed, or at least a flotilla of bomb vessels which could stand off and bombard the forts into submission.

The discussions were in earnest and they continued for several weeks. On November 15, Secretary Welles arranged a meeting at General George McClellan's house at 14th and H streets. President Lincoln was there, as well as Assistant Secretary Fox and Commander Porter. There was argument as to the necessity of reducing the forts, and the view that the bombardment squadron must be taken was finally adopted. The plan was ready.

What was needed at this point — November, 1861 — was a commander for the expedition. The logical candidate was Flag Officer William W. McKean, but he was ill.

In the search the name of Farragut came up, along with many others. He was not particularly noted as an officer of dash or daring; indeed, his mainstay was his solid capability, which had appealed to Commodore Joseph Smith when Farragut was chosen to head the new Mare Island Navy Yard. But as the days rolled by, the case for Captain Farragut grew stronger. Assistant Secretary Fox favored him because of the manner in which he had left Norfolk on the day that he learned Virginia had seceded from the Union. Secretary Welles was aware of this action, and he had also been in the Navy Department during the war against Mexico when Farragut had come forth with his plan for the capture of the Castle of San Juan de Ulloa. Welles had been favorably impressed with the daring of the plan, if Secretary Mason had not been, and he remembered the officer who suggested it.

Welles began talking about Farragut within the department. Captain Joseph Smith spoke highly, as did several other senior captains. (Captain was then the highest grade in the navy, the terms commodore and flag officer simply designated jobs or tasks to which captains were put, or became honorific, as in the case of national heroes. But all senior officers were captains and received the same basic pay and treatment.)

Commander Porter was consulted, and he spoke highly of Farragut. But Farragut had a good but not well-known record, and some of the politicians were horrified to learn that an officer of so little renown was to be given so grand a task. The fact was, however, that the United States Navy had no heroic figures in it. The closest to a hero was Flag Officer DuPont, who was much in favor because of his recent exploit; Secretary Seward, among others, thought he ought to have the New Orleans command.

In December, Porter went to the Brooklyn Navy Yard to see Farragut and held a long conversation with him at the Pierpont House in Brooklyn. What the Navy Department really wanted to know was the extent of Farragut's belligerence against the Confederacy. Porter asked the captain how he felt about fellow officers who had joined the Confederate Navy.

"Those damned fellows will catch it yet," Farragut replied.

"I am glad to hear you talk that way," Porter said. "Would you accept a command, such as no officer in our navy has ever held, to go and fight those fellows whose conduct you so reprobate?"

"What do you mean?"

"I will tell you nothing until you have answered my question," said Porter. "I am empowered to offer you the best command in the navy, if you will go in against the rebels and fight them to the last."

Farragut considered, and his face grew long, and the crow's feet at his eyes tightened. "I cannot fight against Norfolk," he said slowly.

"Then you are not the man I came after, for Norfolk will be the very place to be attacked first, and that den of traitors must be wiped out," said Porter.

That remark might have ended the conversation, but Porter was exceeding his instructions in every way in his effort to ascertain the exact state of Farragut's feelings. Actually, had the black-bearded Porter been ten years older, with another rise in rank accomplished, he would have had the appointment himself, for Assistant Secretary Fox thought he was the man for the job. It was established that Porter would have an important part in the task ahead, and he was already playing the role of devil's advocate in the interests of the decision-makers.

The conversation continued for two hours, Porter ruthlessly forcing Farragut to examine every aspect of his own feelings and his own position about fighting old friends, and even relatives of his wife's family—the Loyalls were a navy family and had many members in the ranks of the South.

Finally Farragut jumped up from his chair. "I will take the command; only don't you trifle with me," he said heatedly.

Porter showed his pleasure as he prepared to leave. "You will hear in twenty-four hours what your fate will be," he said, and departed to telegraph Assistant Secretary Fox.

Farragut was asked to come to Washington. Nothing was decided, but he knew that he was being considered for a vital post. On December 21, he was breakfasting at the home of Postmaster General Montgomery Blair with Assistant Secretary Fox. Fox explained the New Orleans plan to Farragut and asked what he thought of it.

Farragut did not hesitate. "It will succeed," he said.

Fox pulled out a piece of paper on which were listed the ships that were being made available for the expedition, and asked if Farragut could do the job with this force.

"I will engage to run by the forts and capture New Orleans with two-thirds of the number," he said.

Fox smiled. "More vessels are to be added to these, and you are to command the expedition," he replied.[*]

Farragut could not conceal his elation at securing the command. In his own hotel room, he wrote a note for his family: "Keep your lips closed, and burn my letters; for perfect silence is to be observed—the first injunction of the Secretary. I am to have a flag in the gulf, and the rest depends upon myself. Keep calm and silent. I shall sail in three weeks."

Because Farragut was not well known to the leaders of his nation, Blair had second thoughts after the interview.

"Don't you think Farragut is too enthusiastic?" he asked Fox.

[*] *Ibid.*, pp. 11-12

"No," replied Fox shortly, "I was most favorably impressed with him, and I am sure he will succeed."

That day the decision was made by Welles that Farragut would have the command. The moment the word was out, the second-guessers were complaining to the Secretary of the Navy. Secretary Seward expressed his doubts. At least one Senator questioned Farragut's loyalty because he was a southerner married to a southerner. But the appointment stood. Farragut went to New York to get ready for the expedition and to spend Christmas at Hastings-on-Hudson.

The day after Christmas he, his wife, and son took the train to Philadelphia to see the U.S. steam sloop *Hartford*, which would be his flagship. She was much like the *Brooklyn*, a little shorter, a little broader, a little heavier. He was satisfied.

The Farraguts went to Washington, where the appointment was confirmed and his orders were issued: Captain Farragut was to command the Western Gulf Blockading Squadron, which would operate from the mouth of the Rio Grande to the eastern shore of St. Andrew's bay in East Florida. He was to proceed to Philadelphia and hoist his flag aboard the *Hartford*. Additional orders would be sent to him there.

Before he left Washington, Farragut called on President Lincoln, taking his son Loyall along. The purpose was to secure, if possible, a commitment for Loyall's appointment to the United States Naval Academy at Annapolis, seemingly a slight enough favor for an officer who had already served for fifty years and who was now entrusted with the navy's most important command. Lincoln smiled, asked Farragut to make his request in writing, and shook hands with them. The appointment never came through.

But the orders did. Farragut and his family went to Philadelphia and put up at the Continental Hotel. He began making preparations for the fight ahead. He added six 9-inch Dahlgren shell guns to the *Hartford's* sixteen, and another 30-pound Sawyer rifle, which gave the ship three such guns, two on the forecastle and one on the poop. On January

19, the *Hartford* was commissioned and the square blue flag of Flag Officer David Farragut was run up the mizzenmast. On January 25, Farragut boarded, along with Captain Henry H. Bell, who would be his fleet captain, or second in command. Captain of the ship was Richard Wainwright.

The ship moved under steam and sail to Hampton Roads, making as much as thirteen knots when under both, but only eight knots under steam alone. At the Roads Farragut received extra men for the crew and his final orders, which named the thirty vessels he was to have for the mission and gave the details about the bomb vessels that would be assigned to the squadron. Commander Porter would have charge of these bomb vessels and the armed ships that would tow them into position to bombard the Mississippi forts.

Farragut's primary task was the blockade, but he was ordered to collect the vessels he could spare from blockade duty, proceed up the Mississippi, reduce the fortifications, and take New Orleans and hold it until troops could be sent to relieve him. He was also to take Mobile Bay.

Farragut steamed south, with a growing load of worries on his mind. He did not have a hospital ship, and he knew he would need one. At Key West he discovered that some of the gunboats were in such poor shape that they must be sent north for major repairs. Worse, he found that none of the vessels attached to his squadron were suitable for work in shallow water, and he knew that the waters of the gulf were indeed shallow. Postmaster General Blair would have been less concerned about Farragut's "over-enthusiasm" had he read the letters the commander of the blockade force began sending back to Secretary Welles.

From Key West the *Hartford* went to Havana, then filled with French, British, and Confederate ships. The officials at Havana were not particularly friendly, and when the *Hartford* arrived off Morro Castle after dark, they tried to stop her from coming into harbor. Farragut paid no attention, but steamed in boldly under unfriendly eyes, his fingers itching to throw "a dose of 9-inch shells" around the harbor. At Havana, his fears were realized; he learned from the American consulate there of the continuous arrival of small ships loaded with cotton that were coming in from the southern states, originating at little places on the shore where it would seem that nothing larger than a rowboat could get in. Again, the need for small, shallow-draft blockade vessels was made clear, and again he communicated with Washington about the problem.

Then the *Hartford* left Havana and steamed to her point of rendezvous with the blockade force, Ship Island, thirty miles south of Biloxi. This was familiar water to Farragut, for as a boy he had often sailed hereabouts with his father, going through Mississippi Sound from New Orleans to the family plantation at Pascagoula.

The other ships had not arrived, but on the day after coming to Ship Island, Farragut took command of the district and the squadron from Flag Officer McKean, and got down to work. He attacked the mountain of paper before him; he sent to Secretary Welles for more coal; he sent for more tools for the repair shops; he sent a hydrographic expert out to survey the passes into the Mississippi. He sent his old ship *Brooklyn* on a mission to seize the telegraph station and the operator at the head of the Mississippi passes and cut communications with New Orleans. Captain Thomas Craven, the commander of the *Brooklyn*, was also instructed to raid the river pilots' headquarters, capture the pilots who should be there, and bring them to Ship Island.

Farragut also sent orders out to his ships to meet him at the Southwest Pass into the Mississippi, and the ships soon began to assemble there. It was an impressive flotilla. The ships available and called up for the passage included: the *Brooklyn*, twenty-four guns; *Mississippi*, seventeen guns; *Pensacola*, twenty-four guns; *Cayuga*, six guns; *Oneida*, nine guns; *Varuna*, ten guns; *Katahdin*, four guns; *Kineo*, four guns; *Wissahickon*, four guns; *Winona*, four guns; *Itaska*, four guns; *Kennebec*, four guns; *Iroquois*, nine guns; *Sciota*, four guns; *Colorado*, fifty guns. (The frigate *Colorado* drew too much water to cross the bar and as a sailing ship was not fit for the work at hand, so her guns were distributed among the other ships.) The mortar division included twenty merchant schooners, each with a 13-inch mortar. They were drawn by three ferryboats, the *Clifton, Westfield,* and *Jackson,* the revenue steamer *Harriet Lane,* the gunboat *Owasco,* and a double-ender, the *Miami.*

Farragut worked at his plans. To lighten the ships, lower their center of gravity, and increase their fighting power, he ordered topgallant masts taken down and extra spars and rigging put ashore. This move also increased the field of fire of all ships, as did his decision to put howitzers in the tops. He and Bell prepared a detailed general order to cover conduct during the coming battle. Ships were to keep bows-on to the enemy at all times. If injured, they were to back down the river, not turn and run. Grapnels were to be ready for towing off fireships that might be sent against the fleet.

All the while, the ships were coming in. The *Pensacola* arrived on March 2, just ahead of a norther—that worst-feared of Gulf of Mexico storms. She brought intelligence from Secretary Welles, including a sketch map of the Confederate defenses drawn by the engineers from memory. A half-dozen more ships and 18,000 soldiers were on their way, said the Secretary, but Farragut was not to wait for them. He was to go on with what he had when he was ready to move.

By March 5, much of the fleet was assembled, but Commander Porter's bomb fleet was not yet on hand. Farragut was feeding information ashore and making every effort to appear ready to launch an attack on Mobile, to throw the Confederate forces off in their defense planning. But there were new, serious problems, and most serious of them was a difficulty that no one had considered.

On paper the matter of approaching the Mississippi River seemed to offer few obstacles. The engineers who had maintained the Mississippi delta in years past reported that the bars of the channels were at nineteen feet. The frigate *Mississippi* drew about twenty feet, the *Colorado* drew twenty-two feet; the frigate *Wabash* drew some twenty feet after and sixteen feet forward, and none of the other ships drew so much. Referring to the *Wabash,* Secretary Welles wrote Farragut:

> This would indicate a very easy passage for this noble vessel, and, if it be possible to get these two steamers over, and perhaps a sailing vessel also, you will take care to use every exertion to do so. The powerful tugs of the bomb flotilla will afford the necessary pulling power.[*]

How easy it was for even the best-intentioned and most benign leader in Washington to sit in his chair and spin the stuff of victory!

Everything Secretary Welles said was true; the bars at the mouths of the Mississippi Delta *should* have been relatively simple for Farragut to cross with his fleet. A little lightening here, a little adjustment there, and whoosh—they would be over. The *Wabash,* for example, could be made ready for a nineteen-foot passage by shifting stores and equipment amidships, giving her an even keel level of eighteen feet and four inches, or eight inches above the bar depth.

But what the navy men and the engineers in Washington forgot was that North and South had been at war for nearly a year. With the retreat of federal power north to Washington, many things had changed, among them the condition of the delta of the Mississippi. That delta consisted of five mouths or passes: Pass a L'Outre, standing at the extreme east side; then came Blind Bay, a *cul de sac*; Northeast Pass, Southeast Pass, South Pass, and Southwest Pass.

These passes were fingers of muddy but free-flowing water, spread out like a hand and surrounded by muck, mosquito swamp, and jungled lowland filled with roots, vines, and creepers. Every ripple of water into these mouths brought its hanging screen of erosive particles of the land, and these were deposited as silt at the entrances to the five passes. In better days the engineers kept the passes open with dredges, although, even in 1860, it had been difficult to maintain correct

[*]*Ibid.,* p. 212

knowledge of the daily conditions of the delta because the mud was so subject to change. Pilots sounded constantly as they went down the river, changed the buoys and landmarks nearly every week, and the dredges came and went.

As Pass a l'Outre was supposed to carry nineteen feet across the bar, Farragut tried to put the *Brooklyn* across. She drew only sixteen feet, and it should have been an easy job. But in the year of war no big ships had moved up the Pass a l'Outre, stirring the bottom and pushing aside the top silt with their passage, and the *Brooklyn* went aground—so hard that she lay on the bar helpless for seventeen hours until Farragut took the *Hartford* in to pull her off. Fortunately, the Confederates had abandoned the mouths of the Mississippi as indefensible. At least there was no danger from human enemy.

Having failed at Pass a l'Outre, Farragut reconnoitred and made the final decision that Southwest Pass would be used when he discovered that the *Brooklyn* could get across the mud bar there. She grounded once, was stuck for an hour, but shook loose. The day was March 12. The next day, the *Hartford* struggled across and joined the *Brooklyn* inside. Farragut then moved his two warships up the long finger of Southwest Pass to where the five passes converged and one could see the whole mighty Mississippi. Here stood Pilot Town, whose handful of questionable inhabitants (scoundrels mostly) were already in custody and whose miserable village of a dozen houses built on piles on a mudbank had been turned into a storehouse and hospital. Farragut wrote proudly to Secretary Welles that he had hoisted the flag permanently on Louisiana soil, or at least he hoped so.

Farragut was troubled by the necessary politics of war, and he resented it. He had known almost from the beginning that the bars would give trouble, but two of his friends in the Navy Department had been unable to resist giving their unasked-for advice and had told Secretary Welles that they were sure the *Colorado* could be lightened and taken across the bar. Farragut wasted several days fooling with the *Colorado*, shifting her weight, lightening her, and sticking her in the mud, before all around him could see what he knew,

167

that she must be left outside the bar and out of the action. But Farragut's care in making the effort was an indication of how far he had progressed in his ability to play the game of self-protection. Twenty years earlier he would not have bothered to cover his own actions, secure in the mistaken belief that success was its own justification; by 1862, he realized there were considerations other than the blacks and whites, rights or wrongs, that had seemed so clear to him in his youth and that the other considerations were as important as success or failure. He took the *Colorado* back to Ship Island and let his captains convince him that the frigate had best be left outside. Those who made the argument included the two friends who had originally told Secretary Welles that the *Colorado*'s movement would be easy.

Slowly, steadily, the preparations continued for the assault on New Orleans. The *Mississippi* and the *Pensacola* were stripped of everything that could be taken off them and sent to the Southwest Pass. The pass was found to be seventeen feet deep; the ships drew eighteen feet, but they could be dragged through a foot of the soft Mississippi mud by tugs.

On March 19, Commander Porter began moving his mortar flotilla through the Pass a l'Outre, and in two days that task was accomplished. On March 20, Major General Ben Butler arrived at Ship Island, and Farragut, who was there, was delighted to learn that Butler would give him no particular trouble. The army general seemed content to follow the navy in and hold what territory Farragut took for him. An aggressive naval commander could ask for no finer support.

One by one the other ships of the flotilla were moved past the bar, but the *Pensacola* and the *Mississippi* could not make it, and the expedition was hauled up short because their combined forty-one guns could not be left behind. The *Mississippi* was ten days in passage, and the *Pensacola* was even more stubborn—it was two weeks before she managed to cross the mud. Old Admiral Mud, said the navy men, threatened the expedition before it really even got under way.

Fortunately for Farragut, wireless telegraphy was not yet

a part of the naval picture because at this point in the operation he was subjected to backbiting from a source he would not have expected. Commander Porter was an indefatigable schemer and troublemaker. He had Assistant Secretary Fox's ear, and as matters were delayed he began complaining about Farragut to Washington.

One of the Union's most serious problems in conducting the Civil War was interference from political leaders in Washington who did not trust their field commanders, and although this problem was more serious in the army's operations, it existed in the navy, too. Secretary Welles and Assistant Secretary Fox misread Farragut's call for shallow-draft vessels (which Farragut wanted for the blockade of the coast) and panicked, believing they had chosen a man who did not understand how to take the fortifications ahead of him and the city of New Orleans. Had wireless been in use, Farragut might have been stopped or even recalled. Fox and Porter kept up a stream of correspondence that was most denigrating of Farragut. Welles joined the worriers and queried Farragut as to why he wanted more vessels, when he had said the number given him was more than enough. Porter wrote a long, debilitating letter to Fox just three weeks before the operation began, saying that it was too late to change, that he had little confidence in Farragut, but that he, Porter, and the mortars would save the day. Ten days later he repeated the claim. "If I can get all my shells here shortly, I think the game is ours," he said confidently.

Farragut knew nothing of this intrigue, and so it did not harm him in the least. As to the ability of the politicians to run the war: even had Farragut been ready to move across the bar and into the river-proper by the first of April he could not have moved. In spite of his many letters to Washington about the need for coal, and speed in delivering it, the supply division of the navy did not bring coal. He was reduced to borrowing coal from General Butler's transports. Without an adequate supply he could not move upstream. Finally, at the end of the first week of April, the coal lighters and colliers began to come in. He still did not have the medical supplies he had requested months earlier, but at least he had the coal.

At the end of the first week in April, the fleet was very nearly ready for action. Farragut had his four big ship-rigged steam sloops—the *Hartford,* the *Brooklyn, Richmond,* and *Pensacola.* These were the heart of his flotilla. The *Mississippi* was an old side-wheel steam vessel, carrying a 10-inch gun, fifteen 8-inch smoothbores, and a 20-pounder rifle. She was only about half as heavy as the four bigger ships, although nearly as long. She was valuable, but certainly not in the class of the others. The other vessels of the flotilla could be classed as gunboats, from the ten-gun *Varuna,* which was two hundred feet long but weighed only one thousand tons (compared to *Hartford's* three-thousand tons), to such little craft as the *Katahdin,* of five-hundred tons, 158 feet long, and carrying only four guns. Altogether, counting all sizes of guns and the howitzers, the fire power of the fleet was 181 guns, plus the strength of Porter's highly touted mortar flotilla. Porter had twenty ships, each carrying its 13-inch mortar, fifteen of them carrying a pair of 32-pounders, and eleven carrying a pair of 12-pounder howitzers. Porter's seven steam gunboats had twenty-seven guns among them. There, in total, was the force that would move against New Orleans.

As Farragut and the men in Washington knew, the city and the river were very stoutly defended in 1862. Twenty miles above the point where Farragut and his fleet assembled at the head of the passes, the Mississippi turned northeast, and then south again in a great bend. At this bend were located the two forts that protected the river and New Orleans—Fort Jackson, on the south bank, and Fort St. Philip, on the north bank. Fort Jackson was a large five-sided structure, each side one hundred and ten yards long, its thick brick walls standing twenty-two feet above the bottom of a huge ditch, or moat, which ran five feet deep around all sides of the fort. At its nearest point the fort stood a hundred yards from the levee, and here the river was seven-hundred yards wide. The fort's center was given over to barracks, built strongly of earth and timbers, and the walls held galleries and casemates for some of the ninety-five guns.

Fort St. Philip was irregular in shape; its brick walls were seventeen feet high above its moat. It held only fifty-two guns, and far less than half the 1,100 men who made up the Confederate garrison of the two forts.

Between the forts in the river lay a huge obstruction, located just below Fort Jackson. It consisted of a line of eight dismasted schooners anchored bow upstream, secured to two great chains that extended across the river. The interstices between the schooners were filled with cypress logs, some of them forty feet long and five feet in diameter. A stronger barrier had been built earlier, consisting of a larger chain and many more logs, but it had broken loose in a storm in March, and the lesser barrier, which would remain, had been substituted. The whole was anchored in the river to seven big anchors and to trees on the banks.

Along the banks ranged a company of two hundred sharpshooters, who were part of the garrison. Above the forts and the barrier stood a Confederate fleet of a dozen armed vessels of various kinds and several unarmed craft. There were half a dozen towboats that had been converted to gunboats. Each carried a 32-pounder pivot gun, or two of them. There were two Louisiana State gunboats, converted side-wheel steamers, the *Governor Moore* and the *General Quitman,* each carrying two 32-pounders. The Confederate Navy had four ships in this fleet: the steamer *Jackson,* with 32-pounders fore and aft; the steamer *McRae,* armed with six 32-pounders and one 9-inch shell gun amidships on a pivot; the iron-plated ram *Manassas,* with one 32-pounder, with turtleback of oak twelve inches thick, covered by an iron plating an inch and a half thick; and last, the dangerous *Louisiana,* an ironclad of the *Merrimac* type, armed with three 9-inch and four 8-inch guns, and two 7-inch and seven 30-pounder rifles. The *Louisiana* was not quite finished when she was moved down to position; her engines were defective and she had to be towed into place, while the Confederates worked on her propellers.

171

On April 14, Farragut began moving his fleet upriver. Earlier he had gone up to make a reconnaissance and had been fired upon by the forts. But the Confederates were not certain that he intended to attack New Orleans. The officials in New Orleans were now sure, of course, but in Richmond, the politicians were playing the same game that those in Washington played, and President Jefferson Davis did not really believe that the Union Navy would launch an attack. Consequently, New Orleans was not reinforced, as it should have been; instead its strength was dissipated, and guns and men bound for the city and the river were diverted elsewhere. On April 17, three days after Farragut began to move, President Davis indulged in a hot interchange of telegrams with Louisiana Governor Moore because the President wanted the *Louisiana* moved upriver to guard Fort Pillow against an attack from the north.

On that day Farragut was issuing orders for the attack.

According to the orders issued by Secretary Welles, the forts were to be destroyed or reduced to surrender by Commander Porter's mortar flotilla. Experts had surveyed the river below the forts and marked out the positions where the mortar vessels should be placed. On April 16, Porter had brought three of them up and begun trying the range. The firing started, popping from both sides in a desultory manner. The next day the rest of the mortar fleet was brought up to assigned positions, near the western bank of the stream, just below the bend, protected from view of Fort Jackson by a thick woodland. Branches of trees were tied to the masts of the bomb vessels to protect them further from view and to keep the forts from ranging in on them, for they would be stationary.

The battle was about to begin.

16. THE BATTLE OF THE FORTS

Commander Porter had told Secretary Welles and Assistant Secretary Fox confidently that if he was given forty-eight hours and a sufficient force, he could reduce the forts of Jackson and St. Philip to rubble. There had never been the slightest doubt in his mind that he would be the hero of the battle, that his force would make it possible to move upstream, and that thereafter any idiot could finish the job. The events of the previous weeks had only strengthened Porter's belief that if New Orleans was to be captured, he must capture it. For two weeks Flag Officer Farragut had been charging back and forth among the ships, talking incessantly, smiling and joshing with officers and men, making a fine impression on most, but not on Porter.

"He is full of zeal and anxiety, but has no administrative qualities, wants stability, and loses too much time in talking. Everyone likes him personally. He is as brave as anyone, but is neither a Nelson nor a Collingwood," Porter wrote to Fox.

Farragut, on the eve of the battle, was like a boy. He confided to the midshipmen aboard one vessel that he was still young, and he knew it because he always turned a handspring on his birthday, and as long as he could do that he did not consider himself old. He went to dinners with his captains and dominated the conversation. He went upstream to test the Confederate defenses and shouted excitedly when the enemy fired on them.

"There! There!" he said, as the shot splashed nearby. "Ah, too short; finely lined, though!"

The first phase of the battle was to be Porter's, and before dawn on April 18, the mortar flotilla moved to final position. The gunboats *Iroquois, Cayuga,* and *Wissahickon* traveled up the river about their chores: they were to divert the Confederates by drawing their fire away from the stationary bomb ships.

Light began trickling through the trees and reflecting along the water. Still the ships were silent. Nine o'clock came and with it the breakfast hour for the men. The guns were loaded. So were the mortars.

At 9:45 the noise began, the shells with short fuses bursting in air, the bombs lobbing over toward the forts and some of them falling to explode in the river or the marsh with huge splashes of muck and water.

Farragut allowed the gunboats *Sciota* and *Kennebec* to go into action and begin firing. Soon the firing was general from ships and shore. Direct hits on the wooden barracks in Fort Jackson set them on fire, leaving the officers and men without sleeping accommodations.

The mortar schooners were hidden about three-thousand yards from the fort. Also, because Farragut had suggested that branches be tied to the mastheads, the Confederates did not have any idea as to the precise position of any ship. But that lack of knowledge cut both ways. The bend and the forest hid the fort from the Union naval men as well, and they lobbed their 285-pound shells into the fort by calculation, not by observation.

The crashing and the eerie whining of the shells continued. At one o'clock in the afternoon, a lucky shot from one of the Union ships struck the flagpole at Fort Jackson and brought down the Stars and Bars, which raised an enormous cheer among the men of the North. Later shells set fire to the wooden citadel of the fort and it burned and smoked heavily, raising the morale of the attackers. In the middle of the afternoon came news that General Butler's men had landed safely downriver and captured their first objective, the town of Norfolk. By the end of the first day 1,400 "bombs" had been lobbed by the mortar ships, and the gunboats had fired hundreds of shells. Some guns on Fort Jackson had been disabled, but not very many; some men and officers had lost their belongings, but Fort Jackson was still strong and ready to continue the fight.

The battle ceased for the night, and the cleanup began. But next morning at 6:30 the shells began crashing down on the fort. The Confederates were careful and accurate with their fire this second day. At about nine o'clock one of the mortar schooners was sunk when a shell from a Confederate rifled gun passed through the deck, magazine, and bottom of the ship, tearing a huge hole in her. Two men were wounded in the sinking. More—nine in all—were wounded a few hours later when the *Oneida* was struck by two 10-inch solid shot from a smooth bore gun. Still, the exchange of shot and shell continued all day. The heat grew intense and the wind died out, which meant that the smoke from the guns hung above them and only slowly drifted upward and away. The firing grew tiresome, even monotonous, and the men soon exchanged their enthusiasm for weary determination. They sweated and spat and fed the guns, held their ears, sweated and spat and cleaned the bores, loaded and fired and began the process all over again.

By late afternoon it was determined at Union headquarters that they were doing much damage to Fort Jackson. So it seemed from afar, but actually the fort was practically unhurt in terms of its firepower and holding power. Barracks were burned, other woodwork was destroyed, and a shell passing through a casemate had done considerable damage. Seven guns were knocked out at the end of the second day, but seven guns represented very little of the fort's firepower.

On the second night, the firing continued desultorily from both sides, but without noticeable result. On the next morning, Sunday, April 20, Commander Porter came aboard the flagship, bringing a Confederate deserter who had been captured when he brought a small rowboat down the river. The two days that Porter had prescribed as adequate for the reduction of both forts had ended and Fort Jackson gave no signs of despair, while Fort St. Philip was virtually untouched.

Commander Porter's uniform jacket was dirty and streaked,

his slender body was weary, and even his bristling black beard was bedraggled. He was tired and dispirited, and his state of mind was not helped by the weather, which had suddenly taken a turn for the worse. The blue sky of the day before had clouded over and the clouds had begun spilling showers of rain. A cold wind blew down from the north, chilling the men who had been sweating over the guns only hours earlier. As they approached the flagship, the Confederate deserter told the story he hoped the Union officer wanted to hear—that the men inside Fort Jackson were losing hope. But Commander Porter was no fool, and he knew from the sound of firing that the Confederates were still far too strong inside their fortifications and that the deserter was making up the story he sensed would do him best. Porter yearned to believe the enemy soldier, but was too good an officer to be trapped into such frivolity.

He brought the deserter to the flag officer's cabin, and there the man told his story over again.

Farragut was not impressed. He and Porter talked for a while; then the commander left with his deserter, and Farragut pondered the problem. At ten o'clock Flag Officer Farragut signaled his captains to come aboard the flagship for a council of war.

The captains came, with the exception of three who were covering the mortar schooners and could not be spared from action. They came, most of them convinced that their flag officer needed their advice because he had not the ability to make up his own mind about the next step. Farragut then brought out his charts and maps, and began discussing the tactical situation.

Commander Alden, captain of the *Richmond*, said he had a communication that Commander Porter had asked him to present at the meeting, since Porter was back at work on his bombardment of the forts. Farragut said it would be proper to read it. By reading it, Alden also gave his endorsement to the ideas mentioned.

Porter's plan had obviously been drawn much earlier, in the belief that he would have to do the planning for the

176

expedition (since he had so low an opinion of Farragut's abilities). It detailed what had in essence been done already: the vessels had come upriver and begun the bombardment of the forts. The bombardment was to continue, doing grave damage to the enemy. Then, there were two possible methods of attack: either the larger vessels would run the gauntlet of the forts by night or in fog, or the big ships would lie in close and fire point blank into the fort from such angle that the guns could not be brought up to bear by the defenders. But as to running the gauntlet and bypassing the forts, Porter had objections:

> It is not likely that any intelligent enemy would fail to place chains across above the forts, and raise such batteries as would protect them against our ships. Did we run the forts, we should leave an enemy in our rear, and the mortar vessels would have to be left behind. We could not return to bring them up without going through a heavy and destructive fire. If the forts are run, part of the mortars should be towed along, which would render the progress of the vessels slow, against the strong current at that point. If the forts are first captured, the moral effect would be to close the batteries on the river and open the way to New Orleans; whereas, if we don't succeed in taking them, we will have to fight our way up the river. Once having possession of the forts, New Orleans would be hermetically sealed, and we could repair damages, and go up on our own terms and in our own time.

Porter suggested a combined attack of army and navy on the forts. But his entire argument, as before, was in favor of the reduction of the two forts before going on to take New Orleans.

Alden read to the end, then put the paper back in his pocket. Fleet Captain Bell suggested that it be given to Farragut, and it was. Farragut began to talk to the other officers. It was apparent that nearly all of them agreed with Porter that the forts ought to be reduced, either by mortar

177

fire, by a frontal assault by the big ships, or by a combined army-navy assault.

Farragut said he thought they ought to break the boom that night, destroy those schooners and the chain, and that he wanted to go upriver past the forts. His commanders argued against the action, several of them, at least, thinking that Commander Porter was the man who knew what he was talking about and that the affable, quiet Farragut was not sufficiently capable to lead a major action.

The council of war ended. The ship commanders were in for a rude shock. Flag Officer Farragut did not waste time. He ordered distribution of the general order he had drawn before the meeting, holding up his decision only to hear what specific ideas his captains might have to add.

> The flag-officer, having heard all the opinions expressed by the different commanders, is of the opinion that whatever is to be done will have to be done quickly, or we shall again be reduced to a blockading squadron, without the means of carrying on the bombardment, as we have nearly expended all the shells and fuses and material for making cartridges. He has always entertained the same opinions which are expressed by Commander Porter; that is, there are three modes of attack, and the question is, which is the one to be adopted? His own opinion is, that a combination of two should be made, viz., the forts should be run, and when a force is once above the forts to protect the troops, they should be landed at quarantine from the Gulf side by bringing them through the bayou, and then our forces should move up the river, mutually aiding each other as it can be done to advantage.
>
> When, in the opinion of the flag-officer, the propitious time has arrived, the signal will be made to weigh, and advance to the conflict. If, in his opinion, at the time of arriving at the respective positions of the different divisions of the fleet, we have the advantage, he will make the signal for close action, No. 8, and abide the

result—conquer, or be conquered—drop anchor or keep under way, as in his opinion is best.

Unless the signal above mentioned is made, it will be understood that the first order of sailing will be formed after leaving Fort St. Philip, and we will proceed up the river in accordance with the original opinion expressed.

Accompanying this general order was the program of sailing for the ships. The captains could expect to move upriver the next day under fire from the forts, which were to be left, in spite of Commander Porter's advice, unless some drastic change came in the next few hours.

Farragut's next action was to give Fleet Captain Bell the ticklish job of breaking a hole through the chain and line of schooners, making a passage for the fleet through the barrier. His second action was to sit down and write a letter to Secretary Welles, complaining about the shortage of shells and other ammunition, and indicating that it was almost impossible to fight a war without supplies.

As he issued his orders and as he wrote, the booming of the mortars continued. The noise did not stop in the evening, but increased.

As darkness fell, Captain Bell began his desperate mission. He boarded the gunboat *Itaska* with orders to take that boat and the gunboat *Pinola* up the river to the raft. At ten o'clock they set off. The mortar fleet was firing heavily to distract the Confederates, and for a time the ruse seemed to succeed; but as the two gunboats approached the boom, the forts opened fire on them, too.

Bell planned to blow up one of the hulks with two petards, or torpedoes, and a barrel of powder. The petards and powder were placed aboard one of the hulks and the wires were run back to the gunboat, which backed away to protect herself from the explosion. The wires caught, broke, and the attempt failed.

Lieutenant C. H. B. Caldwell, commander of the *Itaska*, then ran that gunboat up to one of the hulks and threw lines around her railing. The *Itaska* backed off and tried to drag the hulk away from her mooring, but the railing broke loose. Caldwell took the *Itaska* to the east end of the line of hulks and managed to cast the ship loose from her chain. But as he was moving the hulk away, the current caught the *Itaska* and carried gunboat and hulk hard aground. Captain Bell was hoping to burn one or two of the hulks, but with one of his gunboats aground, the burning ships would simply become torches to light the Confederate fire on the *Itaska*. Bell gave orders to hold off.

The *Pinola* came up to help her companion ship. A hawser was thrown to the men of the *Itaska* and they made it fast. *Pinola* began backing off; the hawser tightened—and snapped. Another hawser was thrown over, and the process was repeated. Again the rope snapped, strand by strand. However, a third hawser held and pulled the *Itaska* free of the mud.

Itaska was headed upstream as she came free. Lieutenant Caldwell looked at the barrier-raft and saw that the removal of that last hulk had caused the others to shift, clearing a passage around the end of the raft large enough for his gunboat, but not large enough for the big warships. He drove the gunboat ahead, upstream, past the raft, until he could swing around (all the time under fire from the forts) and turn downstream. He ordered full steam ahead, and drove as hard as engine and current could carry him down on the center of the raft, striking the chain between the third and fourth hulks.

The curved stem of the gunboat rose in the water until her bow stuck out three feet above the Plimsoll line. The chain went down; the hulks pulled it upward, the *Itaska*'s weight and force pressed it downward until, finally, the chain broke with a crash and the third hulk swung back one way, while the fourth, fifth, and sixth hulks swung the other, hanging from the ends of their chains in the current, pointing downstream, and leaving an opening quite large enough for Flag Officer Farragut's flagship to negotiate without the slightest trouble.

Upstream the Confederates had thirteen vessels at or near Fort St. Philip, including the ironclad ram *Manassas* and the *Louisiana*. They soon learned of the break of the defense raft. Commodore Mitchell, the commander of the Confederate flotilla, had feared that such a break might come and had asked his captains to guard the raft, but they had decided they did not have the force to try to prevent a Union break. When the break was made, however, they were not long in responding.

Aboard the *Hartford*, Flag Officer Farragut fretted about the danger into which he had sent his executive officer, Captain Bell: "I was as glad to see Bell on his return as if he had been my boy. I was up all night, and could not sleep until he got back to the ship."*

But if he had wanted to sleep, it would have been difficult. The Confederates pondered their problem of defense once the raft was broken and decided to send a fireship downstream to prevent the Union Navy from coming up and, hopefully, to strike one of the major ships and set it afire, creating confusion in the fleet.

At 2:30 in the morning, the fireship was seen from below the raft, and the emergency signal "fire quarters" rang out through the fleet. Then came the confusion: the *Kineo* fouled the *Sciota* and knocked down her mainmast. Both ships drifted down on the big *Mississippi*. The *Westfield* struck the *Iroquois*, and the fireship drifted down between the *Hartford* and the *Richmond*, its flames shooting up mast high, and the heat so intense it scorched the faces of those aboard the Union vessels who turned to look at the flames. But the men of the fleet went out in small boats and managed to tie to the fireship. Finally, when fifty boats had hooked on, they were able to tow the blazing wreck ashore, where it burned itself out harmlessly.

Commodore George N. Hollins, of the Confederate Navy, once a midshipman under Stephen Decatur, had earlier suggested an attack on the Union fleet. He wanted to take all the forces on the lower Mississippi downriver to fight the battle at the barrier of the hulks. He would load forty coal barges with firewood, and take about a dozen ships and

Ibid., p. 228

181

gunboats downriver, towing the barges. Just before reaching the barrier, he would fire the barges and push them down on the Union ships. In the confusion, the Confederates would come racing downstream, ramming the Union ships that were not beset by fire. Hollins outlined this plan to Richmond, but the bureaucrats were at work day and night there, too, and instead of being given permission to make this valorous attempt, he was ordered to the Confederate capital as president of a board to examine midshipmen for the Confederate Navy.

In the early morning hours of April 21, seeing the confusion and damage caused by one Confederate fireship, Flag Officer Farragut would have been pleased if he had known of the consequences of Confederate bureaucracy, for it was mid-morning before order was restored to the fleet. What forty such ships might have done!

17. THE BARRIER

All day long on April 21, Commander Porter's mortars boomed away, maintaining the bombardment of the forts, while Flag Officer Farragut shivered in his cabin from the norther that blew down on them and waited. He had arranged his fleet in two divisions, with Captain Theodorus Bailey, of the *Colorado*, in command of the second division. He, Farragut, would attack Fort Jackson, while Bailey would direct his fire against Fort St. Philip.

But as Farragut considered his problem, he cut his fleet into three parts, giving Bell a third command. Bailey was to lead off in the *Cayuga*, *Pensacola*, *Mississippi*, *Oneida*, *Varuna*, *Katahdin*, *Kineo*, and *Wissahickon*. Bell would take the *Sciota*, *Iroquois*, *Kennebec*, *Pinola*, *Itaska*, and *Winona*. Farragut and the *Hartford* would lead the *Brooklyn* and the *Richmond* into battle.

At first Farragut had planned to move into battle on the morning of April 23, but at nine o'clock on the night of April 22, he learned that the carpenters' crews of two of the big ships were not aboard their vessels, and for damage-control reasons he did not wish to run into battle without these essential workers. He waited again. That night another fire raft came down the river, but otherwise the Confederates were quiet. They, too, were waiting.

On the morning of April 23, Commander Porter came aboard the *Hartford* and again suggested that they wait until he had bombed the forts into submission. Farragut sent a man into the mizzen-topmasthead to count the mortar shells as they fell and measure those falling inside the forts against those falling outside. The number falling outside was far greater than those falling inside.

"There, David," Farragut said, "there's the score. I guess we'll go up the river tonight."

That afternoon Farragut visited every vessel under his command to be sure that all were ready and that there was no misunderstanding of his orders or the specific instructions issued to each commander. Captain Bailey's lead division would be the blue, Farragut's division would be the red, and Bell's division would be the red and blue. The ships would be ready to get under way when the *Hartford* hoisted two perpendicular red lights to her peak. They would then move upriver, the blue division constrained not to use its port guns for fear of firing into the ships of the second division, and the red division forbidden to fire starboard guns for the same reason. This order meant that Farragut and his division would fire on the left bank where Fort Jackson lay, Bailey's blue would fire on the right bank and Fort St. Philip, and Bell with his smaller ships would be free to fire at will, coming up last.

The Confederates knew that something was coming. The mortar fire had slacked off that afternoon, and the fort commanders were uneasy about it. The *Louisiana* had come down to Fort Jackson, and they expected the ship to come forth and drive off the mortar schooners. General Duncan tried to persuade Captain Mitchell, of the *Louisiana*, to move his ship into action that evening, but Mitchell said the ship was not ready and would not be ready until the evening of April 24.

As the sun lowered, the Union ships began to move into position, screened by the bend in the river, so that the Confederates in their forts could not tell exactly what was happening. Bailey's blue division anchored in column on the right-hand side of the stream, heading upriver. The red anchored on the left, and behind it the red and blue.

The *Cayuga* would lead, not because she was largest or most important of the blue, but for the far less noble reason that Captain Henry Morris, of the bigger *Pensacola*, wanted no divisional officer aboard his ship to steal his glory, so Bailey accepted the invitation of Lieutenant N. B. Harrison to raise his flag aboard the gunboat. Porter came aboard the flagship that afternoon for his instructions: he was to increase the tempo of fire of the mortars as the fleet moved past the forts, bring his squadron of gunboats up within range to fire on Fort Jackson, and take the fire of the forts at long range, thus drawing off shot and shell that would be far more damaging against the ships passing.

Darkness descended across the river banks, and in its cloak Captain Caldwell, of the *Itaska*, took a ten-oared boat upstream to the barrier to see that all was well and that the Confederates had not repaired it or planned any trickery which would hurt the Union vessels.

The officers cleaned and shined the swords, looked to their pistols, and nervously passed away the time writing letters home. Farragut paced his quarterdeck, deep in thought. Suddenly he turned to his clerk: "What do you estimate our casualties will be, Mr. Osbon?"

"Flag Officer, I have been thinking of that, and I believe we will lose a hundred," said the clerk.

"No more than that? How do you calculate on so small a number?" Farragut asked, for there were four-thousand officers and men in the fleet.

"Well," the clerk replied, "most of us are pretty low in the water, and being near, the enemy will shoot high. Then, too, we will be moving and it will be dark, with dense smoke. Another thing, gunners ashore are never as accurate as gunners aboard a vessel. I believe a hundred men will cover our loss."

"I wish I could think so," Farragut said heavily, pacing the deck. "I wish I could be as sure of it as you are."

Of one thing, Farragut was certain, and had been since the moment that he accepted the command back in Washington. The bombardment of the forts by mortar was useless and wasteful, and would never succeed. Farragut had said nothing before because he knew that in the minds of Secretary Welles and Assistant Secretary Fox, the mortaring was the thing; that had he argued against the mortar bombardment he would never have been given the command; that had he argued successfully against it, the entire expedition might have been abandoned in the planning stages. Farragut's distrust of the mortars was based on his own solid experience in watching the French reduce the Mexican fortress in Vera Cruz many years ago. The damage there had been done by the explosive shells from the ships, not by the mortars, which had proved relatively ineffectual. Here on the Mississippi it would be only after the battle that the effects of the mortars might be estimated, but Farragut knew their work had been nearly useless, and by this time so did Porter. But it was essential that the fire continue this night, if for no other reason than to keep the enemy lulled, and it did keep on, the blackness of the night split here and there by the red and yellow flash of the explosions.

The hammocks were piped down and the men were told to go to sleep, that they would be awakened at midnight. There would be no drumming, bugling, or any of the noises of battle. They would be awakened silently, and silent they were to remain, moving to their action stations in the darkness, and remaining ready from that point on.

The quiet preparations continued.

At about eleven o'clock, the lookout high in the top of the *Hartford* caught Caldwell's signal that the passage through the barrier was unobstructed. The Confederates caught the signal, too, and opened fire on the boat, while Caldwell's men rowed swiftly downstream, their mission accomplished.

The Confederates were aroused. Fire rafts were lighted and sent down the river, but they passed well away from the fleet and beyond. Huge piles of logs and branches on the banks were lighted in an attempt to forestall any running of the barrier this night. But they were lighted too soon.

At one o'clock on the morning of April 24, the quartermasters and the boatswains and their mates began passing through the lower deck, awakening the men, and the sailors rolled out of their hammocks and began stowing them. An hour later, the two red lanterns that were the signal were hoisted up to the mizzen peak of the *Hartford* and hung there, swaying in the black, chilly air. Moonrise would not come until 3:30 that morning. There was time.

In the darkness the men moved as quietly as they could, so quietly that on the quarterdeck of the *Hartford* could be heard the calls of animals and the croaking of frogs along the shore. Except for the red lights on the flagship masthead, and later the blue, red, and blue and red lights of the divisional lead ships, not a light burned in the fleet.

The capstans creaked and the pawls clacked as the anchors came up from the sucking mud. Below, the steam hissed and the fires crackled in the boxes beneath the boilers, but the clanking and the crackling were muffled by the bulkheads. Just after three o'clock, the blue division began to move, and by 3:30 all the Union ships were in motion. The men stood at their battle stations ready for the hot work ahead of them, their monkey jackets loosely knotted around their waists, or tied around their necks as shawls that could be ripped off quickly.

Just at 3:30, as the long, undulating snake-line of ships moved forward, the *Cayuga* passed through the broken barrier of hulks and logs and chains. Next came Morris' proud *Pensacola* and then six other ships, bound for the right bank and Fort St. Philip. In the rising moon the Confederates were not long in spotting the line of gray-white silhouettes as they passed through the boom. A gun fired from the bank, then another, and in a moment the firing on the *Cayuga* became so intense it nearly blinded Lieutenant George Perkins, piloting from the forcastle. The Confederates were anything but asleep; they were waiting for a run up the river.

In a flash Lieutenant Perkins saw that the guns of the forts were trained on the center of the stream, and he steered to starboard, passing close under the walls of Fort St. Philip, while the starboard guns of *Cayuga* fired their grape and canister, hoping to knock the men off the walls or away from their guns.

At 3:35 the *Cayuga* was passing the walls of Fort St. Philip. The din was deafening. Every gun in both forts was firing, the guns of the ships were firing back, and Commander Porter's mortars were blasting away as quickly as they could fire and load. The air was filled with the smoke of the guns, and above it the curving lights of the flying shells. The black sides of the ships belched more flame and smoke. Then down the river from the shores came fire rafts, lighted and loosed by the Confederates above.

The plan called for the blue division to steam in line through the barrier, and the red to follow. But in the smoke and fire and flame, there was confusion, and the bigger ships of the red division caught up to the end of the line of the blue and had to wait.

Ahead, at the front of the long line, *Cayuga* sped along the east bank of the river, and at 3:45 she was beyond the range of Fort St. Philip. But, suddenly, Bailey saw that he was out of the frying pan and into the fire, for no fewer than eleven Confederate gunboats were closing on him. He looked behind, but all that could be seen in the rear was a moon rising above a fog of smoke with the shooting stars of shells punctuating fog and flashing across the face of the moon. He was alone.

Three of the rebel gunboats bore down on the *Cayuga* and tried to board her all at once. An 11-inch shell was sent flying from thirty yards away; the gunboat ran aground and began to burn. On the forecastle, the long rifle began to speak, and it drove off a second boarding party. Bailey gave orders that the *Cayuga* was to turn and close with their third tormenter, when suddenly out of the darkness and the smoke appeared the *Oneida* and *Varuna*.

Oneida's captain, Commander Lee, saw the plight of his divisional leader and came charging up to one gunboat, ran her down, cut her in two, and sent her downstream, a floating, helpless wreck. *Varuna* moved up, engaged the *Governor Moore* and the *Manassas*, and was maneuvered into running aground, where she lay, apparently a helpless victim of the two Confederate ships. But *Oneida* moved in to help, over to the left bank, where the *Governor Moore* was ramming the grounded Union ship, while *Manassas* moved away, having already done so. *Varuna* was wrecked now and taking water fast. She would never get off the bar afloat, and her crew knew it, but they continued to man the guns and sent three 8-inch shells into the *Governor Moore* at close range, so crippling the Confederate ship that she surrendered to *Oneida* as Captain Lee came up. *Varuna* was still fighting: she sent five more shells into another Confederate gunboat and drove it ashore. Then she sank.

Meanwhile, the *Hartford* led the second division of the fleet through the barrier and at 3:55 opened with her bow guns on Fort Jackson. Moving through the barrier, *Brooklyn*, which was second in line of the red division, collided with *Kineo*, which was seventh in the line of the blue, and this confusion slowed the ships.

Ahead, under the guns of Fort St. Philip, the *Pensacola* and *Mississippi* were steaming slowly and making a fight. So close was *Pensacola* that as the smoke swirled about them, the men of the ship could see the gunners in the fort and could hear the curses and watch the clenched fists shaken at them. *Pensacola* fired slowly and deliberately; the gunners in the fort fled for cover from the 11-inch pivot gun and the 80-pound rifle. But the Confederates were anything but cowards —they fought and they fought hard—and the results aboard the *Pensacola* were proof of it. The *Pensacola* took the worst beating of any of the big ships, losing thirty-seven men in this encounter with the fort.

As the shot raged back and forth between ship and fort, on the other side of the river the flagship was in trouble of her own. At 3:55 she was taking heavy fire from both forts, and at 4:15, maneuvering to escape a fire raft, she went aground off Fort St. Philip. Farragut had climbed into the port mizzen rigging to see better, and stood with his feet on the ratlines, back against the shrouds, looking around him through a pair of opera glasses he had borrowed from Signal Officer Osbon, which was his clerk's official title.

Suddenly a shell struck the mainmast.

"We can't afford to lose you, Flag Officer. They'll get you up there sure," Osbon shouted.

Farragut said nothing, but continued to sweep the battle scene with his glasses.

"They'll break my opera glasses if you stay up there," the clerk yelled.

Farragut looked at him and extended the glasses. "Oh, damn the glasses," he said.

Osbon, who cared for the glasses no more than Farragut, grew very serious.

"It's you we want," he called. "Come down."

Farragut clambered down obediently, having seen what he wanted to see—and a few moments later a Confederate shell struck where he had been perched, carrying away shrouds and ratlines.

The *Hartford* had her problems, but so did the *Brooklyn,* which had grazed the shore on the right bank and come under fire from Fort St. Philip. She moved upstream, guns blazing, and above the fort set fire to the river defense steamer *Warrior.* She fired then at the *Louisiana,* without apparent effect. The *Louisiana* returned the fire and sent one 9-inch shell into the *Brooklyn's* bow a foot above the water line. Fortunately, the shell did not explode or the steam sloop might have gone down. In the darkness and the smoke, Captain Craven lost his sense of direction and went straight across the river, ending up almost on the left bank, under fire of the guns of Fort Jackson. She was attacked by the Confederate ram *Manassas,* which fired her single gun into the *Brooklyn's* hull five feet above the waterline, ramming her with the special ram that gave the ship her reason for being. Fortunately again, the captains of the big ships had all hung out heavy chains along their sides to act as armor, and the *Manassas* ram did not penetrate the hull, although the shock of the ramming knocked a dozen men off their feet and was felt throughout the *Brooklyn.* Then the *Manassas* was astern, lost in the smoky darkness, and the *Brooklyn* was moving above the forts.

The *Hartford's* troubles really began when the Confederate tug *Mosher* came alongside, pushing a fire raft into the flagship. In a moment, the raft's flames had caught the planking and rigging of the port side, and the fire was blazing as high as the main tops.

Farragut thought for a moment his ship was doomed. He raised his hands above his head and clasped them. "My God," he murmured, "is it to end in this way?"

Signal Officer Osbon, standing beside Farragut, noticed 20-pound rifle shells on the deck and rolled some of them over near the port rail. It was hot and he was forced to shelter his head with his jacket as he knelt; he made a ridiculous figure, kneeling, hiding under his jacket.

Farragut turned to Osbon. "Come, Mr. Osbon," he said, "this is no time for prayer."

Osbon, whose hands were busy taking the caps off the hot shells under him, did not answer for a moment. He was just uncapping the third shell. "Flag Officer," he said, "if you'll wait a second, you'll get the quickest answer to prayer you ever heard of." He rolled the three shells over the side into the burning raft that threatened the ship.

There was a terrific blast, and the flames slackened, because the raft had a huge hole in her bottom. The damage-control teams of the *Hartford* were in action, too, and soon had the fire on the ship under control and the raft pushed away. The *Hartford*, still smouldering aport, backed off into deep water and moved upstream.

The *Richmond* had come through third in line, and she came straight as planned, moving toward Fort Jackson. To protect themselves, the men of the *Richmond* lay flat on the deck as the ship came through the barrier and until she was opposite the fort. Then they jumped up and began firing their guns. The ship was so close at this point that a man could throw a stone from deck to the fort.

"Load and fire at will," Commander Alden ordered from the quarterdeck. The *Richmond* moved ahead slowly, her guns flashing and crashing in the darkness. The captain of one gun was decapitated by a shell, but as he fell his hand pulled the lockstring and fired the gun. A master's mate came to the quarterdeck with a message, saluted sharply, and fell dead, a bullet in his brain. A junior officer felt a sharp tug at his right arm, looked down, and found his arm shot away. The *Richmond* crossed the river, fired a few shells at Fort St. Philip, and moved above the forts.

Having ordered the *Hartford* backed away from the burning raft, Farragut ordered his men to fire at the *Mosher*, which was sunk with all hands in a few minutes. The *Hartford* backed around, put her nose downriver, and had to struggle to turn back upstream. Farragut stood on the quarterdeck, a small compass in his hand, apparently timing and watching the action of the turn—cool as a cucumber, his men said. He pointed, a boat black with men was heading for the flagship as if to board. The pivot gun on the forecastle went to work, manned by its marine guard. A shell exploded amidst a knot of men on the bow of the enemy boat, and the boat drifted away.

Of all the vessels in the engagement, the Confederate ram *Manassas* was the most active. She seemed to be everywhere, going upstream and down between the forts. She came across the *Mississippi,* rammed her, and moved away, as the *Mississippi* fired and struck her repeatedly without doing vital damage. Then Flag Officer Farragut saw the *Manassas* again and hailed Captain Smith, of the *Mississippi,* to run her down. The *Mississippi* rushed at the ram. The *Manassas* put her helm hard aport and dodged, but ran ashore. Broadsides from the bigger ship poured into her and set her afire. The crew escaped through the mud to go into the woods. The *Manassas* worked free and slid down the river, wrecked, and sank.

At the head of the column, the *Cayuga* steamed on in the growing light of false dawn, and behind came the other ships, all but *Varuna,* which had sunk. Fleet Captain Bell led the third division in the *Sciota.* She steamed by the forts, firing as she passed, and up above caught and burned two of the Confederate steamboats. The *Iroquois* passed within fifty yards of Fort Jackson without harm, but was raked by Fort St. Philip and then by the Confederate ship *McRae,* which fired heavily into her and did much damage. The *Pinola* came up, fired on both forts, and took fire from them, but by the time she reached the upper waters, most of the Confederate defense fleet was sunk or routed. She was the last ship of the Union line to make it past the forts, because after her passage the light came up too fast. The *Kennebec* got off course in the darkness, tangled in the barrier, and did not get free until too late to try the passage. The *Itaska* steamed up to Fort Jackson, but the light was then full, and the fort's fire was deadly and accurate; she got one shot in her boiler and turned downstream. The *Winona* went astray among the hulks and was too late to try the passage. She learned this sad truth the hard way, coming within range of Fort Jackson in daylight. The first three shots from the fort swept away all but one of the crew of the rifled gun. The *Winona* kept on. The lower battery of Fort St. Philip opened up on her at point-blank range, and she turned, heading back downstream.

Upstream, as the light became stronger, *Cayuga* discovered a Confederate regiment camped on shore about three-and-one-half miles above the forts. She opened up on the troops with canister at close range. Lieutenant Perkins shouted for the regiment to surrender and the officers to come on board with their swords. Down came the Confederate flag, and the commander, Colon Szymanski, surrendered his seven-hundred troops to a gunboat.

By 5:30 in the morning it was all over. The *Hartford* moved up to the quarantine station in New Orleans, which had been designated as their anchorage. He ordered the fleet to anchor. Marines went ashore to take possession of the buildings. The men began to clear the decks and clean up the debris of battle, washing the sweat and powder from their faces and hands, and swabbing the bloody decks. Late breakfast was served all hands, and preparations were made to bury the dead. The casualties were counted and found to be twice as high as Signal Officer Osbon had estimated: 37 dead and 149 wounded men. The *Hartford* had taken eighteen shots, which disabled two of the guns. The *Brooklyn* was hit sixteen times, the *Richmond* thirteen times, the *Mississippi* eleven, and the *Pensacola* nine. The *Cayuga* had forty-two holes in her, but only the masts and stack were seriously hurt. The *Itaska* was out of action with a shot in the boiler. The *Kineo* was hit by the enemy, but serious damage had been caused in the collision with the *Brooklyn*. The *Brooklyn* and the *Mississippi* both suffered damage from the *Manassas'* ram.

The Confederate casualties in the forts were light: eleven

killed and thirty-seven men wounded in both forts. Aboard ship the losses were heavier: seventy-three killed and seventy-three wounded; but eight of the Confederate ships were destroyed and only two escaped upriver. The *Louisiana*, being under the guns of Fort St. Philip, was at least temporarily safe from the Union fleet. Flag Officer John Mitchell, the Confederate commander of the river, was Farragut's cousin-in-law, and for the moment Farragut was glad not to meet him. The *McRae* had also reached the protection of the forts, and she lay there, damaged but intact.

After the battle, General Butler was the first to congratulate Farragut for "the bold, daring, brilliant, and successful passage of the Forts by your fleet this morning. A more gallant exploit it has never fallen to the lot of man to witness."

"I am so agitated that I can scarcely write," Farragut said in a letter to his wife the next day, "and I shall only tell you that it has pleased Almighty God to preserve my life through a fire such as the world has scarcely known."

Summing up the accomplishment years later, General Viscount Wolseley called it a "splendid achievement." It was made possible, he said, first by the inadequate preparation of the New Orleans defenders, second by the want of harmony between Confederate army and navy men, and finally by Farragut's clear appreciation of the moral effect he would produce by forcing his way past the forts. "In other words, Admiral Farragut's attack was based on a knowledge of the superior importance in war of moral over material force. One can hardly offer a higher compliment to any naval or military commander."

The higher compliment was offered by the officers and men of the Confederate Navy who faced him at the forts and in the ships. They *knew* Farragut would steam past the forts. Captain John Wilkinson, executive officer of the *Louisiana*, had served with Farragut during the Mexican War, when Farragut suggested to Perry that he take San Juan de Ulloa by *boarding*. Wilkinson had been certain all along that Farragut would come after them.

The enemy, not his friends, had really appreciated Farragut's mettle right down to the moment of his victory.

18. CAPTURE OF NEW ORLEANS

The dead buried, the decks cleaned and cleared for action, and the ships pronounced ready for battle—if battle was to come again–the Union fleet of Flag Officer Farragut was ready to take its next step.

The Confederate forces of New Orleans were not long in learning of the battle of the forts. On the morning of April 24, the newspapers of New Orleans carried a dispatch from General Duncan at the forts, which described the mortar bombardment but spoke of "ultimate success" of the defenders against the shooting of Commander Porter's bombers. By that time, more than 7,500 bombs had been fired at Fort Jackson. Of these, a thousand had exploded in the air and 3,400 had fallen in the marshes around the forts. But the real proof was that only four guns had been dismounted in the fort and eleven carriages injured. General Butler was later to characterize the bombing as "that superbly useless bombardment which Farragut never believed in from the hour when it was first brought to his attention to the time when the last mortar was fired."

The Confederate commanders were also confident of the puerility of attempting to knock out the forts by bombing. As Farragut had noticed many years earlier in Mexico, the big charges thrown by the mortars exploded either just above the surface or at the surface, and even when they struck a vital spot, they penetrated only a few inches, if at all. The devastation of a fort depended on burrowing into the protective materials, then creating an explosion that would tear a hole in brick or masonry, shatter timbers and throw them askew, and destroy the foundations of the fort itself. Delayed action explosive shells might accomplish this; mortar bombs would never do so.

The people of New Orleans were confident as they read their morning newspapers on April 24 that the Yankees would never come up their river. But the newspapers were scarcely set down and the business day begun when the word came that the forts had been bypassed. Disbelief, uncertainty, confusion, and finally terror were the reactions that raced through the city.

What would Farragut do next? That was the question on the lips of every southerner in the Queen City.

Farragut seemed to do very little. He planned a day of prayer and Thanksgiving for April 25, being a religious man. He settled down to giving his men rest and making ready to take New Orleans.

In New Orleans, the word of the Union victory had permeated the city by 9:30 and the church bells were pealing out everywhere to call the military men to duty. Business houses closed. The schools were dismissed. Along the river, the boats got up steam, preparing to carry their cargoes upstream. The army began evacuating the city, and the cotton in hand was ordered burned. The fires began. By noon they were burning high and by nightfall the city was ringed with fire.

On April 25, Flag Officer Farragut led his fleet from the quarantine station toward the city. He left two gunboats at quarantine to cooperate with General Butler's land forces. The military men and the mortars of Commander Porter were given the task of keeping the forts surrounded, at bay, and securing their surrender. The ships began moving at five o'clock in the morning.

Farragut began to see the evidence of his victory. A burning ship came floating downstream, cotton blazing on its decks. Then came another, and another, until they passed twenty such ships, and straggling everywhere in the river they saw a thousand burning bales of cotton, which the people of the South had sacrificed rather than give to their enemies.

Farragut moved upriver slowly, and his fleet did not reach

English Turn for five hours. They slid around that bend and confronted Chalmette fortifications, the last shore defense of New Orleans, a system of earthen embankments on both sides of the river, one mounting five 32-pounder guns and the other mounting nine.

The Confederates opened fire on the *Cayuga*, which was again leading the van. She fell back. Farragut brought the *Hartford* up and at a range of about a thousand yards began blasting the revetments with high explosive shell. The *Pensacola* moved up, and with the twelve guns of her starboard battery, put the right-hand bank's guns out of action. Soon the *Brooklyn* moved up on the other side and silenced the battery on the left bank. So eager were the men for the fight that Farragut's main worry was having his ships fire into one another (in the confusion of the previous day, the *Varuna* had fired into the *Cayuga*), and the Flag Officer paced from one side of his deck to the other, shouting himself hoarse in directing the men to take care.

In twenty minutes it was all over. The guns ashore were broken or bent or out of action. The Confederate gunners fled their fortifications and headed for the forests to escape landing parties and capture. The fleet reformed in two columns, the lead ships of the first division hugging the port shore, and those of the second and third divisions moving up the starboard toward the wharves on the New Orleans side of the river.

Below Slaughterhouse Point, a fieldpiece fired on the *Richmond* from a large white building. Commander Alden gave the order, and the *Richmond* turned a broadside on the building. Pieces of masonry fell away and smoke rose from the rubble, and the firing stopped. A few rifle balls struck on the bridge of the *Pensacola* and she fired a broadside in the general direction of the offenders. On they came, the silent fleet, men standing at their guns, while ashore the town was alive with rage; men shook their fists at the warships and vowed vengeance.

This conduct was an indication of the disruption of life in New Orleans. Government had broken down completely on April 24, when the first courier arrived bearing the dreadful news of the passage of the forts by the warships. General Mansfield Lovell, commander of the district for the Confederacy, had been at the fort and knew what had happened there. He returned to New Orleans and began immediate preparations for evacuation of the Confederate Army and all its supplies from the Queen City—no easy job since New Orleans was a major base and supply center for the Confederacy. Mayor John T. Monroe and his city officials retired to protect their own families and property, and in a matter of hours the thugs of New Orleans had taken control of the city streets. The thugs represented the dregs of the city, the waterfront, and the surrounding suburbs. They were the gamblers, the prostitutes and pickpockets, confidence men and thieves, and the low saloon keepers and hoteliers, and all who profited from vice in this Queen City of vice.

Mobs, assisted by the city firemen, ran to the waterfront and set fire to the ships at wharves, instead of trying to man them and take them upriver to safety. Writer George W. Cable, then a boy, remembered seeing the mob grab one man and begin to hang him from a lamp pole, simply because he looked like a foreigner and might be a spy. Cable went to the store where he worked and found that his employers had left the city, along with nearly all others of means who had somewhere else to go. While he watched from the rear door of the store, men set fire to the cutter *Washington* and the gunboat moored beside her in the river. Soon he closed the doors to the store and ran to the river to see the sights. As he wrote later in *Century* magazine:

> What a gathering! The riffraff of the wharves, the town, the gutters! Such women—such wrecks of women! And all the juvenile ragtag. The lower steamboat landing, well covered with sugar, rice, and molasses, was being rifled. The men smashed; the women scooped up the smashings. The river was overflowing the top of the levee. A rain-storm began to threaten.
>
> "Are the Yankee ships in sight?" I asked an idler. He pointed to the tops of their naked masts as they showed

up across the huge bend of the river. They were engaging the batteries of Camp Chalmette—that old field of Jackson's renown. Presently they come slowly round Slaughter House Point into full view, silent, so grim and terrible; black with men; heavy with deadly portent; the long-banished Stars and Stripes flying against the frowning sky. Oh, for the *Mississippi!* The *Mississippi!* (The Confederate warship, not Farragut's); Just then she came down upon them. But how? Drifting helplessly, a mass of flames. (This new ram, unfinished, was set ablaze to keep her from the hands of the Yankees.) The crowds on the levee howled and screamed with rage. The swarming decks answered never a word; but one old tar on the *Hartford,* standing with lanyard in hand beside a great pivot gun, so plain to view that you could see him smile, silently patted its big black breech and blandly grinned.

Farragut brought his ships up into a long line opposite the levee, broadsides trained on the city, and the crews busied themselves with the work of anchoring. At three o'clock in the afternoon, Farragut dispatched Captain Bailey and Lieutenant Perkins to the city hall to secure the surrender of New Orleans.

They were rowed ashore in a small boat to the wharf at the foot of Laurel Street, the heavyset, red-faced captain and the slender young lieutenant. Farragut would never have sent less than a company of marines had he realized the city was completely out of control.

Almost immediately, the captain and the lieutenant picked up a following of mob men and women, who walked alongside them and behind them, shouting for Jefferson Davis and Beauregard, and blackguarding Lincoln. Some began to throw rocks and debris at the Union officers, and the shout "Hang them" arose. They might indeed have been hanged, and New Orleans then leveled by the guns of the fleet, if two respectable citizens had not rescued the officers from the mob and taken them to the mayor's office.

Mayor Monroe was inclined to stall. The city was under

martial law, he said. General Lovell must be consulted. The general came riding up in about half an hour, a lithe horseman, proud and arrogant, who said he would never surrender, but he would withdraw and the mayor could do as he pleased.

The mob grew brave outside and began banging on the walls and doors of the city hall, threatening to hang the Union officers. They were hustled back to their ship, where they reported to Flag Officer Farragut.

Later that day, the *Mississippi* moved in close to the levee, and a crowd gathered. The ship's band played "The Star Spangled Banner," and some of the crowd began to cheer. Out of the depths of the city, a band of cavalry came riding up. They rushed through the crowd and fired into the helpless civilians who had been bold enough to cheer the enemy anthem.

The provocation for Farragut to fire on the city and land troops was great, but he did not yield to it. He realized how serious the situation was and he cautioned his officers to conservative action. But that night every man aboard the Union ships was armed with revolver and cutlass, and the watches were doubled to be sure that no Confederate troops attempted to board or fire the ships.

On the morning of April 26, the mayor sent an emissary to the flag officer, reporting that the council would meet at ten o'clock and consider the demand for surrender. The emissary was Marion Baker, an old acquaintance of Farragut's, and the flag officer took the courtesy and time to show him around the ship and outline the battle they had fought with the forts.

Officers were sent to the council chambers to confer, and a contingent of marines from the *Pensacola* went off in two boats to seize the United States Mint. They succeeded and hoisted the American flag over it. But later that morning Confederates, led by a man named Mumford, brought down the flag, carried it to the city hall, tore it up, and hurled the pieces in the window. A few days later, Farragut told General Butler about this incident in describing the tensions in the city at the time of the capture. Butler became enraged and promised to hang the man. Farragut was more tolerant. "You, know, General," he said, "you will have to catch him before you can hang him." Butler was grim about it; he made a special case of the incident and pursued it with that same grimness. Mumford was captured and was hanged as a horrible example of what became of those who defied the Union forces.

There was the proof—were any needed—that no war is as horrible as civil war, and no commander as diligent in pressing the enemy as he who has *not* fought the battle.

Nothing definite came of the negotiations. The mayor indicated that Farragut would have to take the city by "brutal force."

Farragut had other strategy up his sleeve. His officers were talking loudly of giving the people of the city "a whiff of grape"—firing into the streets from the ships—but Farragut refused to provoke hatred thus. The people were in such a state of hysteria, he said, that they were not responsible for their actions. To add to the incendiarism, a British frigate, the *Mersey*, came upriver and anchored near the American fleet, and the British seamen sang Confederate songs loudly and irritatingly; Farragut finally had to take cognizance of the racket and ask the captain to desist in order to prevent an incident. Instead of allowing himself to be provoked into an incident, Farragut set about sewing up of the victory he had won. He moved the *Hartford, Richmond, Brooklyn, Pensacola,* and *Oneida* twenty miles upstream to destroy the batteries at Carrollton. The report had reached Farragut that two forts existed there, but when he arrived, he found the guns spiked and the carriages in flames. The Confederates had deserted the position.

While on this mission, Farragut marveled at one of the most imposing labors he had ever seen—an incomplete Confederate barrier, which was being built to prevent Union ships from passing through the Mississippi. It consisted of units formed by placing three immense logs together, each three feet in diameter and thirty feet long, and attaching a two-inch chain to the two ends of the center log. The three logs were wrapped crosswise, three or four times around, with one-half-inch or one-inch chains. Farragut found ninety-six units assembled into a raft three-quarters of a mile long.

Back in New Orleans, he found the city authorities as unwilling as ever to surrender to a handful of warships. The newspapers, still in Confederate hands, spoke openly of the "freak of luck" that had permitted Farragut to swoop down on them and bring about this embarrassment. It appeared that he would have to prove that the fleet could take the city.

Farragut and his major fleet units had returned to New Orleans on the morning of April 27. It was Sunday and the city was as idle as might be expected, even without the presence of the enemy in the middle of the city. At noon the Union fleet was joined by the Confederate ship *McRae,* which came in under a flag of truce, bringing wounded from the Confederate forts to the hospital. Along the levees, people took their choice, cheering the Union fleet or the Confederate vessel, and while there were no more incidents involving troops, there were many private fights that day.

Downriver, Commander Porter and General Butler fretted, each in his own way, about the behavior of Flag Officer Farragut in bypassing the forts and leaving them behind. Butler began moving his troops; he landed men at Sable Island, east of Fort St. Philip, and then brought them by boat to the east bank of the river. He was not happy, however, and complained in a letter to his wife about Farragut's "unmilitary proceeding" in leaving manned enemy forts behind him. He attributed the Farragut move most ungenerously to the flag officer's "race for the glory of capturing New Orleans between him and Commodore Foote."[*]

Porter was equally displeased, with perhaps more cause, since he had been proved wrong. He thought he saw the *Louisiana* making ready to attack his force of mortar schooners and gunboats, and called for help. He wrote Secretary Welles, complaining that Farragut had left him to face the enemy, steaming on to glory. He congratulated Farragut on the breakthrough, but added waspishly that Farragut would now find the forts much harder to capture than they had been before. He placed six mortar boats in the shallow water behind Fort Jackson.

[*]*Ibid.,* p. 74

On April 24, Porter sent an emissary to General Duncan at Fort Jackson, demanding the surrender of the forts. The general refused. The next day army and navy forces down the river began to move, and on April 26, Commander Mitchell (Farragut's in-law) was in touch with the Union forces under flag of truce and received the misleading information that New Orleans had surrendered. That day, too, the smoking wreck of the uncompleted ram *Mississippi* floated past the forts, mute evidence of the turn affairs had taken.

On April 27, Butler landed troops above Fort St. Philip, and again surrenders were demanded and refused. But that night, the Confederate defenders of the forts rose against their officers, declined to fight further, spiked the guns, and marched out of the forts. Two hundred and fifty of the men of Fort Jackson marched to Union lines and surrendered to General Butler. Others disappeared into the forests. The officers managed to keep enough men in hand to make a formal surrender the next day, and they surrendered to Commander Porter aboard his flagship, the *Harriet Lane*.

Three days after penning bitter complaints about their "desertion" by Farragut, Butler and Porter were competing for the credit of victory, each claiming he had won the battle of the forts with only an assist from the other—and not mentioning Farragut at all. Porter showed his political ineptitude by not including Commander Mitchell in the surrender talks, so Mitchell took advantage of his anomalous position to blow up the *Louisiana* and thus deprive the Union of a valuable asset.

While all this was occurring thirty miles downriver, Farragut was negotiating patiently with the New Orleans authorities for the surrender of the city. He threatened to fire on the city if surrender was not forthcoming, and the bold mayor countered with the threat that he might slaughter the 140,000 people of New Orleans, but he would not lower the flag. The mayor's representative delivered this message personally. Farragut listened and replied very patiently:

> I am a plain sailor, and it is not expected that I should understand the nice points of international usage. I am

simply here as the commander of the fleet, and I aim only to do my duty in this capacity.

The result of the negotiations was the mayor's tacit acceptance of Farragut's seizure of the city. The flag officer sent ashore the entire force of marines at his disposal. They marched to the customs house, bayonets fixed, raised the Union flag, and then marched to city hall and lowered the flag of Louisiana.

The marines brought howitzers, which pointed up and down the street, and a mob swarmed around. At one moment, when it appeared the mob might try violence, Mayor Monroe placed himself directly in front of a howitzer, as if to say that if the people attacked the marines, he would be the first man killed.

The surrender was complete. To read about it in the Union newspapers of Washington, New York, Philadelphia, and Boston, one would have believed that the surrender was brought about either by Porter or by Butler. Farragut's name was not mentioned. Captain Craven of the *Brooklyn* had earlier predicted that if they won, Porter would get all the credit, while if they were defeated, Farragut would get all the blame, and for a time it appeared so. It was a week before Farragut's name came to be known at all to the American reading public, and many months, even years, before the public came to know how important Farragut's victory was in the course of the Civil War. Nor did Farragut know or suspect that in seizing New Orleans, the primary port of the South, he had changed the tide of feeling in the chanceries of Europe.

As far back as the Tyler and Polk administrations, Britain and France had expressed more than slight concern at the growing power of the United States of America on the North American continent. Each nation in its own way had done its best to prevent further American expansion, particularly to the south. British and French diplomats haunted the capitals of Texas and Mexico on the eve of the Mexican War, hoping to persuade Texas to remain a republic. When the Confederacy declared its independence, Napoleon III of France and

Britain's Palmerston were inclined to assist the Southern government and help make it permanent, if possible. On the day that the bombardment of Fort Jackson began, Napoleon III told an English member of Parliament that he favored opening the blockade of the Confederacy by force. Confederate Commissioner John Slidell worked unceasingly for just such an end and was later told by one French minister that if New Orleans had not fallen to Farragut, French official recognition of the Confederacy would have been simply a matter of time. When New Orleans did fall, even a succession of Union defeats, Confederate victories, and Union military lassitude did not persuade the big powers that the Confederacy could win its war, and the chance to secure independence by foreign support was gone. This was a primary value of the capture of New Orleans; alongside that effect, all the importance of destruction of ships, elimination of a major port of entry, and establishment of a cancer in the heart of the Confederacy were secondary.

Also, almost unrecognized in terms of military and naval strategy, Flag Officer Farragut had proved a point that would be of immense value for his country in this war and in a war that began nearly eighty years later. His victory at the big bend in Mississippi was proof that a strong point bypassed became a liability rather than an asset to a defense force and that it would soon either fall or lapse into uselessness. When General Butler entered forts Jackson and St. Philip he discovered that they were virtually untouched, in a military sense, by the long days of bombardment from Commander Porter's mortars. They surrendered because their soldiers lost courage to fight on, and even the officers knew there was no point in holding out once New Orleans was taken.

The lesson of New Orleans was to be vital in American history when General Douglas MacArthur and the naval commanders of the Pacific agreed on a strategy that called for the bypassing of Japanese strong points—which included entire atolls and island chains in the Pacific. Flag Officer Farragut had added a new dimension to naval warfare.

205

19. VICKSBURG

The naval plan for control of the Mississippi had been drawn by the armchair experts sitting in Washington, and their anxieties, eagernesses, and incompetencies showed through. A naval expedition had been launched from Cairo, Illinois, to head south on the river. Farragut, having passed the forts and taken New Orleans, was to move up the river, while General Butler consolidated the victory and spread the Union troops as far as they might go in holding the territory they now occupied in the heart of the Confederacy. But the Cairo expedition, or Mississippi flotilla, was bogged down outside Fort Pillow, part of the defense ring around Memphis, eight-hundred miles from New Orleans. Farragut was to launch an assault northward in the rear of the enemy and pick off his defenses one at a time.

A few days in New Orleans brought the war very close to David Farragut. Although the family of his brother William lived in New Orleans and he had other friends and relations in the South, not one of them made himself known to the Union commander. Once on a streetcar a woman spat angrily in his face. It was a war that aroused fight and sentiment more severe than war among strangers, and Farragut's resolutions, always strong, did not suffer in the treatment he was accorded by the citizens of the Queen City.

Farragut sent men and ships to capture Baton Rouge and Natchez. He went up the river to Vicksburg to examine the defenses, which he found formidable, consisting of ten guns mounted just below Vicksburg and two above, with two gunboats lying beneath them. He ordered five of his own gunboats to take the two Confederate vessels, but could only find two of his timid captains who were willing to risk their lives. Brigadier General Thomas Williams, of the army, was delegated to take the army forces up the river, but he balked when he heard that the Confederates had 8,000 men while he had only 1,400. It appeared that the assault on Vicksburg would not be carried out at the moment.

Farragut went back downriver to Natchez to join the *Hartford*, and it was generally believed that he would launch an assault on Mobile, where the reports of great naval construction activity were giving him much cause for concern. Had he done so, as he wished, he might have jeopardized his career, because Lincoln was eager to have the river battle pursued for the moral effect it would have on the Confederates. Farragut did not know that a great pile of letters and telegrams were awaiting him in New Orleans, demanding his movement upstream.

On May 24, Farragut anchored four miles below Vicksburg, with the *Hartford*, *Brooklyn*, *Richmond*, and eight gunboats. A look at the defenses showed that he could not destroy the guns on the bluffs overlooking the city with his guns, and the military men said they did not have the personnel for an assault. They came downriver, leaving a blockade force behind them, and narrowly made a safe voyage. They were short of coal and had no way of getting coal along the river, for they were in enemy territory. Landing parties were fired on by Confederate troops or guerillas. They were in constant danger of running aground, particularly with the larger ships, and on one earlier occasion the *Hartford* was almost stranded at high water, which meant she might have been lost entirely if they had not been lucky enough to pull her free.

Coming back to New Orleans, Farragut learned how strong were the Administration's feelings about the need for capturing Vicksburg. He reluctantly decided to try again. General Butler offered him 7,000 men. He decided to take some of Commander Porter's mortars.

Porter was on Ship Island waiting for orders, backbiting

and dreaming dreams of his own glory. Having failed to take the forts before New Orleans with a strong fleet of gunboats and mortars, he now proposed to Assistant Secretary Fox that he be given a monitor and four gunboats and sent to take Mobile. (Farragut wanted a monitor, too, but had not been successful in getting one.) But Porter did dispatch twenty mortars.

On the trip back upriver, the *Hartford* went aground again ten miles north of Union Point, below Natchez. Farragut stayed on deck all night long until the ship was freed.

On June 25, Farragut was in position for the attack. At the same time, four army rams and a tender came downriver from Memphis, the defenses there having been destroyed in May. Thus the Union had naval forces above and below Vicksburg, and the attack was to begin.

Vicksburg's main line of defense was its bluffs. The east bank of the river was high there, two-hundred feet above the water. Guns atop the bluffs could fire down on ships that tried to come upriver, but the ships could not elevate their guns high enough to fire back. These Confederate batteries consisted of twenty-nine old and new guns.

Farragut's solution, outlined in his orders, was to use the mortars sent him by Porter, and on June 27 they began bombarding the batteries and the town.

At two o'clock on the morning of June 28, the old signal was raised—a pair of red lights hoisted in vertical line at the mizzen of the flagship. The fleet lay on two columns and began moving upriver. Two hours later the mortars, on opposite sides of the river, began to open up, but as always their fire was erratic and badly aimed.

The *Richmond* was the first of the steam sloops to go through, under the Confederate guns, and she moved into the heart of their fire by 4:30. All the ships going upriver were damaged: the *Wissahickon* and the *Sciota* were badly hulled; aboard the *Hartford,* the captain's cabin was shot to pieces, and Farragut was almost killed in his favorite spot in the mizzen rigging, where he liked to climb to get a better view. The captain of the gun on the poop deck called to the flag officer to come down because he wanted to fire in that general direction, and Farragut moved down to the deck. Just then a Confederate shot struck the mizzen rigging, just above where he had stood, cutting away the ratlines and the halyards that controlled his pennant. Although he was unhurt, the flag dropped to half mast, and some in the squadron thought their flag officer was killed.

At five o'clock in the morning, the sun rose and, by that time, the *Richmond* had passed around the bend and was out of range of the Confederate guns. An hour and fifteen minutes later, the *Hartford* had also run the gauntlet of fire and was safe behind the trees three miles above Vicksburg. Only the *Brooklyn*, *Katahdin*, and *Kennebec* failed to get through.

Farragut went to breakfast and sent messages to Washington announcing that he had passed the barrier and could pass back and forth at any time he was called on—but to what end? If the War Department would assign 12,000 or 15,000 men to capture Vicksburg and carry out Lincoln's orders to clear the river, it could be done. But he could not do it with seagoing forces that were completely out of their element in these shallow river waters. Altogether, in ships and mortar ships, there had been sixteen killed and forty-five wounded.

Soon Porter was up to his old snarling, complaining that Farragut could have captured the Confederate batteries had he been inclined and that Porter could certainly do it, given a little help. The Confederates reported that *not one gun* had been put out of action, and that they had 10,000 troops on hand to fend off the land attack they had expected to follow the river passage. There was no honor or victory in the successful move, as Farragut had seen. The Confederates were contemptuous of the action. Farragut was forced to reprimand Captain Craven for not bringing the *Brooklyn* through.

Yet what Lincoln wanted was accomplished. On July 1, Flag Officer Charles Davis' Mississippi flotilla arrived above Vicksburg and the two Union fleets met. The flotilla from the north consisted of four great ironclads—which looked more turtle than ship to the saltwater sailors—river steamers, tugs, mortar steamers, and hospital steamers.

Davis took Farragut out to the Confederate batteries to show how the *Benton* behaved under enemy fire. She was an odd boat, a converted snag boat that had been used to clear debris from the river in happier times. She had two hulls for snag-clearing. Now the spaces between the two hulls had been planked over and she had a beam of forty-five feet to a length of two-hundred feet. A slanting casemate covered the upper works and was topped with three-and-one-half inches of iron plate. Ports were cut through for seven 32-pounders, two 9-inch rifles, and seven 7-inch rifles.

The *Benton* steamed into position, Farragut below decks, and the ironclad opened fire on the shore batteries. The Confederates had a new Whitworth rifle, which they began potting at the ram, and they soon put a shell through one of the *Benton*'s bow ports, causing a number of casualties.

"Damn it, Davis," shouted the excited Farragut, "I must go on deck! I feel as though I were shut up here in an iron pot, and I can't stand it."

Farragut did go on deck, but was persuaded to leave this dangerous position and seek the comparative safety of the pilot house.

This adventure was Farragut's way of celebrating the Fourth of July. That same day, he wrote Secretary Welles, asking for instructions. If the vessels were not to be stranded in the dropping river, something must be done soon. General Halleck was in the vicinity, but he could not spare troops to assault Vicksburg or to hold it if it was taken. There was a rumor that Richmond had fallen, but it was discovered that General Robert E. Lee had made victory of defeat at the Seven Days campaign, and that McClellan had been defeated and Richmond saved for the Confederacy. Lincoln and the generals became alarmed and asked Welles for naval strength. Porter was detached from the Vicksburg campaign and sent two-thousand miles to Hampton Roads with a dozen mortar boats.

Farragut was soon to be relieved of the onerous duty of attacking Vicksburg without troops; but beforehand, down the river from the Yazoo, came storming the Confederate ironclad *Arkansas.* She beat her way through the sleeping Union fleet, damaging several ships, and steamed safely into the pier at Vicksburg under the Confederate batteries. She had suffered 12 dead and 18 wounded of her crew of 232 men and officers. The thought at Vicksburg was that she would be repaired (she had been damaged in her run) and would then assault New Orleans and drive away the Union men.

Actually, the *Arkansas* had been very lucky. The Union fleet was at anchor and did not have steam up as she came downriver. Farragut was immensely agitated and wanted to get up steam and go into Vicksburg to destroy the enemy ram right then. Flag Officer Davis thought Farragut overwrought and impulsive. But that night Farragut ran downstream under the Confederate guns again. His force did not find the *Arkansas,* whose silhouette was very low. But at least, at the end of the day, he was below Vicksburg once again.

While Farragut was worrying about Vicksburg and the ram, Washington was heaping honors on his head. Two months earlier, Lincoln had asked Congress to give thanks to Farragut and his men for the capture of New Orleans. Finally, Congress had done so, and the nation at large learned the name of the hero of New Orleans. Congress went further in July and created the new rank of Rear Admiral in the United States Navy for the purpose of commissioning David Farragut America's first admiral.

Farragut knew nothing of such honor those hot July days. He knew only of his duty and, in pursuing his duty, he was driven by the patriotism and feeling for victory that had been the impetus for Commodore Porter and those men of the days of America's great little navy.

Two flag officers were on the Mississippi: one with the rams of the navy of the interior, counseling patience and reserve; the other, with ships of the line, counseling action. Farragut knew that his country and Washington would never forgive him or the navy if the *Arkansas* managed to break its way south through his ships to reach New Orleans and perhaps even the sea. Such a victory by a single ship would undo nearly all that he had done. Davis, above the ram, was not as concerned.

They exchanged letters and Farragut counseled with his officers. Nothing happened. On July 21, the day that turned out to be the hottest of the summer of 1863, Farragut went across the river's bend to see Davis personally and persuade him to participate in an attack to take the *Arkansas*. Davis agreed.

In effect, the battle was Davis' and that of his rams, and they failed. One shot was driven into a gunport and several men were killed and wounded, but that was all. The attempt came on July 22. The next day, Farragut was released from the problem, ordered by Secretary Welles to take his big, deep-draft ships downriver while there was still time. The river was split up; Davis would control above Vicksburg, Commander Porter was placed in charge of the blockade from Baton Rouge to Vicksburg, and Farragut was going back to New Orleans. But, in fact, the *Arkansas* was in control of the river between the Yazoo and the never-land below Vicksburg. The whole country soon learned of the daring feat of the Confederate ram, and the fortunes of the navy reached a low ebb. Secretary Welles had written Farragut a letter demanding that he destroy the *Arkansas*. Perhaps fortunately for Farragut's career, the letter did not arrive until he was back in New Orleans, for the commanders in their swivel chairs in Washington again did not know what they were talking about when they pitted rams against seagoing ships, and seagoing ships in narrow waters against shore batteries two-hundred feet above them.

Yet Farragut was far from finished with the *Arkansas,* as he learned on August 1 in an alarming dispatch that said General Breckinridge was advancing on Baton Rouge with 6,000 Confederate troops and that the *Arkansas* was on her way downriver to assist in the attack.

Farragut was persuaded that the news was untrue, but it was fact. On August 3, at two o'clock in the morning, the *Arkansas* cast off her lines at Vicksburg and headed south to raise the blockade of the river. She broke down twenty-two miles above Baton Rouge about midnight. The next day, she arrived in sight of Commander Porter's *Essex* and gunboats, and again broke down.

Breckinridge launched his attack on Baton Rouge at two o'clock on the morning of August 5 and almost succeeded in all he tried. General Williams was killed with a ball through the heart. His troops were driven back. Only the gunboats in the river saved the Union forces from disaster; their guns were concentrated on the Confederate positions by spotters in the State House.

News of the attack did not reach Farragut until midnight, and his organization was anything but what he might have wished at that moment. Several of his ships were in drydock; the *Brooklyn's* engines were cold and a hundred members of her crew were on liberty in the city. Farragut and the *Hartford* managed to get away by 5:30 in the morning, but the *Brooklyn* was five hours longer in getting her men back aboard and making way.

Farragut arrived at Baton Rouge at noon on August 7 and learned that the *Arkansas* had fallen—by her own hands, one might say. She had come downriver to attack whatever Union vessels might appear, but she had broken a connecting rod and gone ashore when about to engage the *Essex* and the *Cayuga*. The crew had set the ship on fire, cut the mooring lines, and let her drift, alone, down the river.

William Porter, David's brother, had gone up in the *Essex* to battle with the *Arkansas*. The *Arkansas* came floating down, and as the fire reached her guns, they discharged, for they were fully shotted. The *Essex* fired back furiously. Suddenly, the fires reached the magazine and the *Arkansas* blew up. Porter took full credit for the destruction in an extravagant and wordy report, and for a time it was believed that he had destroyed the ship in combat. But the final result was to hurt his claim rather than help it, because the Confederates would not have destroyed the *Arkansas* had he not been about to attack her.

The Porters of this second generation were strange men. Both seemed to believe they must walk to promotion and success over the backs of their fellow officers. William Porter complained in letters to Washington about Flag Officers Davis and Farragut. At first Welles was inclined to believe much of what Porter said, particularly because he was annoyed and upset with Davis and Farragut over the *Arkansas* affair. Then Porter went too far; he sent a letter to Secretary Stanton at the War Department abusing the conduct of the military officers in the area, and Stanton took exception to it. Welles was forced to act—to send Porter before the retiring board to explain himself and to reprove Porter personally.

David Porter was more successful with his backbiting. He managed, because he had the ear of Assistant Secretary Fox and Secretary Welles, to besmirch the names of Davis and Farragut and win for himself the command of Davis' squadron on the upper Mississippi. But all this intrigue was behind Farragut by August. He had been raised from number thirty-one on the captain's list to become the single rear admiral of the United States Navy, and although his pay was still $5,000 a year, the pay of a captain commanding a squadron, his rank was the highest of any officer in the navy. The word reached New Orleans just before the middle of August. He was saluted by the army and by his own ships, and he enjoyed a brief day of glory, before moving on to battle elsewhere.

20. BLOCKADE

In August, Rear Admiral David Farragut, the senior admiral of the four in the United States Navy, was ordered to devote his attention to the blockade of the gulf ports of the Confederacy. President Lincoln and Secretary Welles had seen their plans torn awry by Confederate shot and shell, and although they knew the Southerners controlled the Mississippi from the mouth of the Red River to Vicksburg, there was very little to be done about it until some new development brought them an opening.

Farragut's fleet was badly in need of refit, but the blockade vessels on duty were scarcely in better shape, and the Confederates were quite successful in running the blockades of the ports.

The blockade was a strange business, one Farragut did not entirely like. He kept his headquarters at Pensacola, the old naval base. During the opening months of the war, the Confederates had held the base, but were forced to evacuate for lack of troops to protect it. They destroyed most of the port facilities, but they could not destroy the good harbor, and the blockade fleet pulled in for its major repair work.

In one way, Pensacola and blockade duty brought major relief—the malaria menace was nearly ended for the time. On the river, the mosquitos were so thick that many nights the men did not go to bed, preferring to stay awake than be bitten, walking the decks and swatting insects. The ocean breeze tended to blow the mosquitos away from the shore, and the saltwater inhibited their reproduction. The incidence of fever dropped as soon as the fleet was stationed off Pensacola. It was too late for some, such as Commander Wainwright of the *Hartford,* who died of fever on the river.

Farragut's attitude toward the war continued to be his straitlaced patriotic view. He came to know, although he had been almost entirely in the field, of the "shoddy" merchants who cheated the people in purchase and sale of war equipment. The price of coal for the blockaders rose from $4 to $8 per ton, although coal was in good supply and the ships bringing coal from the northern ports could pick up cargo at New Orleans. The increase was sheer profiteering at the expense of the government. Farragut angrily wrote Secretary Welles about it: "This may not be any of my business, but when my country is bleeding at every pore I feel it my duty to prevent impositions as far as practicable."

In these days of the modernization of the navy, Farragut was buried in paper work. The trappings of bureaucracy grew, but the mechanics had not caught up. He spent most of his life plowing through papers with the aid of clerks and amanuenses, professional copyists whose task it was to make all the copies necessary of his letters for various naval commanders, army commander, higher authorities, and lower authorities.

If paper work was not enough, the matter of war politics kept intruding into the orderly conduct of military operations. The Confederate steamer *General Rusk* became a blockade runner in the South, changed its name to *Blanche,* and was fraudulently declared an English ship. She was destroyed on the high seas by Commander Charles Hunter in the *Montgomery,* after he recognized her for what she was. But the British objected, and to appease them the civilians in charge of the navy dismissed Commander Hunter from the service, to the irritation of Admiral Farragut, who claimed that Hunter was not only right, but that he was doing his duty and serving his country in sinking the blockade runner.

Washington chose not to listen to the admiral's complaints. Then, in September, 1863, came another incident of the same nature, at least from the sailor's point of view. On the morning of September 4, the new armed-steamer *Oreto* pulled in toward Mobile Bay. She looked like one of the English gunboats

216

that frequently came to inspect the blockade forces, a practice the British had adopted to be sure the Union navy was living up to the rules of warfare and neutrality. She was of the type, she was sporting the red ensign of Her Majesty, and nothing seemed amiss. But actually, the *Oreto* was a Confederate ship manned by a Confederate Navy crew, led by Lieutenant John N. Maffitt. She was coming into Mobile Bay in broad daylight because Maffitt was afraid that if he did not get into port this day he would lose his ship. Most of his crewmen were down with yellow fever. As he did not even have a pilot aboard, he had to run in during the daylight hours—and that meant disguising the ship.

The *Oreto* was observed by the blockade commander on duty, Commander George Henry Preble, in the *Oneida*. Since she was obviously British, he let her come near before hailing. But she did not stop to ask permission to pass through the blockade, as was the practice of British ships, nor did she answer Preble's hail, but increased her speed and headed straight for the opening to Mobile Bay, on a parallel course. Preble manned his guns. The blockade runner was only a hundred yards away on a similar course, and he scored four hits that damaged her seriously. But the ship with the red ensign was making fourteen knots to Preble's seven, and she slid inside the harbor and under the protecting shore guns.

Preble had been as cautious as a commander might be, recalling the fate of Commander Hunter who had pursued his orders faithfully. But now the wrath of the civilian managers of the navy fell on Preble's head, and he came to suffer what was all too often the trouble in the Union war effort—interference from higher authority that did not know what it was talking about. Preble was dismissed from the service for "inexcusable neglect" in permitting the *Oreto* to run into Mobile Bay. Farragut was furious and fought the battle until President Lincoln finally reappointed Preble to his post. The blockade was a series of victories and disasters, each capture being accounted a victory and each escape of a Confederate ship a disaster. The disasters were as well known to the American public as the victories because the blockade runners almost always put in at Havana after coming out of Mobile

Bay, and there the officers and men told their stories, which immediately percolated back to the United States.

In the summer and fall of 1863, the constant intriguing of men like the Porters gave Farragut concern that he was about to be relieved, as had been his friend Flag Officer Davis of the flotilla above Vicksburg. General Butler heard the rumor and asked Assistant Secretary Fox about it. Fox denied it— not hotly but in what was apparently real surprise. The navy had not thought of relieving the one commander who had brought dash and glory to the navy side of the Civil War, he replied. But it was Butler, not Farragut, who was to be relieved. He was replaced by General N. P. Banks, with 20,000 men and instructions to open the Mississippi River and take control of Mobile Bay—a large order.

Farragut began getting along as well with General Banks, in a military sense, as he had gotten on poorly with General Butler. Banks agreed to reoccupy Baton Rouge and did so. He agreed to cooperate in the capture of Mobile Bay and plans were laid. But in January, 1864, the Confederates made a daring raid on Galveston, knocked out the Union fleet of gunboats, captured the *Harriet Lane,* and took control of the port.

In Washington, Assistant Secretary Fox panicked, as he usually did, and began hurling recriminations at the officers in charge—accusing Farragut, by innuendo, of not doing his job. Secretary Welles was more restrained. He had confidence in himself and in Farragut. He complained that Farragut was lax about keeping him informed, but he expected Farragut to retrieve the situation.

Farragut sent Commodore Bell down with the *Brooklyn* and a number of smaller ships. He made a halfhearted attack on the Confederates inside the harbor—halfhearted because of the shallow water that threatened his ship more than did the enemy—and then settled down to blockade Galveston harbor.

Soon there was another disaster: the Confederate blockade-runner *Alabama* caught the light steamer *Hatteras* off Southwest Pass and sank her. The *Florida* (formerly the *Oreto*) escaped from Mobile Bay and was at large. In the waves of public criticism that followed, Farragut tended to become discouraged. More disasters came along: the Confederates captured the Union ships *Morning Light* and *Veolocity*—both sailing ships, to be sure, and captured by Southern steamers, but such facts meant little to the newspapers at home that were howling for victories on the sea because affairs were going so badly on land. Farragut worried incessantly about the failures of the officers in his command. He worried about the ships, whose boilers (as on the *Brooklyn*) were so thin that the engineering officers feared they would explode unless time could be taken to replace them. He worried about shortages of ships and shortages of competent commanders. He worried about reports that the Confederates were readying a large-scale attack on Pensacola. He wrote and read and worried so much that his weak eyes gave out.

Fortunately, he had at least one person as loyal as he could wish: his son Loyall, who had come down to join him as clerk at the age of nineteen, partly because his mother feared that he was about to be drafted as a soldier in the army. Loyall Farragut took up writing many of the admiral's letters and such unofficial ones as those to his mother, but Farragut continued to write to his wife, however, at least part of the time. And throughout his correspondence came the steadfast note of belief in country. No one could convince him that the cause was wrong or even that the men at the top were unequal to their task. As for Galveston, which Mrs. Farragut tried to explain away in her letters south, he admitted that no one could blame the politicians for once—it was a bad navy show.

The uncomfortable days became weeks and months, and the situation of the blockading force grew weaker. Still two matters, the only important matters, dominated David Farragut's thinking: the need to take control of the Mississippi and the need to seal off Mobile Bay as a port for the blockade-runners. In all his worries, the admiral never lost sight of these objectives.

21. PORT HUDSON

Early in 1863, Farragut and General Banks were thinking of the situation on the Mississippi and of the need to take control of the river to enforce the blockade against the Southern armies. The disasters at Mobile Bay and Galveston were serious in terms of morale and the public mind; the fact that one or two blockade-runners escaped was not as important as the suppression of free trade into Mobile, and nearly all other ports of the Gulf, and Galveston was a long way from the heart of the Confederacy—the wrong way in fact.

Yet the name Galveston pointed up the deficiencies of the Union blockade of the heart of the Southland. As long as the Confederates could control enough of the Mississippi so that supplies could be shipped across that river from Texas, the blockade could never be effective. Farragut could close off every inlet in the Gulf, not a single blockade-runner could pass, not one man or one boatload of material might enter the South—and yet the blockade could fail. Why? Simply because Mexico was neutral, and ships might call at Mexican ports with any goods, deliver them, and then the goods could be shipped up overland through Texas and taken across the Mississippi River into the heart of the Confederacy. A long trail, but it was a pipeline: it did not matter how long it was or how much it took to get the pipeline feeding out the delivery end; if the flow was constant, it would be very effective.

And this was precisely what was occurring in the winter of 1862-63 as Farragut blockaded the South. Farragut was worried, but more than that he was unhappy with the series of disasters that had befallen his force, not only because of criticism that fell on him but equally because he was a warmhearted man. When the *Alabama* sank the *Hatteras*, he was very much distressed, as he wrote on January 13, 1863:

> Yesterday was a sad day for me. I went to see Banks, and he handed me a dispatch from the bar, announcing the loss of the *Hatteras*. When I came on board I read another, telling me of the death of one of my bravest and most dashing officers, Lieutenant Commander Buchanan, son of Paymaster Buchanan, and nephew of Frank. But we drove the enemy from his position and silenced his batteries. Well, I hope we shall soon have some good luck, for I am sick of disasters. . . .*

Hoping for victory and a turn in the tide, Farragut toyed with the problem that faced the Northern forces. Until, by combined action of military and naval forces, the Union could control the Mississippi, the Confederacy could not be said to be blockaded. In a way, the dependence of the Confederacy on the breadbasket of Texas worked in favor of the Union, if the Mississippi was theirs. Texas alone produced the South's supply of beef cattle. Texas produced sugar. Texas produced wheat and rice and other grains. Texas contact with the Confederacy must be ended, that great thumb of the South must be detached. The task could be accomplished only by a combined operation, and while above Vicksburg General U.S. Grant and Admiral David Porter worked to this end, below Vicksburg the job belonged to Farragut and General Banks. When Porter encountered disaster on the upper reaches of the river and lost his finest ironclad, the *Indianola*, Farragut decided to move without the help of the army. He had not told Welles; he had not told anyone except his new flag captain, Captain Thornton Jenkins, in February: "The time has come; there can be no more delay. I must go—army or no army." Exerting what Welles described as a mind that was "firm and impetuous but sagacious and resolute," Farragut set out to act.

Ibid., p. 307

The fleet was readied. Bell was ordered to come up to New Orleans. Commander C. H. B. Caldwell was ordered to take the *Essex* up to Baton Rouge and with that command ship to take control of the mortars. They were to be moved into position to shell Port Hudson. Farragut turned over command of New Orleans and the lower Mississippi to Commodore Henry Morris, and took the *Hartford,* the *Richmond,* and the *Monongahela* upriver. The latter had just arrived, a welcome addition to the force of big ships. On March 11, they reached Baton Rouge, where they met the *Essex,* three gunboats, six mortar schooners, and a dozen more steamers of various kinds and sizes.

Farragut immediately began preparations for an engagement, taking down the running rigging, which was essential only for sailing, then rigging splinter nettings along the starboard sides of the ships, since their attack would be against shore installations on the east bank of the river.

Farragut examined his intelligence reports that night. The Confederates at Port Hudson were reported to have nineteen modern fieldpieces and thirty-five old-fashioned ones. What he wanted at the moment was a diversion by the military around the rear of the area so that the thirty-five mobile pieces would be moved out, and he would not have to contend with them, or at least not with all of them.

At four o'clock on the afternoon of Friday, March 13, Farragut lifted anchor and the fleet steamed fifteen miles upriver from Baton Rouge. At dawn the vessels got under way again. Their progress was impeded but their security was maintained by a heavy morning mist and high overcast. By eight o'clock the fleet arrived above Profit Island and through the clearing mist Farragut could see Port Hudson squatting on the yellow clay banks of the Mississippi, its guns with their ugly snouts turned toward the fleet, and several Confederate steamers briskly moving about the river.

At ten o'clock Farragut called his captains together for one last council to be certain they understood their instructions. He appeared in his faultless uniform with its gold braid and heavy epaulets of rank, his hair neatly combed across the bald top pate, and his eyes sparkling with the excitement of the coming action.

He had issued his general orders; his experience and his command of tactics had immediately shown him the most profitable course for running the batteries. Each ship took a gunboat on her portside, secured aft, thus leaving the port battery of the bigger ship free to command the left bank of the river. This move was to give the ships fire power after they passed Port Hudson because the river turned there and the starboard guns would no longer bear. Farragut had the gunboats tied to the steam warships, thereby protecting the smaller ones from much of the fire that would be directed against them if they ran the river alone, without significantly increasing the target presented by the bigger ships.

As for the protection of the ships, he said, "I think the best protection against the enemy's fire is a well-directed fire from our own guns." He ordered shell and shrapnel used from a distance; the gunners were to use grapeshot when within four-hundred yards.

Just before ten o'clock that night all was ready, and the *Hartford, Richmond,* and *Monongahela* started upriver, each lashed to a consort. The *Mississippi* brought up the rear; the ship was old and the side-wheel rig made it impractical to pair her. As they were starting out, a message arrived by steamer-courier from the army force, indicating that it would be delayed. The army was camped five miles behind the Port Hudson batteries—just far enough away to be sure that the Confederates would guess of the coming of an attack and just far enough away to be utterly useless to the ships trying to fight their way upstream.

Farragut showed his irritation at the army failure, but only briefly, because he had too many other things on his mind this night. As had been arranged, the mortar boats moved upriver to concealment beneath the river bank and at the appointed hour began their barrage.

The ships began moving into battle.

Fleet Surgeon J. M. Foltz had suggested that Loyall Farragut be sent below to help him during the battle, thus removing the young man from at least some of the dangers of battle. He was not, after all, a navy man.

"No, that will not do," Farragut said. "It is true our only child is on board by chance, and he is not in the service; but being here, he will act as one of my aids, to assist in conveying my orders during the battle. . . ."

The ships steamed on, and the men prepared.

The Confederates were anything but surprised. The movement of the mortar vessels, twice that day, had given them a definite clue. The movement of the force of General Banks gave them another. Yet the Confederates played a waiting game, watching the dark shadows of the ships steam slowly up the river. Up they came to a point a thousand yards from the batteries, which were on the bluff eighty feet above the surface of the muddy water. The current was very strong and the ships moved slowly. The town was a little cluster of fifty houses on the bluff, enclosed on the land side by a line of entrenchments seven miles long, and along the river side were the batteries, seven of them. Furnaces stood in the batteries for the heating of the shot.

Up the river the ships came, 900 yards from the batteries, 850 yards, 800 yards . . .

From the stern of the *Hartford* hung a red lantern, the guidon of the fleet. On the deck of the *Hartford* stood Admiral Farragut with Captain Jenkins, his fleet captain; Captain Palmer, the commander of the *Hartford;* Flag Lieutenant J. C. Watson; and other staff officers. Farragut paced the deck as always. Around the deck stood the men at their guns, tense and quiet. At their posts stood the marines, eyes watchful, guns ready. Engineer Speights was at the control of the engine-room bell, ready to transmit any orders from the deck below. The pilot, Thomas Carroll, towered above all others in the mizzentop, conveying his instructions to the wheel through a trumpet attached to a speaking tube.

Thus the Union fleet moved up the river, until the *Hartford* was opposite the batteries, 800 yards away. At that moment a rocket flared above the west bank, and another, and another. The Confederate guns began to open up on the fleet. Fires were kindled, first on the left bank, then on the right, and the scene about Port Hudson suddenly lost the blackness of dark night, with the outlines of man-made objects breaking the smooth flow of landscape on water and on sea.

The *Hartford* fired back, first with the Sawyer rifle on the forecastle, and then with a broadside when the ship could be turned so the guns would bear. As her guns barked, aboard the *Mississippi* Lieutenant George Dewey smiled in pleasure. "There!" he shouted. "Just as I expected. I knew the old sea dog would bark. He couldn't help it." Dewey was referring to Farragut's own orders—that the ships were to refrain from returning fire because to do so would reveal their own positions.

Faced with action, Farragut grew excited as always. He paced more rapidly, and his son Loyall could scarcely keep up with him. In the dark he stumbled over a tarpaulin covering a small hatchway that led to the relieving tackles. Loyall caught his arm and steadied him. Farragut scarcely noticed. In a moment he was at the mizzen rigging, and up, where he could gain a better view.

The ironclad *Essex* and the mortars began to fire in their deep, grumbling way, and soon the scene was overpowered by sounds, the hissing, booming, screaming, crashing sounds of war—made all the more terrifying by alternating flashes of light with deep jets of darkness that closed around the ships, and the smoke that rose from all the shells and all the guns.

The smoke was always the problem in a confined space, and soon pilot Carroll reported that he could not see ahead. The *Hartford* stopped firing to let the smoke clear away, and as it cleared, Carroll shouted excitedly for left rudder because the *Hartford* had turned in the current and was running in toward the batteries, where she would surely ground and become a sitting duck.

In they came, far too close for safety or even bravery. A Confederate officer aimed a gun filled with grape at the poop deck of the flagship, where the men stood out so clearly, but the gun misfired.

"Back, back on the *Albatross*" was the order, and the little gunboat lashed astern added her pulling power to the engine

225

strength of the flagship in order to bring her about and head her safely upstream and away from the dreadful enemy guns she had approached too closely.

As the flagship swung around, pulled by the engines of the *Albatross* and pushed by her own, there came the cry of a new danger.

"Ram on the port bow!"

A ram, an ironclad, a ship built for close action and boarding. The only way to take her in these waters was to board and set her afire.

"Man the port battery, and call away the boarders!" shouted Captain Palmer.

"I am going to have a hand in this myself," yelled Admiral Farragut, and he seized a cutlass lying on a signal locker and sprang toward the port rail.

But the ram did not appear, and with the swinging of the engines, in a moment they were around the point, behind the trees, and safe from the batteries of the Confederates atop the bluffs on the eastern bank. At 12:15 Captain Palmer brought her to anchor above the town.

But here, instead of giving the admiral comfort, the turn of battle frightened him, for they were alone.

"My God," he exclaimed, peering back into the flashes of the battle. "What has stopped them?"

The others were taking a worse beating from the batteries than had the flagship. Not only had the *Hartford* been protected by the admiral's "well-directed fire" from her own guns, but by being first to go through.

Second came the *Richmond,* lashed to the *Genesee.* Her executive officer lost a leg, taken off by a round shot. As she reached the bend and neared safety, she was hit almost simultaneously by a shot in the boilers and one in the steam drum, while the *Genesee* took a shell below that set her on fire.

But the real damage done was to Captain James Alden's morale. He had developed a terrible fear of "torpedoes" and saw them bursting all about him. The technical problem at the moment was that the steam was escaping from the boilers of both vessels and they were losing power. The executive officer, remarking on the south wind, suggested that at least they could use the sails. Captain Alden was quite beyond such thoughts, as the ship's journal showed: "Torpedoes were exploding all around us, throwing water as high as the tops. We were, for a few minutes, at the rebels' mercy; their shells were causing great havoc on our decks, the groans of the wounded and the shrieks of the dying were awful. The decks were covered with blood. . . ."

The *Richmond* turned and headed back downstream. Three were dead and two were seriously wounded, while ten others were slightly hurt.

Behind the *Richmond* came the *Monongahela,* lashed to the *Kineo.* The *Monongahela* ran aground at the bend, smashing on the bank and tearing the lashings from the *Kineo.* She was, indeed, a sitting duck, and for twenty-five minutes lay aground, while hawsers were snaked to the *Kineo* and the tugging was begun. Finally she was off, without hysterics, with six killed and twenty-one wounded, including Captain J. P. McKinstry. The *Kineo*'s rudder was shot awry and made useless, and in the pounding from the guns, the *Monongahela* was so weakened that she was lucky to be able to turn tail on the battle and get downstream without sinking.

Last came the old *Mississippi,* alone. She went aground on the west shore just before the last battery. Captain Melancton Smith ordered the engines reversed, full. She tugged and pulled at the mud, but it did not help. She was stuck fast. For thirty-five minutes she was pulled and hauled, while Captain Smith looked to her firing, and Lieutenant Dewey wracked his brain to find a way to get her off. But she would not come off, and at the end of those terrible minutes she was little more than a shooting gallery for the Confederates. The pilot said mournfully that she would never come off. Captain Smith agreed that chances were not good enough to continue to risk the lives of the crew; he gave the order to abandon ship.

The men began clambering over the sides, away from the dreadful batteries—three of them—which had zeroed in on the ship. There was no disorder. Sick and wounded went first and were put into the boats. The able-bodied stood at their stations, and at the call, they went about the ugly business of setting their own ship afire; she would not become an asset for her enemies. She was fired in four different places, and the boats were ordered away. The last boat away was the captain's gig, and in it Captain Smith and Lieutenant Dewey sat, mournful but straight and proud, as should be men who had done their unpleasant job to the best of their ability.

All this while, as the ships so ill-made for river fighting came acropper, Admiral Farragut strained his eyes and spent unhappy minutes in the mizzen rigging, trying to discover what was happening below. Obviously, the news of the battle was bad, for the *Richmond* and the others should have been with him long ago, and there was no sign of them.

For half an hour the sounds of battle persisted, but then they trailed off. Suddenly a light brighter than all the others split the sky and Farragut's eyes were opened wide.

"Ship afire," came the cry from the top. Too soon came confirmation that it was the *Mississippi*.

Farragut would have liked nothing better than to take the *Hartford* back downriver to aid his comrades, but he was an admiral, not a ship's commander, and the task was to go above the batteries, not to endanger the mission by defiance.

As he stood, eyes on the *Mississippi's* fires, the light grew until the whole river was visible for several miles downstream. The fire began to reach the ship's guns and they went off, one after the other. The burning lightened her and brought her off the bank. She swung slowly around and headed down-river blazing, keeping near the right bank, passing the *Richmond* and her own officers, drifting until 4:30 when she blew up and the embers scattered about the river and sank.

Admiral Farragut's eyes roved from one fire to another, and he kept turning over in his mind the various explanations for the failure of his fleet. The *Hartford* was scarcely hurt, with one man dead and two slightly wounded; several shells and much shot had holed her, but no vital damage was done. Putting her to rights was not a serious problem, but the flagship must remain immobile until the admiral discovered what had happened to his fleet and devised a new plan.

On Sunday morning, March 15, Farragut dropped down to a point just out of range of the batteries and fired three shots to indicate that he had passed the batteries safely. He could not immediately communicate with the fleet because both banks were held by active groups of Confederates. He could see the cavalrymen, their sabres gleaming in the sun as they shouted defiance to the ship.

22. VALOR

Valor, not victory, is the key to the success of a naval commander in time of war, and just as the career of Commodore David Porter in the War of 1812 was marked as much by valor as by victory, so it was now with his namesake, David Farragut. No one could call the fight at Port Hudson a victory for the Union. General Banks kept his troops outside Port Hudson by a good five miles, never did advance, and skulked back to Baton Rouge muttering about Farragut's "premature commencement of the action."

With eleven men killed and wounded, the *Mississippi* totally lost, some of her officers and men captured, and a major effort frustrated, Farragut felt considerable concern for his own position as he sat down to report to Secretary Welles in Washington: "Sir: It becomes my duty again to report disaster to my fleet. . . ."

But in Washington the opinion was quite the opposite. Lincoln and his cabinet had been embarrassed by the defeat at Galveston and by the successful blockade-running of Confederate vessels far beyond the strategic damage done the Union cause by these efforts. Now the cabinet was cheered far beyond the warrant of circumstances simply because here was an action of which every man in the Union could be proud, and although it was a failure as an attempt to secure control of the upper Mississippi, Farragut, with the *Hartford* and one gunboat, had run the gauntlet of fire and did stand above the Confederate defenses at Port Hudson. Lincoln, Welles, and the rest chose to regard the affair as a victory, and while Farragut knew moments of despair for his command

and for his future, in Washington, his name was again cleared and his reputation soared. Captain Melancton Smith suffered the horrors that beset a commander who has lost his ship, but Assistant Secretary Fox glossed over the loss and actually wrote a letter of commendation for Smith's record that made it an asset rather than liability to his future. Nor was any fault found with others, including Captain Alden, and even as high an official as the President found no complaint at all with the action.

Farragut moved upriver, sometimes under fire, near Grand Gulg, where the Confederates killed two more men and wounded six in an exchange with a battery high above the river. But this price was not high, considering the effect his presence on the river had, even with only two warships for patrol duty. A steamer loaded with 300,000 pounds of bacon was suddenly cut off from Port Hudson, where it was to land supplies for the 16,000-man army there. Four other steamers were cut off. And, as long as Farragut was on the river, the Confederates simply could not use the Mississippi as their artery of transportation. It was not at all like an ocean-port situation in which the chance of running a blockade was always worth the taking. In the narrow confines of the river, one warship could control a transportation system.

During the rest of March, Farragut attempted to secure support for his position. He went north and conferred with General U. S. Grant. He asked for help from Admiral Porter with the fleet above Vicksburg, but did not receive it, and it was only after he came back downriver to Port Hudson that Porter had word from Welles indicating that help should be given. On April 7, Farragut sent his secretary, Edward Gabaudan, downriver in a camouflaged skiff to try to reach New Orleans and communicate with the command. Then Farragut went north to the mouth of the Red River, captured a Confederate steamer, and began systematic destruction of all craft on both sides of the river that could be used to ship supplies across.

On April 15, he returned to the point north of Port Hudson.

This time the *Richmond* was on the other side, for Gabaudan's mission had been successful, and communications between the admiral and his fleet were possible.

Farragut quickly put another scheme into motion. He turned over command of the *Hartford* to Palmer; in other words, he removed his command flag. In the interim, Porter had run below Vicksburg with part of his fleet, and Grant had besieged the place, which changed the tactical situation completely and relieved Farragut of further responsibility for the river run. Farragut made his way in a gunboat along the Red River to Grand Lake and Brashear City, and then by rail to New Orleans. On the day he arrived, the newspapers issued extras, calling attention to the coming of "the gamecock," even though he had left behind the flagship the Confederates now called "the black devil."

Farragut was soon at work bombarding Port Hudson for General Banks, who had launched a campaign against the area—and worrying about his future in the navy. His wife did not help a great deal, for in her fervent correspondence she reported that Dahlgren, the inventor of the rapid-firing gun, was to replace him in the Gulf, and Farragut believed her. He was certain that Washington looked with as much disfavor on his actions in fighting his way above Port Hudson as Washington had despised the debacle at Galveston; and the repercussions of Galveston were still felt in his command.

The months wore on, months of worry and uncertainty. The action against Port Hudson palled. He was short of ammunition and there was neither glory nor clear victory to be gained. Yet Farragut remained himself, a heroic and legendary figure, very dear to the men of the navy for a thousand reasons, such as this one:

One day Lieutenant Winfield Scott Schley, the executive officer of the *Richmond,* was in command of the ship when she went into action, shelling the citadel at Port Hudson with a long rifle. During the shelling, a signal was hung from the yard of the flagship, calling her back, and Schley purported not to understand it. When he returned from the mission, he called at the flagship to report and on the quarterdeck encountered Farragut.

"Captain," said the admiral stiffly, "you begin early in your life to disobey orders. Did you not see the signal flying for near an hour to withdraw from action?"

Schley made an embarrassed explanation. His signalman had seen a flag, but it was hanging limp and he did not read it.

"I want none of this Nelson business in my squadron," said Farragut.

Then the admiral invited the lieutenant to his cabin, and when the door was shut, he turned to Schley, smiling: "I have censured you, sir, on the quarterdeck, for what appeared to be a disregard of my orders. I desire now to commend you and your officers and men for doing what you believe right under the circumstances. Do it again whenever in your judgment it is necessary to carry out your conception of duty."

Thereupon the admiral asked the lieutenant to drink a glass of wine with him.

During the summer of 1863, the course of the Civil War moved south and east, and from time to time it appeared that the Confederates would attack New Orleans in force. Farragut was constantly off balance, devoting his time and presence to defenses that never materialized and to the siege of Port Hudson, which was a long, tiresome affair. In July, Vicksburg fell. Farragut learned of it on July 7, and Port Hudson surrendered the following day. It was an army affair; Farragut was only informed of the surrender late and without ceremony. But one thing was certain, New Orleans was no longer in danger, and there was no longer need for Farragut's services on the river. On July 15, 1863, he turned over command of the river as far as New Orleans to Admiral Porter. On July 16, the steamboat *Imperial* arrived in New Orleans from St. Louis, signaling the end of the waterway as a Confederate highway and the beginning of a new era in the war of the West.

In the *Hartford*, Farragut again left the Queen City and went south, but this time with a purpose. All his big steam sloops were desperately in need of repairs, and now they could have their refits. He was sick with fever and nervous exhaustion, and he could have a furlough. His prestige had never been higher, and with light heart he turned the *Hartford* northward for Brooklyn Navy Yard. She arrived on August 12, and the admiring crowds came to inspect the two hundred and forty holes that represented her wounds from shot and shell during nineteen months of actual service in the war.

Farragut had left Brooklyn a few months before as an unknown professional naval officer in a nation that had long ceased to lionize its navy. He had headed for an important assignment, but with so little prestige that when he had asked President Lincoln that his son be given an Annapolis appointment, the request was ignored. But now, he was met as a hero. Mrs. Farragut came down from Hastings-on-Hudson with Loyall (who had been sent north shortly after the *Hartford* ran the gauntlet at Port Hudson). She had good news of her own: Loyall had been given an appointment to West Point, had passed the examinations shortly after his return from the war, and was soon to enter the academy. The newspapers saluted Admiral Farragut with the welcome of a returning warrior chieftain. Secretary Welles had a message for him—offering congratulations, an unlimited furlough, and advice to stay out of Washington until the hot summer was over. A publisher was dickering with Virginia for a biography of her husband, and eighty-one citizens of New York and dozens of the other leading businessmen signed a testimonial to the admiral.

There was a time for rest, and Farragut went to Hastings, where he was out of the heat of battle, the heat of the Southland, the heat of the city. There were several weeks of peace and recuperation, but it was not in Farragut's nature to seek peace when his nation was at war. He was still commander of the United States naval forces in the Gulf of Mexico and had left Bell in charge while he took this needed rest—but it could not be for long. By September, he was in Washington, where on the eleventh of the month he called on Welles.

In the course of the call, dispatches from Bell were received in the Welles office and the two men went over them. Bell reported that General Banks had asked for ships to support

234

an attack on Sabine Pass and that Bell had given them.

Farragut read and laid down the papers in disgust. The attack would fail, he said. Banks was like the other generals—without a notion in his head of the true use of naval force in land warfare:

> The army officers have an impression that naval vessels can do anything; this call is made for boats to accompany an army expedition; it is expected the navy will capture the batteries, and, the army being there in force with a general in command, they will take the credit.

But there would be no credit here, he said; the army wanted too much, and the expedition would fail.

Welles hoped this would not be the case; Farragut hoped not also, but eleven days later they learned that instead of attacking from one side while the ships attacked from the other, Banks had tried to use the ships as his only assault weapon. The expedition had failed and two gunboats had been captured by the Confederates.

So much for Farragut's judgment. As for valor: a few days later, Secretary Welles was talking with President Lincoln about the men who led the American Union defense effort, and in the presence of one he trusted, Lincoln was frank. The army commanders had given him much trouble and he had little respect for most of the old professionals, including McClellan. As for the navy men, the President classed Admiral DuPont with McClellan (and DuPont would be relieved by Dahlgren). The President considered Porter a scheming busybody of a type he had grown to know and abhor so much in the war. As for Farragut, Lincoln complimented Welles on the best appointment in either branch of the service that had been made during the war. "No man surpasses Farragut in his estimation," said Welles.

23. MOBILE BAY

In October, Farragut was ready for action once again, and so eager that he proposed that he go south in the *Richmond* from Brooklyn Navy Yard since the *Hartford* was not quite ready for sea. He was restrained by Welles and waited for his flagship. He was tired of the attentions of the New York Chamber of Commerce and others who would lionize him. He was upset about the failure at Sabine Pass even though he knew Bell was not at fault. He warned Bell that the army was trying to run everything by the technique of placing everywhere an army officer in command who was superior in rank to the navy counterpart. To Assistant Secretary Fox, he put it a little differently:

> I am very anxious to get to my station as I perceive that General Banks is beginning to take the field, and it may be in my power to render him assistance.*

He had learned much in the last few years about dealing with politicians and interservice rivalry, and he played his cards carefully and wrote his letters even more carefully. His popularity continued to increase; finally, he complained that he had no time for himself. And time dragged, the repairs were delayed, and Farragut fretted. He had many friends now. Admiral Lessovsky, of the Imperial Russian Navy, was in New York harbor with sealed orders for his fleet (apparently to assist the United States in case of attack by France or England). Farragut and Lessovsky had served together as young officers in the Mediterranean, and their friendship

Ibid., p. 215

236

flourished. There seemed to be no hurry about anything. There were parties and balls, and trips to see the sights, and the atmosphere was gay and stimulating.

But the gaiety ended on December 30, when a messenger delivered a missive from Secretary Welles informing Farragut that a deserter from Mobile had brought out the information that the Confederates intended to make a break through the blockade of Mobile Bay on January 20. Welles was distraught. He wanted Farragut to rush south. Knowing Farragut was having manning problems on the *Hartford,* he authorized the transfer of enough men to her duty so the ship could get away. (Farragut had suggested such a transfer earlier but had been ignored.)

Farragut sailed on January 5, 1864, ran into a heavy northwester that lasted for three days, but arrived at Key West a week after sailing, exchanging heat for snow and mosquitos for frostbite. He took with him Captain Percival Drayton as his new fleet captain, and the new officer commented on one aspect of Farragut's character that the admiral seldom discussed: he was partial to gout, but he never admitted to having gout because he was also partial to Bordeaux wine and it was generally conceived that red wine and gout were good companions.

The admiral's destination was Pensacola, the old naval base, which was then used by Bell as base for the Gulf fleet. Farragut arrived on January 17. He found the base abounding with rumors and misinformation. Most of it was caused by the preparations in the harbor at Mobile for the breakthrough of one or more Confederate rams. Everyone, from Bell down, was suffering from "ram fever." The captain's major worry was that the rams might break through at that moment; all his gunboats were in dock having their machinery repaired, and he had only the *Pensacola* and a handful of river steamers with which to stop a ram. He remembered only too well how critical the Navy Department had been of the navy failure at Galveston.

The stories of the plans of the Confederates were unbelievable to anyone who was not infected with "ram fever":

"The rams would break out and destroy the Union fleet";
"The rams would break out and head for the Mississippi
where they would take New Orleans, go up to the confluence
of the Red River, take the gunboats there, and drive the Union
forces off the river."

Within a matter of hours Admiral Farragut learned that
the fever was based more on worries than on facts. Refugees
from Mobile informed him that the major ram in the vast
reaches of Mobile Bay was the *Tennessee;* that while she was
formidable enough, she had not yet been gotten over Dog
River bar; and that she drew two more feet of water than
was ever found over the bar. What might be expected? Admiral
Franklin Buchanan, of the Confederate Navy, was trying to
float the *Tennessee* over by using camels, or pontoons. There
was nothing to fear from the *Tennessee* at the moment.

Farragut did share Bell's apprehensions in general, however,
when he discovered that all the gunboats were out of service
and that when he arrived at Pensacola only the *Richmond*
would be of any use to him.

At some point, Farragut would need a major force to handle
the problem at Mobile Bay. The Confederates were preparing
a desperate sally—that much was known. It was also known
that the force they had assembled was not inconsiderable.

First was the *Tennessee.* She had been launched almost
exactly a year earlier at Selma on the Alabama River, 150
miles north of Mobile. She was 209 feet long, 48 feet in
beam. Her battery, or armament, was carried in a casemate
seventy-eight feet long, with sloping sides (33°), which would
cause shot and shell to bounce off. She was armored with six
inches of iron plate forward, and five inches elsewhere. The
sides beneath the armor were two feet thick. The ram stuck
out two feet forward and was covered with wicked iron
plates. She was armed with two pivoting 7-inch rifles and four
6.4-inch rifles that were fixed two on a side. Her weak point
was the propulsion system: the Confederates simply did not
have adequate engineering works and the engines had been
taken from the steamboat *Alonzo Child.* They were totally

inadequate, and placed in this heavy warship, they generated only enough power to drive her at six knots.

Next in order of importance among the Confederate fleet came two other rams, the *Tuscaloosa* and the *Huntsville*. They were reported to have two-and-one-half inches of armor and to be generally constructed along such a scale in relation to the *Tennessee*. Two other rams were mentioned, the *Nashville* and the *Baltic*. There were also three gunboats, the *Selma*, *Gaines*, and *Morgan*. The latter was the largest, with a length of two hundred feet, carrying two 7-inch rifles and four 32-pounder guns.

Besides this floating arsenal, the Confederates were known to have built strong fortifications in the harbor. How strong became apparent to Farragut on the morning of January 20, when he went to the edge of the harbor and there boarded the gunboat *Octorara*. Accompanied by another gunboat, the *Octorara* took Farragut on a tour of inspection of Fort Morgan and Fort Gaines at the respectful distance of three miles. It was a clear day, and he could see the guns and the men at them, the pilings driven across from Fort Gaines to the channel opposite Fort Morgan.

These two forts guarded the main entrance to Mobile Bay. Thirty miles north of them was the city of Mobile, on the north shore of the bay. Fort Morgan stood on Mobile Point, and three miles west, across the channel, stood Fort Gaines, on the eastern side of Dauphin Island. The channel here had been reduced by the planting of mines, or *torpedoes*, which they were then called. Torpedoes had been placed on both sides to reduce the channel to 250 yards, and this free space of deep water ran directly under the guns of Fort Morgan.

Thirty miles long, the bay was also fifteen miles wide at the lower end, where Farragut surveyed it, and it then funneled north to a width of six miles. At the lower end, the bay was twenty to twenty-two feet deep, which would carry most oceangoing vessels. Inside, however, it was a different story: the channel rapidly grew shallow and was generally from twelve to seventeen feet deep. The bar surrounded the city, making direct contact impossible, for the bar was only nine feet beneath the surface.

The defenses, then, were the shallowness of the water, the heavily gunned forts, the narrowness of the channel, the Confederate fleet inside, and the torpedoes.

Until the Civil War the use of torpedoes had been restricted by public horror and by faulty conception and construction of gunpowder vessels. Petards and torpedo-mines had been used in the Napoleonic wars and since then in various local fights, but it remained for the Confederates to improve these defensive weapons and make them deadly and effective. They were made of many materials and in many ways. One favorite was a beer keg filled with powder, containing a fuse that would explode on contact with the side of a ship. Tins and other containers were also used.

By January, 1864, the federal navy had respect for torpedoes. In December, two years earlier, the ironclad *Cairo* had run onto a Confederate torpedo in the Yazoo River and had sunk. On February 28, 1863, the monitor *Montauk* was badly damaged by a torpedo on the Ogeechee River. Two other Union ships were seriously damaged thus. In Charleston harbor, the Confederates were using torpedoes for protection and torpedo-like petards on the ends of long sticks. Indeed, several torpedo boats and submersible torpedo boats had launched attacks on Union ships, and one such craft, the *Hunley*, would sink the Union ship *Housatonic* in Charleston harbor by use of a petard within a month. Ram and underwater explosives were major Confederate weapons, and they gave serious cause for concern to every Union Navy man.

Farragut was not afflicted with "ram fever," however, but with impatience to get at the job at hand—the destruction of the Confederate defenses in Mobile Bay and the elimination of the port as a blockade-runner's haven.

On the survey trip aboard the *Octorara*, he missed nothing. "I am satisfied," he wrote later, "that if I had one ironclad at this time, I could destroy their whole force in the bay, and reduce the forts at my leisure, by cooperation with our land forces—say five thousand men."

Farragut began waiting and planning. It was comfortable duty for the moment because he went back to the waters of the Mississippi and to New Orleans. There he was given a new barge, made from the launch of the *Mississippi*. Almost every day and sometimes more than once a day, his barge chugged through the river traffic to the levee at New Orleans, for Admiral Farragut was drawn up into the busy social life of the Queen City while he waited.

New Orleans was then the most charming town in North America and also the center of a thousand intrigues. The population was French, Spanish, Southern aristocrat, Northern gentleman, Northern carpetbag, Northern officer—or at least that was the society among which Admiral Farragut moved. General Banks, the land commander, was called "the dancing master" because of his predilection for social affairs, of which there were many in the salons and ballrooms of New Orleans that winter of 1864. The general encouraged them because he believed that by amusing the Southerners of New Orleans he could turn them to the Union cause. He created, of course, a hotbed of espionage and rumor, and Captain Drayton, of Farragut's staff, remarked sourly that the taking of Galveston or Mobile would provide a stronger diversion in the Union favor than a thousand opera performances and balls.

Yet Farragut secretly liked the attention and the amusement he found ashore and he plunged into this duty (it was expected that he would "cooperate") with more enthusiasm than Drayton might have liked. On the Monday following his return to the South, he went to a "promenade concert" sponsored by the general and his staff, and attended by many handsome ladies. The next day, he and Drayton dined with Mrs. Norman Jackson, one of the belles of New Orleans. She was an outright secessionist and said so, much to the amusement of Drayton. A few days later, the admiral was dining with another lady. He noted that masked balls were the order of the day—invitations to personal intrigue—and also excellent cover for spies, although he did not say so publicly. He went to the balls at the St. Charles Hotel, and to grand dinners and parties at private homes. He enjoyed himself thoroughly and often outstayed his younger staff members at the parties. But all the while, he was simply waiting.

Farragut had promised Mrs. Bell in New York that he would send her husband home on furlough, and having made representations in Bell's behalf and taken away the heat that was generated by the Galveston affair, he did send Bell home. Bell advanced in the service to become commander of the East Asia Squadron the next year. Drayton now officially became second in command, and every day the two men worked on the intelligence reports and the plans for the future.

The planning went on even though Farragut was not very well that winter of 1864. He felt impelled to plan because so much was expected of him, and he was well aware of his unique position as a commander. The Administration in Washington had ceased to bedevil him in recent months, so great was his prestige, which continued to rise; no amount of caviling by David Porter or the outright enmity of William Porter seemed to hurt Farragut at this point in his career. The caviling continued, and William Porter spoke of bringing an attorney to New York to file charges against Farragut for his treatment of Porter during the days of the Gulf command. That unhappy and unfortunate affair came to an end in a few months with the death of William Porter.

Farragut's illness was largely his own fault. He was sixty-three years old, yet he insisted on riding horseback in bad weather, drinking more red wine (although he was not intemperate with liquors) than was good for him, and going out and staying out late. The planning did not suffer; indeed, Farragut did what few other commanders were to do during the Civil War: he gave time to helping the army men when he need not have and when he could gain nothing from it but a quicker end to the war. When he learned from Banks of General William Sherman's projected campaign against Atlanta, he did not have any naval force to spare, but he decided he could help Sherman by pretending to force an entrance into Mobile Bay. He sent six mortars, on February 13, to the west of Dauphin Island to attack the small, weak fortress called Fort Powell, which was actually not finished and not much of a threat. The mortars, supported by four gunboats, put up a fierce display.

The threat worked just as Farragut had hoped it would: Confederate General Dabney Maury panicked and asked Richmond for more troops. Thus any intention of siphoning off troops from Mobile to defend against General Sherman was dropped, and Farragut accomplished something with only the cost of a few mortar shells.

During all these feints and operations, the Confederates had been working, quietly, and had gotten the *Tennessee* to the Dog River bar, but still not over. On March 1, however, a small ram was seen in the harbor, and Farragut identified it as the *Tennessee*. Since this information contradicted all the admiral's previous intelligence, he, too, developed a case of "ram fever." But it soon was established that the *Tennessee* was still mud bound and that one of the smaller vessels had been the cause of the confusion.

Farragut waited for the Confederates to move, and for ships and supplies. He needed ironclads, and they were tied up by Porter on the Mississippi, and by DuPont and then Dahlgren at Charleston. As he sat idly, he complained because he was growing fat and his clothes were too tight for him. He expressed amusement in letters to his wife about the excesses of the newspapermen and politicians, who were saying that first he would take Mobile Bay, then he would be sent to destroy the Confederates in Charleston harbor, and then he would be run for President of the United States. It was an election year, 1864, and General McClellan was already openly seeking the Presidency. Why not this far greater hero, Admiral Farragut?

One reason—the best in the world—was that Farragut refused to see himself as a politician. Of Mobile Bay and Charleston, he wrote:

> My own opinion is that if I survived those two engagements, there is little doubt that a presidential campaign would finish me. No, after I have finished my work, I hope to be allowed to spend the remainder of my days

in peace and quiet with my family on the banks of the Hudson.

It is for man to plan, and God to rule, and I am perfectly submissive to His will, but hope He will grant my prayer. I expected from the beginning to fight to the end of this war, or to my end, and I am still ready and willing to do so if my health will permit.

Yet while he spoke of his health, he was no more able to resist the blandishments of the table than before, and one day, after a dinner that included shrimp bisque, lobster salad, soft shell crabs, boiled shrimps in creole sauce, ice cream and strawberries, he developed a boil so severe that he was forced to go to bed. He also admitted to his wife in a letter that he had gained 20 pounds over his usual 130.

Wait. That was the watchword in the spring of 1864. Farragut had about eighty vessels at his disposal, but they were in various stages of repair, and fully a quarter of them were in drydock at any given time. He waited.

Washington was correct in assuming that Farragut knew the situation in Mobile Bay better than the Cabinet or the Navy Department and that he could be counted on to handle it in the best manner. In May, he wrote Secretary Welles about the danger of the military situation once the *Tennessee* crossed the bar, as he now expected her to do at any hour. He expected Admiral Buchanan to attempt a sortie with his four ironclads and three wooden gunboats. He was under the impression that the four ironclads were ready for action (which was not true) and his strategy was based on the existence of superior firepower by the Confederates.

It was a gloomy time throughout the Union. With slender resources, with half their land taken by the Union, the Confederacy fought on and threatened the lines of communications and even the regions north of the Mason-Dixon line. Lee was gaining the power of Chancelorsville. Porter was worried about his position on the Red River. Farragut was worried about all the Union positions, including his own. He asked Welles for an ironclad or two, but said that if he did not get it, the Secretary could still expect him to do his duty; but the tone was such that Welles might read into the letter that Farragut believed that without ironclads the Union fleet was destined to suffer loss of ships and probably of an admiral.

On the night of May 17, the *Tennessee* cleared the bar and was towed out into the bay by two steamers. Admiral Buchanan had long planned to go rushing out of Mobile Bay on the night that the ironclad cleared the bar, speed to Fort Pickens and Pensacola, capture them, and then tell the Union Navy to go to hell. But she had been lightened for her passage over the mud. Ammunition, guns, and supplies had to be restored, but by the time all this was accomplished it would be too late to do the job. Or so it seemed. Although Admiral Farragut was at Pensacola with the *Hartford* and four or five gunboats, that was the total force in the base at the moment. On blockade off Mobile were the *Richmond* and eight gunboats—a force too weak to stop the big ironclad's progress. The *Monongahela* was under repair. The *Brooklyn* was en route from New York. Actually, Admiral Buchanan could not have planned a better day for attack than May 18, but he did not attack. The next morning, the alert Union officers outside the bay caught sight of the ironclad in the harbor, and the element of surprise was lost.

On the evening of May 20, Farragut learned that the *Tennessee* had come out of her resting place and was preparing for a fight. He lost no time in making final preparations of his own. He took a few hours to straighten out affairs at Pensacola, turned over the command to a subordinate, and sailed the next day for Mobile Bay. He was not at all pleased with Washington's refusal to give him the ironclads he needed, but more than weaponry he had the will to fight. "Our fellows are beginning to understand that war means fighting," he wrote two days after his departure from Pensacola. "It is the duty of an officer to save his men as much as possible; but in almost all cases there has to be a certain amount of sacrifice of life."

Farragut, nearing a battle that he knew would be decisive, felt a more general peace than usual and was even happier about the state of his fleet: "I have a fine set of vessels here just now, and am anxious for my friend Buchanan to come out."[*]

On the afternoon of May 24, Farragut and his staff toured the edge of the bay in the gunboat *Metacomet* and steamed close inshore to take a good look at the *Tennessee*. She carried a torpedo fixture at her bow, but was otherwise as advertised by the spies and defectors who had already reported on her to the admiral. With some reluctance, Farragut decided to add such a spar arrangement to his own ships. He did not consider the torpedo a chivalrous weapon, but he was a warrior, not a philosopher, and it would never do to give the enemy a decided superiority. Obviously the circumstances of the sinking of the *Housatonic* were very much in his mind.

Two days after the inspection, Farragut noted the industrious laying of torpedoes in the harbor by the small Confederate vessels and came to the logical conclusion that Admiral Buchanan was as concerned about their moving in to attack him as Farragut was about a potential breakthrough. Both sides were waiting for the results of the great land battles being fought in Virginia and in Georgia.

Again the waiting began.

May slipped into June, and Farragut's letters home indicated his state of mind:

> June 9: I think, after the brush of the *Alabama* in Mississippi Sound, my friend Buchanan will be a little more chary about coming out to visit "Farragut's fleet" as they call it. I wish he would come along and let us have it over. . . .

> June 21: I am tired of watching Buchanan and Page, and wish from the bottom of my heart that Buck would come out and try his hand upon us. This question has to be settled, iron versus wood; and there never was a better chance to settle the question. . . . But I shall have patience until the army has finished its campaign in Virginia and Georgia.

> July 6 [after a successful blockade action in which a blockade-runner was destroyed]: I have never seen a

[*]*Ibid.*, p. 401

crew come up like ours. They are ahead of the old set in small arms and fully equal to them at the great guns. . . .*

Farragut constantly prodded Washington for ironclads, and eventually his requests and pleas bore fruit. The monitors *Manhattan, Winnebago,* and *Chickasaw* were finally sent to him; he learned of their coming in July. Immediately Farragut began planning an attack on Mobile Bay. With three monitors he had no fear of going in to beard the enemy in his fortress.

His plan called for the ships to go in through the channel between the forts, two and two, as at Port Hudson. This time, however, Farragut would have fourteen ships, including the ironclads. The attack would be made at low speed, on the morning flood tide, on a day when the wind was from the southwest to favor the invaders. The ironclads would attack the *Tennessee* and the enemy ironclads. The gunboats would attack the Confederate gunboats. Seven vessels would remain outside to help the army land on the beach and try to outflank the enemy forts and ground troops. Other troops would land on Dauphin Island.

Farragut made his plans and the Confederates made theirs. On July 28, the *Tennessee* cruised around the bay, majestically, calmly, engaged in target practice, and from the decks of the *Hartford,* Farragut watched.

On July 29, Farragut issued General Order No. 11., which covered the procedure of the battle to come. August 4 was to be the day. Major General Edward Canby and Major General Gordon Granger visited the flagship and talked about landing operations. Canby said he did not have the men to take both forts at the mouth of the bay, so Farragut suggested that troops be landed on Dauphin Island to attack Fort Gaines.

The attack was set, but the monitor *Tecumseh* arrived unready, and the navy delayed. General Canby landed his troops anyway, at a very grave disadvantage, and the Confederates immediately began reinforcing against them.

Farragut fretted all day long on August 4, waiting for the

Ibid., pp. 403-04

Tecumseh, which had not arrived from Pensacola. It rained hard about sundown and then the weather began to clear. The wind came up fresh from the southwest, and a pleased admiral announced that in the morning they were going in. It would be Friday, the sailor's unlucky day, and Friday was bringing them a breeze that would blow smoke in the eyes of the Confederate gunners. Furthermore, that Thursday night a comet flashed across the sky. Even the most hard-bitten salt, filled with the superstition of the foredeck, must admit that the heavens were giving David Farragut omens of victory.

24. THE LAST BATTLE

As he had done many times before, Admiral David Farragut stood on the poop deck early on the morning of August 5 and watched—and listened—as the ship came to life around him, making ready for battle.

The old cries—"all hands," "up all hammocks," "quarters"—the shrilling of the bo's'n's pipes, the scuffle of feet moving swiftly across a wooden deck, the sounds of the wind in the rigging, and the rattle of chains and the clanking of metal on gun barrels—all these were sounds he had heard in his boyhood aboard the *Essex*. But the swishing of steam, the tooting of the whistles, the pulsing of the engines, the churning of the screws—these were new sounds, which showed how far he had come since one day fifty-three years before, when, his hand clutched in the horny paw of Commandant David Porter, ten-year-old Midshipman Farragut had trembled on the pier and saluted his captain, passing from childhood into navy life at the moment he went aboard ship as a junior fledgling navy officer.

How long! How far! He was the most admired admiral in the American Navy, the greatest single hero of the war that dominated the minds of all Western men. He was no Nelson, had said an envious Porter, but that was Porter, whose bravery and sterling qualities were always tarnished by his jealousies and unavoidable pettiness. If any man could forgive David Porter, it was Farragut, who knew only too well how badly Porter's father had fared at the hands of equally jealous, equally petty, officers of another day.

Was he no Nelson? Was he the hero of whom the northern

newspapers prated, whose flagship was called the "black devil" by respectful enemies? Was he, who had twice run batteries that no ship was supposed to be able to brave, a man to stand alongside Decatur in the pages of history, or of Lawrence, or of the great Oliver Hazard Perry? Or was he, as his detractors snarled and his enemies sometimes said, just a lucky little man, genial and smiling, who had not the sense to avoid battles he could not win, and so won them by fluke upon fluke?

This day would tell, this day of days, when the future of two squadrons was at stake.

For "Buck" Buchanan, Admiral of the Confederate States of America, and the squadron inside Mobile Bay, the battle to come meant victory or defeat for the entire Southern navy. The Mississippi was lost; Texas ports were of no use unless all of them could be kept free of Union forces; Charleston was bottled up and would stay that way. The South had little with which to work: old locomotive boilers were cut and pressed together in new shapes to serve new purposes, while once-careful mechanics looked the other way in embarrassment at their tired handiwork; the fatigued, worn machinery of memorable steamboats was dismembered and brought to serve purposes its designers could never have foreseen. Most of the men were freshwater men; there were a handful of old salts and a double number of soldiers-turned-sailors. But if there was valor to be shown, these sons of the Confederacy would show it, as they already had on the Red River, on the Mississippi, at Galveston, in Charleston harbor, and in the gallant blockade-runners and raiders. If David Farragut wanted the title of hero, he would have to fight to earn it.

The battle plan was ready, the vessels were ready, the admiral was ready, and soon the scurrying of men aboard the ships assumed purpose and Farragut's fleet began to take a definite form.

The commanders were familiar with the plan, announced in General Order No. 10, nearly a month before, and then implemented in General Order No. 11.

The ships were stripped for a fight. All the topmost rigging and the spars were sent down, the whiskers were triced up, and the splinter nets were out to starboard. The wheel positions were barricaded with sails and hammocks and sandbags. Chains and sandbags had been laid out over the delicate machinery on deck. The sheet chains were hung over the sides of the ships to protect them from round shot and, to a lesser extent, from penetrating shell. Starboard boats were stripped off and landed or towed around to the port to dangle behind the port boats at water's edge. In each ship's port-quarter boat stood a leadsman and the pilot of the vessel, protected as much as possible from the fire they would face.

In the admiral's cabin that morning, Farragut ate his breakfast, talking with Fleet Captain Drayton and Captain Palmer, of the *Hartford*, as he ate. He was worried about the weather and frowned when told at daybreak that it seemed to threaten rain. But the wind was west-southwest, just where he wanted it. At four o'clock, the wooden ships formed into a double column, the *Brooklyn* under Captain Alden leading, and the ship lashed to the *Octorara*. Next came the flagship, the *Hartford*, lashed to the *Metacomet;* then the *Richmond* with the *Port Royal;* the *Lackawanna* and *Seminole;* the *Monongahela* and *Kennebec;* the *Ossipee* and *Itaska;* the *Oneida* and *Galena.*

The admiral's plan had been, as always, to lead his ships into battle, but even in such a plan he was flexible, and since torpedoes seemed to be important in this fight—the Rebels had been sowing them for days—he chose to let the *Brooklyn* lead because she had a sweep apparatus aboard—the only ship to have one—and four chase-guns to explode them.

At 5:30, the admiral looked up from his tea. He took one last sip and spoke. "Well, Drayton," he said, "we might as well get under way."

The Fleet Captain spoke, and the signal was passed to the poop and then to the other ships. Within sixty seconds the answering flashes came from the other ships and the column took form, the wooden ships in their long line and

251

the monitors *Tecumseh, Manhattan, Winnebago,* and *Chickasaw* in a single column to the right of the wooden ships, the *Tecumseh* just opposite the *Brooklyn*.

There was to be no question about this fight being a hard one, as General Order No. 10 indicated.

> If one or more of the vessels be disabled, their partners must carry them through, if possible; but if they can not, then the next astern must render the required assistance; but, as the Admiral contemplates moving with the flood-tide, it will only require sufficient power to keep the crippled vessels in the channel.

These orders had been modified by General Order No. 11 to indicate that any vessel that was so disabled that her consort could not keep her going would drop out to the west, and then take her station at the tail of the line if she could make repairs.

Once inside the forts the heavier vessels might separate from their gunboats and let the gunboats chase the Confederate gunboats toward Mobile. But the commanders were warned about the black buoys that extended across the channel from the piles on the west side toward Fort Morgan. They were to steer east of the easternmost buoy because it was understood that torpedoes were placed between the buoys.

All was ready at 5:30 in the morning with the Union fleet.

The Confederates had not been sitting by idly. They saw the lights on the Union ships and the motion aboard the decks, and they took up position in a single line across the channel, with port batteries bearing on the Union fleet.

The Union line began to move in, Captain Alden, he of the uncertain temper at Port Hudson, was in the lead in the *Brooklyn*. Off to the south and east of Fort Morgan, six smaller Union steamers were firing to distract the defenders.

At 6:47, the *Tecumseh* opened fire on Fort Morgan, and shortly afterward the fort returned the fire. The wooden ships mounted guns of shorter range, and it was some time before they moved up. On his deck, straining his eyes, Admiral

Farragut became irritated with the extreme distances between the wooden ships and gave the order to close up, which was acknowledged and obeyed.

A few moments later, the Confederates opened fire, generally, and for half an hour had the fleet under fire before the broadsides of the Union fleet could bear, but it was raking fire, which did relatively little damage.

All eyes were on the *Tecumseh,* the leading Union ironclad, with her long-range guns, and Farragut's eyes followed the guns of the rest.

The admiral stood on his poop deck, surrounded by Captain Drayton and his staff officers, Lieutenant J. C. Watson, Lieutenant Arthur Yates, Secretary Alexander McKinley, and others. Signal Quartermaster Knowles stood by, awaiting the admiral's messages to the fleet. At the wheel stood the quartermasters, McFarland, Wood, and Jassin, all veterans of every Civil War engagement of the *Hartford.* Soon, the admiral was up in the port main rigging, three ratlines up, where he could see every one of his ships and still yell down his orders to his poop deck and talk with Lieutenant Commander Jouett, the captain of the *Metacomet,* who stood on top of the gunboat's wheelhouse. In the top, above Farragut, was Pilot Freeman.

The Union ships came into firing position and opened up on the forts and the enemy ships. As the men on deck went at their hot work, the smoke rose above the ship, driving Farragut upward, upward, until he rose to the futtock bands and found himself clinging to the futtock shrouds, so he might see.

Above the *Hartford's* mizzen, shaking in the breeze, stood Admiral Farragut's blue pennant, so his position was the more exposed. Below, Drayton saw his admiral's movements, but knew better than to try to bring him down. Instead, he sent Signal Quartermaster Knowles into the rigging with a line to secure the admiral in his perilous perch. Knowles climbed up doggedly with a piece of leadline in his teeth and made it fast to a forward shroud, then passed it around the admiral as if he were a block of wood and fixed him between forward and after shrouds; he could not fall to the deck unless the lines gave away.

"Never mind," said Admiral Farragut, peering all the while at the course of battle, "I am all right."

Knowles, with the sureness of an old and loyal friend, ignored his admiral and did as he was told, then climbed back down to the deck.

The battle proceeded with much noise and relatively little damage done, in the beginning.

The shouts and noises of battle rang out aboard the *Hartford*. Shortly after seven o'clock, with guns elevated to 1,400 yards range, the flagship made ready to open fire on the forts.

"Steady boys, steady," came the shouts from the gunnery officers. "Left tackle a little. So. So."

Then the roar of a broadside smashed out across the decks, and the smoke rose above the deck, shrouding the men as they saw the Confederates driven from their water battery.

But only for a moment. The Rebels were anything but cowards. The shot passed, they manned their guns.

It was boom, whistle, crash, boom, whistle, crash, up and down the line as the shots and shells flew furiously in three directions, from Union ships to forts, from forts to Union ships, and from the sidelong shelling of the Confederate fleet farther on.

At 7:20, the *Hartford* came within range of the Confederate gunboats. They opened up on her, the telltale blue admiral's pennant marking *Hartford* as the special target of the day. A shot struck the foremast. A 120-pound shot hit the mainmast and stuck there. At first the Confederates were shooting high, but moment by moment their shots climbed down the masts and down the rigging, and soon men began to fall and cry out in the smoke.

Aboard the *Hartford* and elsewhere in the fleet, officers complained that Admiral Farragut had no right to expose himself with such braggadocio to the enemy. The question of his insistence on so positioning himself was tested in the moments after 7:25.

Just before the engagement, a number of army signalmen had come aboard the big warships with the assignment of communicating with General Granger's soldiers after the ships passed Fort Morgan. Half a dozen of these men were aboard the *Hartford;* others were aboard the *Brooklyn* and the remaining sloops. Suddenly, from the *Brooklyn* came a strange set of signals that Quartermaster Knowles could not decipher. He guessed that these were signals from the army men, although why Captain Alden should be using army signalers instead of navy men no one aboard the flagship could determine. Army Lieutenant John Kinney was summoned from the lazarette, where he had gone to help the surgeons until his services were needed. He ran to the forecastle and wrote down a message from Alden to the flag:

> The monitors are right ahead. We cannot go on without passing them. What shall we do?

The general orders covered the situation, but in a few moments Farragut had returned a specific reply:

Go Ahead.

The general orders also specified that the ships should stay inside the buoys when passing next to Fort Morgan, and the matter of the torpedoes had been discussed and made quite clear to all the commanders. But instead of following those orders, Captain Craven, in command of the monitor *Tecumseh,* turned his vessel to port, which brought him—and the following monitors—across the line of approach of the steam sloops. Since the monitors were very slow, like turtles chugging along in their plating, while the ships moved like fish in comparison, the whole advance was slowed.

But even slowing was not to be the worst of it. At 7:30, Craven became so eager to move in and engage the *Tennessee* that he forgot his orders, passed to the west of the buoy, and struck one of the torpedoes moored there. Craven simply had not followed orders; later information indicated that he had told the pilot that the admiral must be mistaken to tell him to go inside the buoy, and he directed the ship outside. The captain directed the Union's best monitor to its death, as it turned out, for no sooner had she turned outside, than she struck, and began to heel. Lieutenant Kinney was climbing up the unfamiliar rigging of the flagship, a soldier on strange ground, but a soldier doing his duty with a flair. He reached the fore-top gallant crosstrees and stood—or clung —above the smoke that wreathed the flagship. Below, ahead, he saw the *Tecumseh* sink. A few minutes later came a strange, gloomy message from the *Brooklyn*:

Our best monitor has been sunk.

The message might have been: *Tecumseh* sunk—which would have given all the information the admiral needed, if he needed any at all, but Alden could not resist the panic that overcame him in times of stress. His message told his whole story: he had witnessed the sinking of the *Tecumseh*; he saw now that the Union fleet was deprived of its strongest weapon against the *Tennessee*; and he feared the outcome of the battle.

The shock was worst among the men of the other monitors, for the heavy-laden vessel did not hesitate; she simply raised her stern and plunged bow foremost for the depths so suddenly that the following *Manhattan* could not reverse engines in time and passed directly over the spot where she had sunk, and where men were struggling for their lives in the whirlpools and currents below.

As the *Tecumseh* went down, the iron plating became an iron trap. Captain Craven and Pilot Collins met at the small hatchway in the floor of the pilothouse. The hatch led down into the turret, and only by going down and then out and up could a man escape.

"Go ahead, captain," said the pilot.

"No, sir," said Craven. "After you, pilot. I leave my ship last."

Collins reached the turret, found one of the sliding hatches on the top side, and made his escape. Captain Craven was not seen again.

The *Brooklyn* seemed to be paralyzed. Behind her, the flagship manned a boat and sent it away to rescue survivors. One boat managed to get away from the *Tecumseh* herself in the two minutes of life left between striking and sinking. Some men leaped over the side and swam away from the suction.

Everywhere, for a few moments, the battle stopped as men stared. At the time of her striking, the *Tecumseh* was headed directly for the *Tennessee* with intent to ram and begin firing. The *Tennessee*, posted just inside the line of torpedoes, had her bow gun aimed and ready to fire, but Captain Johnston had ordered the fire held until the ships were touching. As the ship went down, the gun was still trained on the water and on the rescue boats, but the captain forbade firing on struggling men, and the muzzle was raised to send the shot far down the line.

Within the Union fleet, far down the line, the shooting and the movement continued, for no one knew exactly what had happened if they were not in the leading ships. At Fort Morgan, General Page ordered his gunners to hold their fire against the boats because they were saving drowning men.

Then the waters subsided, the boats headed for the safety of the Union fleet, and the battle resumed.

Admiral Farragut watched the sinking of his monitor from the main port rigging of his flagship. At 7:40, he signaled to Alden in the *Brooklyn*:

Tell the monitors to go ahead and then take your place.

Alden panicked.

The lead man of the *Brooklyn* reported shoal water ahead. The captain saw a strange line of buoys directly under his bows, which meant that he had gotten off course and was leading the fleet into the torpedo field and disaster. One of the advantages of positioning a gunboat at the port quarter of the steam sloops had been an increase in maneuvering power. As Farragut had discovered in the Mississippi, if the gunboat backed full while the steam sloop's screws turned forward and the helm was put to one side, the turning radius was very short. But Alden had cast loose his gunboat prematurely, just before the sinking of the *Tecumseh*, and it was hard for him to turn the *Brooklyn* when he found her in danger.

Instead of making a neat turn, the *Brooklyn* backed across the line of approach at an angle, and her thrashings were noted by the van of the Union fleet. Resolution was replaced by confusion. The shooting of the Union ships slackened and became less accurate, while the guns of Fort Morgan, seeing the confusion in the enemy ranks, redoubled their effective fire.

Farragut, the religious admiral, clung to his rigging, lashed there, and sought Divine guidance.

"O God, who created man and gave him reason," he prayed silently, "direct me what to do. Shall I go on?"

Immediately a voice came to him.

"Go on," it commanded.

His determination was replenished.

"What is the matter with the *Brooklyn?*" he asked Pilot Freeman.

The pilot did not know.

"What's the trouble?" came the hail to the leading ship as she backed.

"Torpedoes," came the reply from the *Brooklyn.*

"Damn the torpedoes!" shouted Farragut from his lofty perch. "Four bells! Captain Drayton, go ahead. Jouett, full speed."

All morning Farragut had rued the decision his captains had persuaded on him, to allow the *Brooklyn* with her superior anti-torpedo equipment to go ahead. Now he was bound to correct his error in judgment. He, the admiral, would be out in the front of his fleet where he belonged.

The *Hartford* glided past the *Brooklyn,* sped by the twin engines of the steam sloop and the *Metacomet* lashed alongside.

Behind, the captains and officers of the fleet were certain that they were taking their ships to death in the waters of Mobile Bay, running into the beds of the torpedoes about which they knew so little; but seeing Farragut's gallant gesture, they followed him, and the almost certain disaster promised by Captain Alden was avoided as the admiral took the lead and moved in to do battle against the Confederates.

Quickly the *Hartford* moved ahead and was soon out of range of the batteries of Fort Morgan. Not a single torpedo was detonated. Later, some officers claimed they heard the snapping of the primers as they passed through the field, but no torpedo exploded. Later, too, it was suggested that the torpedoes were arranged in lines facing the entrance to the bay and that by changing course as he had to do to avoid the backing *Brooklyn* and lead the fleet around that ship, Farragut had chosen the precise point of entry that would be safe for him.

But getting through the torpedoes meant only that the battle was not lost before it began, because as soon as Captain Johnston, in the *Tennessee,* spotted the admiral's pennant coming through, he devoted his full attention to the flagship and moved forward to ram and sink her. But the *Hartford* had speed if not armor and she moved agilely ahead of the monitor, pouring out broadside after broadside, which glanced off the armor plating of the Confederate ship, until she moved into a line where it became more profitable to fire on the Confederate gunboats. The Confederate's *Selma* had been raking the flagship with a fire that she could not return; Admiral Farragut released the *Metacomet* and ordered Jouett to take out after the other gunboat, which Jouett did eagerly.

Once Farragut had steamed past the *Brooklyn,* Captain Alden seemed to find himself and pushed into line behind the flagship, successfully avoiding the *Tennessee* when she moved forward to try to ram.

The *Richmond* and the *Lackawanna,* the *Monongahela* and the *Ossipee,* all passed by the *Tennessee* with more or less success, but by the time the *Oneida* came up, trailing the column, the Confederate ironclad was waiting in proper position and passed down her starboard side. A shell from Fort Morgan exploded in *Oneida's* boiler and another cut her wheel ropes. The firing from *Tennessee* also did serious damage to her, but the *Itaska* and the *Galena* managed to tow her away before she was wrecked or sunk.

The Union monitors had been standing by, waiting for the wooden ships to go through the passage and protecting them, as they could, from ramming by the *Tennessee.* They opened fire on the *Tennessee,* but a coming storm descended to close off the view.

The *Hartford,* having passed the batteries, moved in to anchor four miles northeast of Fort Morgan and was anchored at 8:35 in the morning, in the heart of the enemy bay. The other ships came up, including the battered *Oneida* under tow, and the men of the fleet cheered their admiral as they passed him in the flagship, for it was apparent that he had led them to victory.

The monitors moved to the east, and the squall blotted them from the view of the fleet.

The Confederate gunboat *Morgan* retired under the guns of the fort of the same name. The Confederate gunboat *Gaines* beached five hundred yards from the fort, for she was about to sink after taking fire from most of the ships of the Union fleet on their way into the bay. The Confederate *Selma* fled, but Jouett chased her in the *Metacomet,* caught her, and began a rousing fight, which ended in the *Selma's* capture as the Union ship *Port Royal* moved up to make the odds completely uneven. Captain of the *Selma* was one of Jouett's oldest prewar friends, Lieutenant Patrick U. Murphy, and when he came aboard the Union vessel, arm in a sling, he tendered his sword to Jouett, saying stiffly that the fortunes of war compelled him to do so.

"Pat, don't make a damned fool of yourself," said Jouett. "I have had a bottle on ice for you for the last half hour."

After the *Hartford* anchored at 8:30, Farragut disengaged himself from his lashings in the rigging, and came down to the poop deck. Drayton approached him: "What we have done has been well done, sir; but it all counts for nothing so long as the *Tennessee* is there under the guns of Morgan."

Farragut agreed heartily: "I know it, and as soon as the people have had their breakfasts, I am going for her."

In a few moments the men of the flagship were sent to breakfast, and the order was shown to the fleet. Farragut stood aside and made his plans to try to capture the strange Confederate warship that looked more like a floating Egyptian tomb than a vessel of destruction. The Union fleet was anchored in the upper part of the deep pocket of the channel. The Confederates were fleeing or were silent beneath the guns of the forts. The rain came down and the sky threatened.

25. THE *TENNESSEE*

As the Union sloops-of-war had come charging through the narrow channel into Mobile Bay, each sloop had fired zestfully on the sharp-angled sides of the *Tennessee*. She had taken a hundred hits from the broadsides of her enemies, but so stoutly was she constructed that no serious damage had been done either to her armor plate or to her machinery. True, she had been hit in the smokestacks several times, and the perforations had reduced her draft so that she could not attain anything like maximum speed, but she had never been built for speed anyhow, and as long as she could move at all, Admiral Buchanan was content. The *Tennessee* could do her job.

Admiral Buchanan knew what he was about. He had led the old *Virginia* (*Merrimac*) in its encounter with the *Monitor* two years earlier and had sustained a wound that dogged him yet—he limped up and down the deck impatiently, waiting to continue the action.

Unlike the officers and men of the Union fleet, the Confederates had come to fight without having their breakfast, so after Farragut had run the gauntlet and retired to anchor, the men of the *Tennessee* also ate. Their fare was hardtack and coffee, simple but adequate to quiet the aching in their guts and the dryness of their throats, a dryness intensified by the heat of the casemate when the *Tennessee* was fighting.

Admiral Buchanan was not long in making his decision. He called Commander J. D. Johnson, the captain of the *Tennessee*.

"Follow them up, Johnston," he said, "we can't let them off that way."

The bow of the ram was turned toward Farragut's fleet up the bay as Admiral Buchanan set his desperate strategy in motion. He would dash in (as quickly as an ironclad could dash), shoot off all his ammunition, and do as much damage as he could do to the Union fleet, then retire to the mouth of the harbor and remain in safety under the guns of Fort Morgan.

As Admiral Buchanan issued his orders, Farragut saw the *Tennessee* begin to move. The Union admiral had been planning his own next move and had come to the conclusion that he would wait for dark, then board the *Manhattan*, and personally lead the Union monitors in attack against the *Tennessee*. As he told Captain Drayton his plan, Drayton looked across at the *Tennessee* and saw that she was moving—outside, he thought—to attack the flotilla of Union gunboats left out in the deep water when the fleet came in.

"Then we must follow him out," the admiral said.

But it soon became clear which way the *Tennessee*'s ram was pointing, and Farragut exclaimed with satisfaction: "No. Buck's coming here. Get under way at once. We must be ready for them."

At 8:45, the crew of the flagship was called back to general quarters, and the signals were flying. Farragut warned the fleet, ordered the *Brooklyn* to prepare to run down the ram and hail the *Manhattan*, the monitor. Fleet Surgeon Palmer was sent around to all the monitors to order them to prepare to attack the Confederate vessel as she came.

The *Monongahela* was the first to attack. She came running at full speed, in spite of two shells that struck in her berth deck and wounded three men. She struck the *Tennessee* so forcefully that her entire iron prow was carried away. Then, the wooden ship fired her broadside at the Confederate ironclad, but without result.

The next Union attacker was the *Lackawanna*, which, in ramming, crushed her stem and sprang a leak forward. She hit the Confederate ram near the after end of the casemate with such force that the two vessels swung head and stern to one another, the *Tennessee* bringing two guns to bear on the *Lackawanna,* but the Union ship bearing only one. The Union crews were close enough to hear the Confederates swearing at them, and from the *Lackawanna* were hurled a spittoon and a holystone to add to the shot and shell.

The *Hartford* was the third Union ship to attack the ironclad. The *Tennessee* turned toward the flagship, and the two rushed at each other head on. Farragut jumped into the port mizzen rigging above the poop deck for a better view. Lieutenant Watson seized the admiral by the tails of his coat and tried to haul him back, but without success. Then he grasped a line and climbed up. "If you *will* stand there," he said, "you had better secure yourself from falling," and he handed the admiral the line. Farragut thanked him, took a turn around the shrouds and around his body. Watson stood by him with drawn revolver, searching the ram for anyone who might fire at the admiral.

The two ships rushed at one another, the *Hartford* striking a glancing blow, which force was further mitigated by the port anchor catching in the gunwale of the *Tennessee.* The ships came port to port so close that an engineer on the *Tennessee* bayoneted a Union man on the *Hartford* and a Union sailor put a pistol ball through the engineer's shoulder at point-blank range.

The *Hartford* then stood off for another go at the *Tennessee,* but the *Lackawanna* crashed into the *Hartford* and cut a deep wound in her side. The *Tennessee* was lucky in a way—at least all who surrounded her were enemies and she fired at will, while the Union vessels had as much difficulty in trying not to kill their friends as they did in trying to destroy their enemy.

The Union monitors came into the battle, the *Manhattan* firing at the *Tennessee,* and the *Chickasaw* doing much more valiant work at close range with much more damage. A shell from the *Chickasaw* wounded Admiral Buchanan in the leg.

That did not bring about the surrender of the Confederate ship, but she was taking a terrible pounding. Her gunports were protected by shutters, which could be closed to prevent shells from coming in, but these were jammed by shell fire from the monitors. Her wheel chains were exposed and were shot away. Relieving tackles were substituted for steering, until these, too, were destroyed.

Captain Johnston saw the Union ships closing in to ram. His casemate was so shattered that it was ready to fall off the ship. He decided to surrender—Admiral Buchanan had realized that surrender was coming soon and had given Johnston his head in the matter. The Stars and Bars were hauled down from the gun scraper, which had been stuck up through the grating for a flagstaff, and a white flag was run up.

As the surrender flag came up, the *Ossipee* was running down on the *Tennessee,* and Commander William LeRoy could not stop the impact of his ram, although he stopped his engines. He struck the *Tennessee* a glancing blow, but it did not do great damage. He hailed then—Johnston was an old friend of his—and sent a boat for the Confederate captain. They disappeared into his cabin to renew old times over a bottle.

For his part, Farragut acted properly although not as generously as he might have. He did not go aboard the *Tennessee* to call on the wounded admiral, and he demanded that the junior officer who did board the ship take the admiral's sword —an insult that years earlier had aroused Captain David Porter to fury when a British junior officer tried the same at the surrender of the *Essex* in Valparaiso Bay.

To the junior Confederate officers Farragut was polite, if distant; yet when Surgeon Palmer visited Buchanan, who indicated no particular friendship for Farragut, the little admiral's feelings were hurt. General Page asked that Buchanan be sent under parole to Mobile, but Farragut refused, and the Confederate admiral was sent to the Pensacola hospital along with the other wounded, traveling in the *Metacomet* under a flag of truce that took them under the guns of Fort Morgan without injury.

The battle was over. Farragut regarded it as the most desperate encounter he had fought since the days of the

Essex. He had lost 52 killed and 170 men wounded in the fight, not including the losses in the *Tecumseh,* which went down with 93 of her 114 officers and men. The flagship had borne the brunt of the fighting, with 25 killed and 28 wounded. He had lost one ship, the supply ship *Philippi,* which had followed the larger vessels into the channel against orders and had swiftly been disabled by a shot from Fort Morgan, then run ashore, where she was burned by the Confederates.

Most of his battle force was badly hit and holed. The *Kennebec* was badly damaged by a shell from the *Tennessee,* the *Oneida* was out of action, and the *Tecumseh* was sunk.

The Confederate casualty list was much smaller, only twelve killed and twenty wounded. The *Selma's* crew was captured, the *Gaines'* crew escaped by small boat, and the *Morgan,* having anchored under Fort Morgan, slipped away on the night of the battle and escaped under fire through the Union fleet.

After the battle, Farragut thanked his officers and men, and mentioned that he had "led in" to Mobile Bay. Captain Alden of the *Brooklyn,* who was supposed to lead in, and who had almost lost the battle for the Union, took offense at the admiral's statement and went aboard the *Hartford* to protest. Farragut took the captain below to his cabin and what occurred there no one knew, but forever afterward there was a coolness between the men, even though Farragut did not prefer charges or carry the matter of Alden's behavior further.

After the battle, in writing to Secretary Welles and to other officers, Farragut was far more gentle in his treatment of Admiral Buchanan than he had been in person. For one thing, he had a personal grudge against those officers who had been trained by the United States government, supported that government and been supported by it, and had then turned against the Union to fight for the Confederacy. He might have friends in the aggregate, but personally his emotions were too involved to allow him to treat Buchanan as he might have treated an enemy from a different culture.

Not quite three hours had passed between the time that Fort Morgan fired its first gun and the *Tennessee* hauled down her colors. Thus ended the great Battle of Mobile Bay, which was David Farragut's crowning achievement as a fighting sailor.

26. THE FIRST ADMIRAL

Events moved rapidly in the next few days. Fort Gaines surrendered on August 7, although Fort Morgan held out against land and sea assault for another two weeks before General Page raised the white flag. By this time, Farragut's health was giving out and it was obvious to his officers that he was living on nerves. During one conversation with a junior officer, he fainted dead away for no apparent reason.

The fleet settled down to the tedious duty of blockade, relieved by incidents both gay and sad: the *Tennessee*, when towed to New Orleans, was shown to have a prize value of nearly $900,000, which meant a large chunk for Farragut; in the removal of the torpedoes from the bay, five men were killed and nine injured when one exploded.

Farragut's reputation was made now, beyond the ability of anyone to denigrate him. Secretary Welles offered him the thanks of the nation. Generals wrote their thanks from New York, Washington, and other points. Lincoln wrote his personal thanks and ordered a special 100-gun salute for the admiral at the Washington Navy Yard and every other Union navy yard. And abroad, navy men in Britain and France recognized the grandeur of Farragut's exploits and numbered him among the great admirals of history.

There was much talk about shifting Farragut from this worn-out command to the next focal point of naval battle, which Welles thought would be along the Atlantic coast. The idea was to form a combined operation between Grant's land forces and the navy to cut off Wilmington from the sea. But Farragut was talking about relief from duty for a time because of his health, and in the absence of telephonic communication and the absence of a conference between the men, they bogged down in correspondence that seemed to be mostly at cross-purpose. The result was that at the end of November, 1864, Farragut went home to New York, into the hands of the adulatory crowds and the social whirl of the nation's largest city. On December 22, the office of vice-admiral was created and Farragut was appointed first vice-admiral of the United States, while the *Army and Navy Journal* approved loudly, comparing Farragut with Nelson and Collingwood. James Parton wanted to write his biography. New York merchants got up a purse of $50,000 in government bonds, which they presented with gusto and much ceremony.

Farragut went home to Hastings-on-Hudson, where the citizens had decided that he was no longer a danger to the Croton Reservoir and gave him a hero's welcome, then were kind enough to leave him alone for a few days of rest. But by mid-January he was in Washington, dining with Secretary Welles, calling on the President, and attending the opera with the Lincolns.

The Farraguts attended the inauguration on March 4 and remained in Washington during the rest of the month. Then they went to Norfolk, where Mrs. Farragut visited relatives. Richmond fell, and Farragut made a quick trip to the former Confederate capital. At Norfolk, he attended several receptions, but he was snubbed by the first families of the city—his old friends—because he had chosen to fight for the Union and against their Confederacy. He left Norfolk after a very brief visit and never returned.

In the spring and summer, as Lincoln was assassinated and the war ended and the nation tried to get back to some semblance of peace, Farragut traveled a good deal to be praised and worshiped as a hero. He served on a special naval commission on promotions that spring, and as summer struck the capital, he went back to Hastings in retreat. But with the moneys from prizes and the gifts from merchants and other admirers, he was able to buy a town house at 113 East 36th Street in New York, and there the Farraguts spent the winter of 1865, the admiral indulging himself in dinners and other aspects of New York's busy social life, which he dearly loved.

In the summer of 1866, Farragut was named Admiral of the Navy, again the first man in America to hold the rank. It was granted him on the same day that Ulysses S. Grant was made the nation's only full general. He became friendly with President Andrew Johnson, and he and Grant accompanied the President on the ill-fated tour of the big cities that year. There was talk that he might be made Secretary of the Navy in a cabinet reorganization that year, but the cabinet was not reorganized. In the spring of 1867, Farragut was appointed to command of the European Squadron and sent on a triumphal tour to show the American flag abroad and recreate the goodwill that had evaporated over the war years.

In the middle of June, 1867, Farragut's blue pennant was raised on the U.S.S. *Franklin* in New York harbor, the four-star flag of a full admiral. The *Franklin* was a 4,000-ton steam frigate, with thirty-nine guns and crew of 750 men. As a signal honor from the President, the naval regulation against wives cruising with their husbands was waived, and Virginia Farragut joined her husband on the cruise.

First the *Franklin* steamed to Cherbourg. The Farraguts traveled to Paris and dined with the Emperor at the Tuileries. He visited Berlin and Cronstadt and renewed acquaintance with his old friend Admiral Lessovski of the Russian Navy. He was entertained by the Grand Duke Constantine, because the Czar was traveling in southern Russia that year. He was honored and given gifts and the finest of treatment wherever he went. The Grand Duke suggested that he visit the Russian ironclad fleet and Farragut offered to accompany him, but the Grand Duke said No, he wanted Farragut to go alone so that all the honors of the visit would fall on the American admiral.

So it went, in Sweden, Denmark, and even England, where the atmosphere was still slightly clouded by the English attitude toward the Confederacy during the war. He was well-treated and occupied the royal box at the Drury Lane Theatre, although he was not received by the Empress because the royal family was at Balmoral Castle in Scotland during this summer when all who could fled London. He was entertained by the Admiralty, by the Duchess Dowager of Somerset, and a stream of eminent Londoners came to his apartments at the Clarendon Hotel to call on the man the London newspapers were characterizing as "the Nelson of the Age"—no mean compliment in England.

Then it was Lisbon, where King Don Luis I received the American admiral and his wife; Gibraltar, Tangier, and Madrid, where Queen Isabella welcomed him to Spain with especial warmth because his ancestors came from that country. He visited Minorca, and a delegation of citizens from Ciudadella, his father's birthplace, came to call on him. He visited the town, spent two days there, and as one of his party said, could have been elected emperor at that moment. He visited Italy and dined with King Victor Emmanuel; he toured the country of which he had once been so very fond. He went to Sicily, and then off to Malta.

While on his triumphal tour in the spring of 1868, approaches were made to him by political bosses about running for the Presidency, but he flatly refused, saying he had no qualifications for politics nor any ambition to become a political leader. His answer was severe and final.

He went to Holland and to Brussels, where he dined with King Leopold II; then to Germany and back to England, where he was received by Queen Victoria at Osborne House. He went to the Mediterranean, to Constantinople, and the Greeks tried to use his visit to propagandize for Greek independence of the islands, which was something of an embarrassment. He visited Athens, found that his Greek visitors at Constantinople had been jailed for urging Cretan independence and successfully interceded for them.

In October, 1868, the tour ended and the flagship started home again. The triumphal tour had lasted seventeen months, during which various officials and politicians all over the world had speculated that Farragut was being sent as an envoy extraordinary to make treaties with the Russians, English, Italians, or any and all of the others that he visited. But the truth was that it was a goodwill visit, pure and simple, and it accomplished precisely that purpose. The unassuming Farragut, recognized as the naval hero of the age by nations that had more respect for naval heroes than the United States of the 1860's, had created an enormous reservoir of goodwill for his country.

27. THE HERO

The admiral who dies on his ship in a wreath of smoke and flame is able to maintain the aura of his heroism more than the admiral who outlives the war in which he earned his fame, as any student of Nelson knows. Stephen Decatur and Oliver Perry died with their boots on, so to speak, and are far better known than Richard Dale, Thomas Truxton, Edward Preble, and Isaac Hull, who were just as grand in stature in their day, but who died quietly in retirement.

Farragut, on return from his remarkable European victory cruise, faced special new problems that came out of the war and the pettiness of mankind. Congress had turned coldly and absolutely against Andrew Johnson because of his view of a need for reconciliation between North and South. The radical Republicans had elected U. S. Grant as President, first convincing this deluded man that he was fit for the task. The vilification of Johnson had come about and culminated in the ignoble attempt to impeach him.

Farragut had missed all this political infighting, and when he came home to America, his old superior, Secretary Welles, hoped that Farragut might secure the appointment as the new Secretary of the Navy in the Grant cabinet. But to seek such an appointment would mean that Farragut would have to shift his loyalties, to demean himself in his own eyes by toadying to a man who had thoroughly disgraced himself personally on the Johnson tour of 1866. Then, although Johnson was charged with drunkenness and other vices, the notable instances of overindulgence in alcohol were all on the part of General Grant. At Cleveland, Grant got roaring drunk and began crying on Virginia Farragut's shoulder with such vehemence that it became embarrassing to all concerned. He was shipped off to Detroit on a steamer to sober him up and get him out of sight.

Farragut returned to New York, now his home, just after the election and attended several dinners at which Grant was also a guest. But Farragut also dined with President Johnson, Secretary Welles, and other old friends and acquaintances of the outgoing administration—which definitely put him in the wrong camp because Grant, goaded by his toadies, refused to appear where the administration appeared or to have any truck with administration friends.

Farragut, as a full-fledged national hero, had a difficult road to walk. He attended the Grant inauguration, but did not stay for the ball. He quietly went home instead.

There was a good reason for Farragut's leaving so soon. The ambitious David Porter, never a man of principle, had devoutly supported Andrew Johnson until he saw how the wind was blowing with the impeachment proceedings, and then he turned against Johnson. Once Grant was nominated, Porter became his toady. Grant chose as Secretary of the Navy an unknown war profiteer by the name of Adolph E. Borie, who distinguished himself by letting Porter run the navy.

So with his junior vice admiral in charge, there was nothing for Farragut to do in Washington. He went home, while in Washington Porter set about denigrating him and his works.

Secretary Borie lasted only three months, and his successor, Secretary George M. Robeson, was a good judge of wines and at least a good enough judge of men to know a bad appointment. It was not long before Vice Admiral Porter was removed from his perch.

Farragut's precarious health failed in the winter of 1869, when he suffered several heart attacks. He traveled that year to California to visit Mare Island Navy Yard and stopped off in Chicago, where he was ill for a time. In January, 1870, he took charge of the naval ceremonial cortege that brought the remains of the famous merchant George Peabody into American waters after the body was conveyed home on a British battleship.

The admiral was growing old and ill. He met Commander Winfield Scott Schley during the Peabody funeral ceremonies and recalled a conversation of years past, at Port Hudson:

> I remember you then said I belonged to that class of men who would preserve their vigor and vitality until ripe old age, and that, when the break comes, would go in a year. It looks to me now that this may be so.

On July 5, 1870, he celebrated his sixty-ninth birthday, very weak, but aboard the dispatch steamer *Tallapoosa* on his way to make an inspection of the navy yard at Portsmouth and to visit friends there. While at Portsmouth he wandered down to the old sailing sloop *Dale,* launched in 1839, which was laid up in the yard, dismantled, outmoded by steam power. He paced up and down the decks, mindful of the sight she had once made at sea, her sixteen guns flashing fire, and he spoke to the old seaman who was her caretaker:

> This is the last time I shall ever tread the deck of a man of war.

Then he climbed shakily onto the wharf and up the steps to the residence of the commandant and sat down heavily on the verandah.

The admiral was right. A few days later, he was too sick to leave his bed at Portsmouth. On August 14, he died of a paralytic stroke. It was a Sunday, a very peaceful day in the navy yard, and the ship's bells were just striking eight.

There was a meaningful funeral service at Portsmouth, attended by Secretary Welles, General Banks, Assistant Secretary Fox, and others with whom he had served. But the administration ignored the occasion. There was a far more pretentious, far less meaningful, service in New York, where President Grant and his cabinet, seeing how strongly the press and public objected to their gaffe in trying to ignore this national hero, made a great occasion of coming up for the services.

Grandiose preparations were made. The body was carried to New York by the frigate *Guerrière*. A procession was to wind its way up West and Canal to Broad, and then to the Harlem Railroad Station at 47th Street. President Grant was to lead the procession, followed by his cabinet, naval officials, generals, New York state officials, New York city officials, and hundreds of representatives of civic and patriotic organizations.

But it rained.

It was not an ordinary rain; it was a torrent, and it continued for hours. The procession was cut in half, and the funerary party marched soddenly through the rain, with the plumes of the military drooping in the wet.

Farragut was buried in Woodlawn cemetery, and when all the eulogizing was finished, that was the end of it. Except for students at the naval academy, naval historians, brother officers, and a few who recalled the famous words, "Damn the torpedoes!" he was largely forgotten, although his life story was written several times, including one brief but strong biography by Admiral Mahan. In 1943, Charles Lee Lewis of the Naval Academy produced a remarkable, detailed biography in two volumes which bespoke months and years of careful tracing of the record, but again, it came at the wrong time, when Americans were bemused by a war as all-consuming as the passion of the 1860's. The Lewis biography was seen and passed on, leaving Farragut largely unremembered.

The admiral's career, as noted by Admiral Mahan, really began, in the heroic sense, at the age when most navy men were ready to retire, or at least to relax and let the younger fellows have the glory. Farragut was nearly sixty-one years old when he steamed past the Mississippi forts with such apparent abandon.

Mahan, the student of naval strategy, compared Farragut very favorably to Lord Nelson, and particularly in one rare respect: "a natural genius for war." Mahan also indicated that

275

Farragut's early training was responsible for his vigorous approach to a fight. How true, for Farragut was lucky enough to serve aboard America's fighting ships of sail at a time when American naval men had a tradition that gave pause even to the English admirals. He learned his trade in the school of "Preble's boys," who conducted a very hard school indeed, teaching by example of bravery and audacity.

There was Farragut's genius, and it was illustrated in his quoting one day from Danton:

L'audace, et encore de l'audace, et toujours de l'audace.

The quotation celebrated Captain Drayton's sense for the audacious, but it showed how much Farragut revered the quality of decision.

Audacity by itself might be no more effective on an enemy than foolhardiness. Yet to Farragut audacity was the fervor with which he took the last step, made the movement to engage. His career shows that he combined the sense of the audacious with a respect for the slogging, tiresome labors of the naval profession that so many young officers hated and avoided where they could. Mahan summed it up: Farragut never went into a harbor that he did not memorize all about it, the depths, the turns, the land, the anchorages—anything he could learn. "Who knows," he said, "but that my services may be needed here some day?"

The castle at Vera Cruz was an example—and if a less brilliant Commodore Matthew Perry could not see it, that was the navy's loss. But the castle at Vera Cruz, and Farragut's close observation of the French capture of that fortress, led him to the knowledge that ships could run by forts. Further, he had been under fire by an American fort in the War of 1812, when he and Captain Downes came sailing up the narrows in the disarmed *Essex Junior*. He *knew*. There was no problem about figuring and estimating. He drew from his experience what was necessary to win on the Mississippi and in Mobile Bay, and to these bits of knowledge he added *l'audace*.

Mahan credits him with a great natural aptitude for war, for knowing instinctively what to do and when to do it.

The more you hurt the enemy, the less he will hurt you.

The *best* protection against the enemy's fire is a well-directed fire from our own guns.

These were maxims of Farragut's. "I believe in celerity," was another, to match Nelson's, "Five minutes may make the difference between victory and defeat."

Above all, however, Farragut was a man of strong character. He was not an easy man. Indeed, he had a hot temper, and his best friends were constantly warning his wife and him to hold that temper. Captain William Bolton, according to Lewis, advised Virginia to "tell him to keep quiet and avoid getting into difficulty" when Farragut was smarting under the doltish treatment he was receiving from the insensitive and recriminatory Commodore Perry during the Mexican War.

Here is Mahan's summing up:

> The acquirements of the accomplished officer may enable him to see the right thing to be done under given conditions, and yet fail to lift him to the height of due performance. It is in the strength of purpose, in the power of rapid decision, of instant action, and, if need be, of strenuous endurance through a period of danger or of responsibility, when the terrifying alternatives of war are vibrating in the balance, that the power of a great captain mainly lies.

And there is Farragut, the young officer, who dared write in his notebooks that his hero, Commodore Porter, had fought the *Essex* improperly in Valparaiso Bay; the officer who had faced up to a doughty old whaling captain when he was twelve years old; the commander who had moved cautiously but purposefully in the San Francisco Rebellion of 1856; and the flag officer who had sent his ships past the forts of the Mississippi while other officers trembled, in 1862.

There is one criterion by which Farragut's greatness as a

captain was shown beyond all doubt. Lieutenant George Dewey began serving with Farragut during the New Orleans campaign and fought with him at Port Hudson. This lieutenant rose to become an admiral himself, with all the perquisites and all the responsibilities. On April 30, 1898, Admiral George Dewey, with a squadron of four cruisers and two gunboats, entered Manila Bay with orders to capture or destroy the Spanish fleet, which was almost double the strength of the American squadron. That night, as he prepared for action in the morning, Admiral George Dewey asked himself:

"What would Farragut have done. . . ?"

And there is the test of history.

INDEX